Contents

INTRODUCTION AND ACKNOWLEDGMENTS

IN THE SUMMER OF 1982, while engaged in a search for feature material to use in the *Barnsley Chronicle* newspaper, I came across a faded, sepia-toned photograph of a group of men in dark coloured 'bus conductor' style uniforms; written in indelible pencil on the back were the words 'Barnsley Pals leaving for the front'. Intrigued, I wondered what the story could be behind that scrawled message. I had heard of the Barnsley Pals of the Great War, but twenty-four years ago there was very little information, in a convenient form, readily to hand. At that time public awareness of the existence of a First World War battalion known as the Accrington Pals was growing, thanks to a then new stage play by Peter Whelan – but it was becoming clear to me that the small Lancashire town of Accrington was not the only public authority to raise men for Kitchener's New Army; where men who volunteered together in response to the call were assured that they could remain in the same battalion and serve, shoulder to shoulder, for the fight against the Kaiser's Germany. That Barnsley had raised two such battalions seemed like a particularly good nostalgia feature story. I decided to include the account of the Barnsley formations the 13th and 14th (Service) Battalions, York and Lancaster Regiment, in one of the *Chronicle* tabloid supplements, but where would the illustrations come from? Someone pointed out that Sir Joseph Hewitt, grandfather of the present newspaper proprietor Sir Nicholas Hewitt, had been the public minded citizen of the day who had helped raise the Barnsley Pals and had been appointed commanding officer of the 13th Battalion. Surely the family would have a snap or two that would illustrate the feature. In the event, three large albums were produced for me to make a selection – they were packed with photographs of the Barnsley Pals in training at a purpose built camp at Silkstone village and of the battalion serving in the desert protecting the Suez Canal from raids by the Turks. During the planning and sub-editing of the feature, along with the reporter who had been assigned to write it up, it became apparent that the material was growing out of the tabloid format. Sir Nicholas decided to run the story broadsheet size in the 'big paper', serialised over a period of weeks during the autumn of 1982. Immediately, the appearance of the feature aroused great interest and back copies of the newspapers carrying the story were quickly sold out. Obviously, Barnsley people wished to read of the exploits of their grandfathers and uncles during the Great War.

After the series had finished its run in the *Chronicle* I was summoned to the boardroom to meet a personable young school teacher with a trendy hair style – Jon Cooksey. Jon was expressing a desire to write the complete story of the two Pals battalions. Sir Nicholas commissioned the book and the Barnsley

PALS

ON THE SOMME 1916

PALS

ON THE SOMME 1916

Kitchener's New Army Battalions raised by local
authorities during the Great War

RONI WILKINSON

Pen & Sword
MILITARY

... imprint of
Pen & Sword Books Limited
47 Church Street
Barnsley
South Yorkshire
S70 2AS

Copyright © Roni Wilkinson, 2006

ISBN: 1 84415 393 2

The right of Roni Wilkinson to be identified as Author
of this Work has been asserted by him in accordance
with the Copyright, Designs and Patents Act 1988.

A CIP catalogue record for this book
is available from the British Library

Typeset in 10pt Palatino by Pen & Sword Books Limited

Printed and bound in England by
CPI UK

For a complete list of Pen & Sword titles please contact:
PEN & SWORD BOOKS LIMITED
47 Church Street, Barnsley, South Yorkshire, S70 2AS, England
email: enquiries@pen-and-sword.co.uk • website: www.pen-and-sword.co.uk

Chronicle Ltd took another faltering step (*Dark Peak Aircraft Wrecks 1 & 2* being the first) into the international book publishing company it has become today.

The design, some additional research, and veteran interviews were to be my responsibility; Jon would author the work. A large format was decided upon which could be printed on the newspaper press, and that would accommodate a same-size reproduction of official forms and selected 'cuttings' from the newspapers of the time.

Jon proved to be a meticulous researcher who would not settle for merely rewriting the published work of others. As a result, the book, *Barnsley Pals* became firmly and soundly established on original and previously unseen material. Documents from various archives in this country and Germany delivered a fresh look at that infamous day of 1st July, 1916 when, at 7.30 am on a Saturday morning and in glorious sunshine, men of Kitchener's New Army, each man loaded down with stores and equipment, walked across the rolling hills, north of the River Somme and into the German barbed wire and chattering machine guns. Enhancing the printed story were rare and previously unpublished photographs and the text was laced with personal accounts as veterans told their stories. An example of the detailed research carried out by Jon was the identifying, naming, locating and marking on a map and aerial photograph every German machine gun position facing the 94 Brigade of the

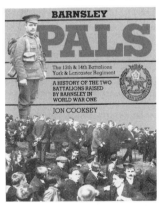

31st Division as it went 'over the top' for the first time on that awful summer's day in 1916. As a direct result of the author's conscientious hard work, and within a matter of months of its appearance in the book shops, teaching establishments in Birmingham and Leicestershire were using *Barnsley Pals* as a text book on the subject of the Great War. Guides to the battlefield were employing maps from the book in their touring enterprises and public speakers on the subject of the First World War were referring to the work on their lecture rounds. Jon has gone on to author several more titles in our *Battleground Europe Elite Operations* and *Images of War* series.

Success of one Pals book drew other authors, who invariably proved to be avid collectors of postcards, photographs and memorabilia of a particular battalion. Usually they had become friends of veterans of a particular Pals battalion. Bill Turner had had published a picture booklet of the Accrington Pals and approached the *Barnsley Chronicle* Newspaper Group in the hope that it would give the Accrington story the same large format treatment. Immediately, a close working relationship was struck up with the author and the team in the newly formed Graphic and Features unit of the *Barnsley Chronicle*. The Lancashire weekly newspaper office publishing the *Accrington Observer*, then owned by the Crossley family, opened its archives to provide illustrations and extracts from printed pages of the newspapers of the relevant years. Cooperation and interest in the Accrington Pals shown by the Lancashire County Library, especially the Accrington Local Studies department, was exceptional then and continues to be so today. As we at the *Chronicle* worked on Bill's book we became good friends with him and it was a pleasure, in 1998, to repeat the experience with the *Accrington Pals Trail*, a guide book in the highly successful *Battleground Europe* series of Pen & Sword Books Ltd (a subsidiary operation of The Barnsley Chronicle Ltd, specifically created to publish books).

The next authors to arrive at our offices in Barnsley were Paul Oldfield and Ralph Gibson. They had the Sheffield City Battalion (12th York and Lancaster Regiment) story and soon we were working on another Pals book, this time with a difference. Whereas the volunteers for the Barnsley and Accrington battalions were drawn from the lower working class (before present-day political correctness it was alright to say this) the young men volunteering to serve in the City battalion were mainly office workers with the benefit of a grammar school education and whose families were further up the social ladder. Perhaps best illustrating the obvious differences

Dare we say 'Band of Brothers'? Laurie Milner signs copies at the book launch of **Leeds Pals** *held at Leeds City Hall, 1991, with fellow Pals authors looking on. Left to right: Ralph Gibson, Graham Maddocks and Jon Cooksey. Presenting his profile is author and militaria dealer Peter Taylor.*

between the miners and mill workers of Barnsley and Accrington and the white-collar workers of Sheffield were the words of one under-age soldier in the Barnsleys, Frank Lindley (incidentally, at the time the youngster was a deserter from the Royal Artillery). He recalled: 'I'll always remember the Sheffielders with their handkerchiefs stuffed up their sleeves and their wristwatches flashing in the sun. They were the elite of Sheffield – they were the 'Coffee and Bun Boys' – we were the 'Ragged Arsed Battalion'.'

We saw little of the main author, Paul Oldfield, who was a serving officer

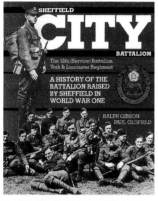

in the British Army, but we saw a lot of Ralph at the office and soon became good friends as we shared the agonies and thrills of book production. Ralph phoned recently from the south coast, where he and his wife Jean are now living, to discuss the reprinting of the *Sheffield City* battalion book in smaller, hardback format. He claimed to being pleased once again to be renewing his acquaintance with the Barnsley office complete with insults and ribbing, as he was missing the experience down south. Ralph is still very much heart-involved in the story of the Sheffield City men of the Great War and frequently visits the site of their first day of 'going over the top' in the Big Push. An area of French real estate from where the Sheffielders launched their assault became the property of the City of Sheffield following the war. Yet another substantial memorial to the battalion is in the village of Serre itself (which was behind the German lines on 1st July 1916). By comparison and in sharp contrast, and echoing the sentiments of Barnsley Pals veteran Frank Lindley, the Barnsleys' memorial at Serre consisted of a simple brass plaque measuring about six inches by twelve, nailed to a tree. That had to suffice as a remembrance device for seventy years.

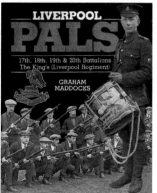

In quick succession there followed two further titles in the Pals series, Liverpool and Leeds. Our Liverpool author was Graham Maddocks, who died 18 July 2003. Graham was a school teacher who in his spare time acted as a First World War battlefield tour guide. For us his Pals' story, the 17th, 18th, 19th and 20th Battalions of the King's (Liverpool Regiment), was different to the other previously published histories as regards the action on 1 July 1916. Instead of being stopped and hung up on the German wire, the Liverpool Pals, took their objectives on that Saturday morning in 1916. We at the publishing office had been used to reading of slaughter and failure on the first day of the 'Big Push' caused by uncut German wire, artillery and machine-gun fire and, it has to said, naive optimism on the part of the British military planners. Here was a different outcome for

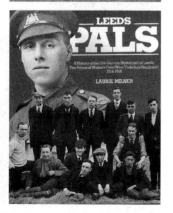

9

the first day of the Battle of the Somme. Another interesting feature of the Liverpool story was the claim that, out of the many Pals or 'Chums' battalions to be formed, the 17th (1st City) Battalion was the very first, officially coming into existence on 31 August, 1914 at the instigation of Lord Derby. In 1994 Graham was the main instigator in the placing of a joint memorial to the Liverpool and Manchester battalions at the Somme village of Montauban, the scene of the successful taking of their objectives on the first day of the Battle of the Somme. His dream, he told us, was to purchase the ground south of Montauban where the Briqueterie (brick yard) was once located and where the 20th Battalion The King's (Liverpool Regiment) attacked successfully.

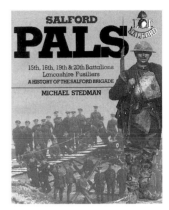

The staff at the Imperial War Museum, London, are regarded by researchers, authors, students, programme makers and book publishers to be the experts on the subject of world conflicts, so it was a pleasant surprise to have a Pals story submitted by a member of that staff – Laurie Milner. With Laurie's story of the *Leeds Pals: 15th Battalion The Prince of Wales's Own (West Yorkshire Regiment)* we were presented with a wealth of photographs and documents and a clean, professionally written script. We were pleased for him when his book sold out and was reprinted and relaunched. Laurie generously offered material to other Pals authors for use in their books and authored another book with us, the story of *The Royal Scots in the Gulf*. We would like to do more books with Laurie.

Likewise with Michael Stedman, author of two Pals books, *Salford Pals* and *Manchester Pals*, his scripts were clean and professional. For over twenty years Mike taught history and economics at schools around Manchester and included trips to the battlefields in his teaching programmes. Mike went on to write four titles in our *Battleground* series of guide books and, as a consequence, we have become good friends. He has recently been involved in putting together the new visitors' centre at Thiepval, and he is working on a DVD project.

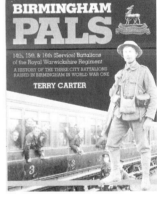

The publishing of the story of Birmingham Service Battalions was next. Working on illustrated books usually means close liaison with writers as, we employ a policy which recognises that expertise on a subject belongs with the author. Therefore their judgement as to what is included or excluded and what goes where, is allowed to prevail wherever possible. Terry Carter arrived at the office with a

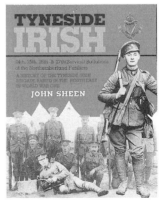

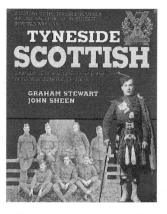

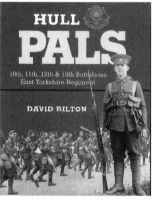

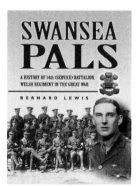

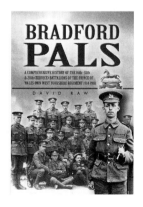

wealth of pictures and documents and we were able to work with him to produce a comprehensive history of three battalions of the Royal Warwickshire Regiment – the 14th, 15th and 16th (Service) Battalions. When it came to good natured leg pulling, we Yorkshire lads had met our match in Terry, who was a master scrounger and skilled in wheeling and dealing. He works/ed at Land Rover, Solihull, and will most likely be involved in selling it off to the Chinese. Terry's choice of what went where in the final product prevailed and we ended up with a highly visual and well rounded history entitled *Birmingham Pals*.

Photographs of British infantrymen actually engaged in 'going over the top' and advancing on the German lines on that Saturday morning in July 1916 are rare. However, a famous series of photographs taken by an official War Office photographer showing British Tommies advancing across the skyline at La Boisselle were of the Tyneside Irish. Understandably, we were delighted when a collector of information on those battalions contacted us with a view to adding a history of the 24th, 25th, 26th and 27th Northumberland Fusiliers – Tyneside Irish – to our expanding series. John Sheen is a no-nonsense ex-regular soldier who, at that time, worked for the Durham authorities as a driver of a corporation sewage truck. He told us, in no uncertain terms, that we either did his book the way he wanted or he would arrive at our offices in his works vehicle, put the hose through the window and select 'blow' instead of 'suck'. Concerning the presentation of his work, we have always listened very carefully to John's suggestions. Likewise it was the case when he followed up with the history of the Tyneside Scottish in the Great War, this time with the help of Graham Stewart. John is working on the history of the Durham Pals and so we were delighted and very much relieved to learn that John now has a desk job with the Durham authority.

As previously mentioned, anyone who collects photographs, postcards and documents in connection with a particular First World War battalion may very well have the material upon which to base a book and to become a published author. David Bilton, a school teacher from Reading, is an example of this. David, an avid collector of Great War illustrative material, proposed the story of four battalions of the East Yorkshire Regiment for our Pals series. We were pleased to go ahead, hence, in 1999, we added Hull Pals to our growing list of battalion histories. Since then David has written other books for us which have included *The Trench* and *Oppy Wood* in the *Battleground* series. For those seeking illustrative material for their books then David Bilton may have some suitable images in his considerable picture archive. David has been especially helpful in the production of this book; nothing is too much trouble for him.

Although the series has certainly been a success, there has been one drawback – the large, coffee-table size. Because of the large format and the fact that, in order to keep the cover price down, the binding was softback, bookshops have not viewed handling of stock with enthusiasm. Admittedly, single books have proved unwieldy and have struggled to remain upright on the shelves without bending, bruising and creasing. Consequently, shop damage and returns to publisher occurred. Too much shelf room taken up, too many copies shop-soiled – no matter how important a subject, or how interesting a story, marketing considerations had finally to be taken on board. After much heart searching and debate it was decided to abandon the familiar, cumbersome large format and publish in a more retailer, user-friendly size in hardback. After a successful experiment with a *Manchester Pals* reprint in 2002, in 2004 we went ahead with the story of the 14th Battalion Welsh Regiment – *Swansea Pals*. Also the author, Bernard Lewis, was dealt with by us in a more conventional (and, dare we say, professional?) manner. Bernard is currently employed as Principal Administrative Assistant in the Environmental and Health Department at Swansea. He proved to be a helpful and amiable writer to work with and production proceeded smoothly. Perhaps contributing to the reason for the trouble-free gestation of *Swansea Pals*, was the fact that the book designer was a woman – for the first time.

In September 2005 we published, at long last, the history of the 16th, 18th and 20th Battalions of the Prince of Wales' Own West Yorkshire Regiment, 1914-1918, – *Bradford Pals*, by David Raw. This was a story that had been long in arriving in the hands of an eagerly waiting public. A proposal for a Bradford Pals book was submitted by David way back in the distant past – as far as we can remember – about fourteen years. Maybe this is some kind of a record in the experience of writer's block? The list of outstanding, preprint orders for the account of men who joined up to serve together from 'Worstedopolis', the wool trade centre of England, was considerable. However, it was a story well worth telling and well worth waiting for. It includes an account of a famous international sportsman who served in the Bradfords. The story of the soccer superstar captured by the Germans who, with some pride, promptly announced the event on a notice board placed out in No Man's Land. It carried the words, '... Dickie Bond. We've got him'. Or the account of two men, Crimmins and Wild, who were convicted of the charge, 'When on service deserting His Majesty's Service' taken out and shot at dawn. The new smaller format did not allow for the lists of men who served, lists of their awards and decorations, or those who died serving in the Bradford battalions. We judged that David Raw's writing could not be cut back to allow room for them – it was far too fascinating a story to be severely edited.

Without a doubt, the story of the Pals battalions raised by local authorities is one rich, not just in action-packed first-hand accounts of men who served, but in social history in a period focused on the first quarter of the twentieth century. The thirteen Pals authors who delivered the stories of those years have done a great service by recording historic events of the times, and it has been a pleasure to work along with them. No doubt there will be more titles published in future, for there are still Pals and Chums stories to be set down. However, the men who fought in the Great War are almost all gone. The story will continue but answers to specific questions put by researchers to those who experienced the Great War has come to an end. Diaries and existing tape recordings will have to suffice.

The Pals story to date, as recounted through the Pen & Sword series, covers the histories of forty Service battalions of the First World War. With roughly 1,000 men to each battalion (rarely did a battalion proceed abroad with a full complement) it means that, taking into account men posted out as replacements for casualties, the service history the units involving maybe 100,000 men is now in print.

This present work strives to pull together a brief outline of those battalions and hopefully, cause the reader to seek out the fuller stories in the respective individual volumes of the Pals books. Thanks go to the authors who kindly gave permission to use material from their books.

Thanks are also due to Peter Taylor, author, collector and militaria dealer, who has amassed a large collection of maps, photographs and movie film covering conflicts in the Twentieth Century. Peter, who is consulted by the large media companies for use of his archival material, has always found time to render unstinting cooperation and assistance, from the time I first began work on the Pals battalions project over twenty-four years ago until now. Seeing the Great War from the 'other side of the hill' has brought a fresh look to the conflicts on the Somme. I would like to thank Jack Sheldon, author of *The German Army on the Somme* for permission to quote from his fascinating book. Nigel Cave, editor and co originator of our **Battleground Europe WW1** series of guide books for, over the years, sharing his encyclopedic knowledge of the Great War and casting his eye over this work.

Then of course there are my Pals at Pen & Sword, fellow designer, Sylvia Menzies, who mysteriously finds everything I misplace and lose during the course of a day, and who respectfully alerts me when I begin to nod off. Jonathan Wright has been courteous and helpful as ever and has done all he can to promote this work. Also I would like to thank my son Jon who designed the jacket with his usual flare for visual appeal and impact.

Roni Wilkinson, Barnsley, 2006

PROLOGUE

SCHOLARS AND HISTORIANS of succeeding generations following after the one which lived through and experienced the horrors of the First World War, have puzzled as to how it all came about. Professor A. J.P. Taylor stated, 'It is difficult, in fact, to discover any cause of hostility between the European Great Powers in the early summer of 1914.' There had been tension between them but the situation had calmed. Justification for nations becoming embroiled in the war, optimistically labelled by some as it got under way as 'the war to end all wars', seems fuzzy and confusing. The Second World War, on the other hand, did have a clear and purposeful reason – a vicious, callous, dictatorial regime was intent on subjugating Europe and peoples were fighting to survive. Students of history usually agree that the seeds for that conflict were sown in the Great War of 1914-1918. The Treaty of Versailles in which the defeated peoples were humiliated by the victors made sure that there would be a return match.

As the twentieth century began, Europe, during the first decade, certainly by 1905, proceeded to separate into two distinct camps forged by alliances between on the one hand, the three centrally located European empires of Germany, Austria-Hungary and Italy, and, on the other, those of the nations ringed geographically around them. The Prussian statesman Otto von Bismarck had he been alive (he died just eighteen months prior to the twentieth century) would have viewed the situation with foreboding. Being the undoubted founder of the German nation he had been well aware of the danger of having potential enemies on two frontiers of his newly formed country and, through clever diplomacy, had averted that threat. True to Bismarck's concerns, and according to many historians, including Professor Taylor, the cause of the war was the system of alliances: on the one hand the German, Austria-Hungary and Italian – the so called Triple Alliance – faced off against a rival power bloc consisting of the French, British, and Russian nations – the so called *Triple Entente*. However, that arrangement could still have made for a peaceful world had the kings and national governments respected each others sovereignties, after all they professed to be stalwarts of the Christian faith. Furthermore, those rulers were often interrelated, one with another, through marriage alliances.

Monarchs such as Kaiser Wilhelm II of Germany, Czar Nicholas II of Russia and Emperor Franz Joseph of Austria-Hungary were adherents to and bound by the signatures of their forebears to what was termed the Holy Alliance, which proclaimed that God had delegated them to oversee parts of Christendom. 'We Christian Kings,' wrote the Kaiser to the Czar of Russia, 'have one duty imposed upon us by Heaven, that is to uphold the principle of the divine right of kings.' Firmly endowed with such an arrogant conviction the supreme rulers in Europe could have been expected to

Royal rulers of Europe gathered on the occasion of the funeral of Britain's Edward VII in 1910. Four years later when tensions between the Great Powers reached crisis point, some of them, instead of seeking peace between their governments, sought further power and signed declarations of war, plunging their subjects into four years of misery. **Seated, left to right:** *Alfonso XIII of Spain, George V, Frederick VII of Denmark.* **Standing, left to right:** *Haakon VII of Norway, Ferdinand of Bulgaria, Manoel of Portugal, William II of Germany, George I of Greece, Albert of Belgium.*

exercise their autocratic authority with benevolence to avert outright conflict between their subjects.

Coupled with belief in the divinely ordered heads of state was the fact that at the start of the twentieth century the churches were well subscribed and attended. The clergy were acknowledged to be representatives of the suppliant laity interceding on their behalf before the presence of the Almighty. Those religious institutions, the various denominations, exercised undeniable influence over the masses and especially world rulers and governmental leaders. The thrust of their message purported to be one of universal love, forgiveness, tolerance and of peace. With such powerful factors for peace in place, how could world war even be contemplated in the twentieth century?

Bearing this out, Winston Churchill wrote, 'The spring and summer of 1914 were marked in Europe by an exceptional tranquility.' The rivalry between Britain and Germany, which had existed in the years leading up to 1914, seemed to have settled down. As the year began 1914 was full of promise and Churchill further wrote with confidence, 'Germany seemed with us, set on peace.' Obviously, then, other factors were involved which caused men to suddenly, in a matter of weeks, abandon the Christian ethic of worldwide brotherhood in favour of hatred, and to subscribe to wholesale slaughter. Patriotism was clearly a factor.

Extreme patriotism, in the summer of 1914, acted like petrol vapour to a smouldering rag. Devotion to their particular nation manifested by citizens of european states, coupled with xenophobia, succeeded in working-up the peoples to enter into what would become four years of human butchery.

Pride is listed as one of the deadly sins and it is easy to see why. Now, over ninety years on, the extreme national fervour experienced in the previous century, the generation of 1914–1918, is an emotion which is embarrassingly out of fashion. It sits uncomfortably with the majority of persons living today. Now it is a more cynical, fault-finding, common man in this twenty-first century who has to be convinced (albeit by carefully contrived propaganda), before sacrifices to the gods of war are countenanced. These are the times of 'political correctness', 'stress' and 'counselling'. And today, woebetide the governmental leaders who are later discovered to have misrepresented the facts in order to justify invading another sovereign state.

Perhaps flavours of the kind of patriotism that fuelled the First World War become evident in this country on the occasion of some sporting event. For example, in the summer of 2005, as it became clear that England would win the ashes, grown men stood and sang the chosen theme tune 'Jerusalem' with tears streaming down their faces. Flags depicting the Cross of St George of England are hung from windows of homes and flown from cars throughout the country during international sports events. Those type of emotional experiences in the present day may provide a fleeting glimpse, and may help us to understand, the sort of intense feeling which swept through the populace of the belligerent nations in the summer of 1914, causing men to abandon their jobs and to descend en masse on the recruiting offices. They appeared eager, if indeed they had thought it through, to be taught how they might shed the blood of foreigners with bullet, bayonet and bomb – preferably on the away ground.

The national fervour of those days, rather than lasting a few weeks over the period of sporting events as in our day, had to be sustained over many months, even years of bitter conflict. That could only be achieved through a relentless vilification of the enemy and, as a ploy which ensured ongoing suport, succeeded as far as the civilian population was concerned. However, those men who took part in the fighting became increasingly disillusioned, especially so after the Battle of the Somme in July 1916. That change of attitude may be discerned in the change of tone in written verse of some of the war poets.

But at the height of unashamed patriotism at the outbreak of war the gallant British Tommy was cast in the role of hero, rescuing defenceless Belgian women and children from the rapacious 'Hun'. There is no doubt that there were atrocities carried out against the civilian population by some among the one million plus German soldiers sweeping through Belgium. In such a situation, and against such acts of foulness, God, it was reasoned, was surely to be on the side of the Allies and would cause Tommy Atkins and his glorious allies to triumph over evil in the end.

Assisting the national cause and to bolster patriotism, clergymen of the day, for their sermons, drew on Old Testament accounts of how the great Jehovah granted outstanding victories to His people Israel, even intervening with hailstones, flashflood and fire from Heaven on special occasions. Therefore, surely the Allies could expect no less. A bogus newspaper report of an angel that appeared over the battlefield of France during the British retreat in 1914, intervening to save some units of the Expeditionary Force from annihilation, was eagerly snapped up and belived by the masses. There

Religious institutions of Christendom failed to halt the progression to war and once it got underway for four years they drove their flocks to the slaughter. At this service on the steps of St Paul's the Bishop of London urges the massed soldiers '...the Church calls upon the nation to say that no sacrifice matters if you win'.

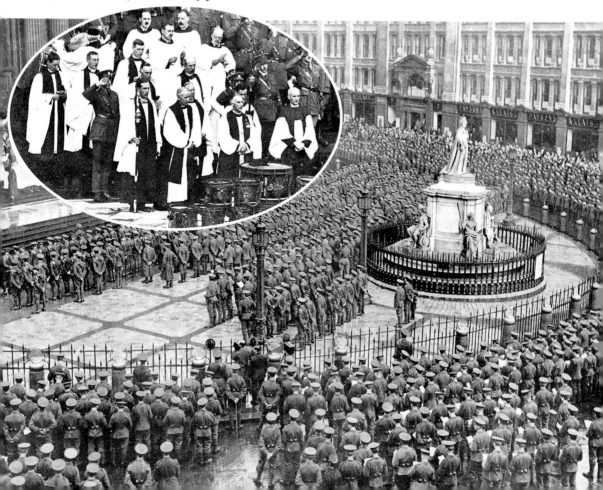

it was, the miraculous appearance of the Angel of Mons confirmed it – the Almighty was 'batting' for the British Empire. One prominent clergyman, Reverend Arthur Winnington-Ingram, Bishop of London, incensed by the news of the alleged crucifiction of a captured Canadian Sergeant on a barn door at St Julien near Ypres, delivered a hate-filled tirade to the London Territorials at a drumhead service on the steps of St Paul's Cathedral in July 1915. Making no pretense at drawing on the authority of holy writ for his bloodcurdling sermon, he urged:

'Everyone that puts principle above ease, and life itself beyond mere living, are part of a great crusade – we cannot deny it – to kill Germans: to kill them not for the sake of killing, but to save the world; to kill the good as well as the bad, to kill the young men as well as the old, to kill those who have shown kindness to our wounded... to kill them lest the civilisation of the world should itself be killed.'

It is difficult to imagine that similiar such bellicose rhetoric by a bishop would have been palatable to the British public during, say, the time of the Falklands War of 1982.

The ones reviled as the detestable invader rampaging through Belgium in

Roman Catholic open-air service held at Sittingbourne in March 1915. Most religious denominations were provided for.

The following religious groups provided uniformed ministers to serve with the British Army:
Roman Catholic Church, Church of England, United Free Church of Scotland, Presbyterian Church of Scotland, Presbyterian Church of Ireland, Presbyterian Church of England, Congregationalist, Baptist, Primitive Methodist, United Methodist, Welsh Calvinistic Methodist, Wesleyan, Salvation Army and the Jewish faith.

Three Chaplains were awarded the Victoria Cross during the Great War: Rev. William Addison, Rev. Theodore Hardy, and Rev. Edward Mellish. Hardy was the highest decorated non-combatant, earning the DSO and MC in addition to the Victoria Cross.

William Robert Fountains Addison VC.

Edward Noel Mellish VC, MC.

Theodore Bailey Hardy VC, DSO, MC.

WOODBINE WILLIE was the nickname given to Yorkshireman Geoffrey Studdert Kennedy for his practice of distributing cigarettes to soldiers. He was loved and respected by the men for his bravery under fire. In 1917 he was awarded the Military Cross at Messines Ridge for going into No Man's Land to provide comfort to those wounded during an attack on the German positions.

German Army belt buckle with the words 'Gott Mit Uns'.

the summer of 1914, the Germany soldier, for his part was sufficiently confident of the Almighty's favour. He was equipped with a slogan carried on his belt buckle that announced millions of times throughout Kaiser Wilhelm's army: *Gott Mit Uns* (God is with us).

Reinforcing conviction of the right of arms were the padres, pastors, and chaplains accompanying, comforting and encouraging the fighting soldier on both sides. Religious worship was carried out behind the battle front as priests celebrated the Mass, heard confession and administered the last Rites. They wrote letters home to next of kin assuring them that their man's sacrifice had not been without purpose in the present 'Christian crusade against a ruthless enemy'. The book *Columbia History of the World* comments on that supportive activity by the various denominations: 'Truth was devalued along with life, and hardly a voice was raised in protest. The guardians of God's word led the martial chorus. Total war came to mean total hatred.' In August 1917, Pope Benedict XV (he had inherited the world-at-war situation having been elected to office 3 September, 1914 when it was well underway) made an appeal for peace to

19

the governments of all the belligerent nations. His overtures were turned down flat by the major powers on both sides. Long gone were the days when religion could exert a force for peace.

We can imagine the depressing effect of the conclusion one nurse arrived at when she considered how, time and again, the military initiatives entered upon by the British Army were ruined: 'Can God be on our side, everyone is asking – when His (alleged!) Department always intervenes in favour of the enemy at all our best moments.' She was referring to the tendancy for the heavens to open and deliver a downpour before every attack launched by the British in the Ypres Salient. As a consequence the Allied soldiers were often bogged down in a morass and cut to pieces by machine-gun and artillery fire. The possibility had to be seriously considered that the diety to whom they appealed for victory favoured neither side.

In the final analysis – that proverbial 'bottom line' – the institutions of monarchs and governments, the churches, supported by big business and applauded by the press, capitalized on the unswerving patriotism and enthusiasm of the masses. National pride was exploited in order to swell the ranks of an army which was to proceed abroad and engage in four years of battles for the sovereignty of the British Empire.

As for the British Tommy, once the initial zeal had disappeared to be replaced by a fatalistic resignation, he carried on a strange day to day existence hoping that the 'Red Tabs' at HQ, and his own officers would somehow manage to bring about an end to the war without killing him or any more of his mates. He came to regard patriotism as a joke and as for the representatives of religion in the battle lines, the padres, they were just sharers with him in the dangers and misery. The individual soldier became resigned to the fact that the representatives of religion appeared to hold no more sway with the mysterious Almighty than any other man.

The story of the spirit of the British Tommy as it underwent a change from the jingoistic optimism of August 1914 to fatalistic stoicism following events of 1 July 1916, is told through the service battalions known as the 'Pals'.

Chapter One

THE BALKAN POWDER KEG AND DECLARATIONS OF WAR

TWO ANCIENT EMPIRES with dominion over numerous Balkan states were in terminal decline. Especially so was the case of the Ottoman Empire which had held sway over south-eastern europe for an incredible six and a half centuries. Traditionally they considered their Christian subjects as second class citizens ('rayas' or beasts) and for centuries had used them merely to work and pay taxes. With the arrival of the twentieth century a more enlightened attitude might have been hoped for by the subjugated peoples. Understandably, a population that had suffered for so long under the Muslim Turkish yoke, seized upon the opportunity to form fully independent states as their masters' once iron grip slackened. On October 1912 the impoverished country of Montenegro declared war on Turkey and was soon seeking aid in its fight from neighbouring Serbia. Greece and Bulgaria joined the fight against the common enemy.

When war broke out, the whole of Macedonia, Albania and Epirus still formed part of the Ottoman Empire. In order to hang on to their territories the Turks were compelled, by the geographical situation, to fight three distinct campaigns simultaneously. The inevitable result of the First Balkan War was that Macedonia and Thrace were freed from Turkish domination. However, after peace was declared, Bulgaria was assailed by her former allies, Greece, Montenegro and Serbia for grabbing the lion's share of the territorial spoils. Yet another conflict, The Second Balkan War, was fought in which Turkey succeeded in recapturing a toe-hold in her old territories, the town of Adrianople in Thrace, which resulted in Bulgaria having to withdraw from her conquered ground. By July 1913 Greece and Serbia were marching on the Bulgarian capitol of Sofia, and when Rumania joined in against Bulgaria, it was soon over.

Meanwhile in the northern territories the ailing Austro-Hungarian Empire had seized the opportunity to annex the formerly Ottoman province of Bosnia-Herzegovina, which it had occupied since 1878. That had brought upwards of a million Orthodox Serbs under the control of the Hapsburg dynasty. As a result of the Balkan Wars Serbia gained the Kosovo region and extended into northern and central Macedonia. Albania was made an independent state under a German prince. Inevitably there were political consequences of the wars. Bulgaria, frustrated in Macedonia, looked to Austria for support, while Serbia, which had been forced by Austria to give up its Albanian conquests, regarded the Hapsburgs with greater hostility

*After the Balkan Wars of 1912 and 1913 the borders of the Balkan states had been drawn.
However, the Hapsburgs had designs on Serbia and sought an opportunity to invade.*

than ever and sought closer ties with Imperial Russia.

Nationalism had produced a volatile mix of states. The Balkans was a powder keg with its numerous small countries and its peoples speaking some fifteen plus languages; added to this were the two rival faiths of Christianity and Islam further dividing men. The bulk of the population of the Balkans professed the Greek Orthodox faith that looked longingly at Constantinople – which they regarded as their sacred city. The stage was set for the most terrible conflict the world had ever experienced, for the increased tensions in the Balkans prepared the ground for the assassination of the Austrian heir-apparent by a seventeen year old Serb student. The spark which ignited the fuse of war occured at the end of June 1914.

Archduke Franz Ferdinand, nephew and heir to the Austro-Hungarian Emperor Franz Josef, and his wife were the victims of a Bosnia-Serb outrage while on a state visit to Sarajevo on 28 June 1914. It was strange that he should have been selected for the revolutionary gesture for he was perhaps the most liberal-minded member of the Hapsburg dynasty, often, it has been said, to his own detriment within court circles.

The Royal couple were to be driven to the Governor's residence and six members of the assassination team dispersed themselves along the route looking for opportunities to commit murder. Within minutes of the motorcade getting under way a bomb was thrown by gang member Cabrinovitch and the Archduke instinctively sought to ward it off. It struck the vehicle and bounced off to explode in the vicinity of the following car where fragments injured two Austrian officers. Immediately the wounded aides were driven to hospital. The Archduke ordered his driver to make for the same place so that he could ascertain the extent of the injuries of his staff. In the

Right: The motorcade prepares to leave for the Governor's residence.

Below: an artist's interpretation of the assassinations taking place.

Below right: a camera captures the action as a conspirator is arrested.

event, the driver took a wrong turn and was reversing slowly when Princip stepped forward, revolver in hand, and fired the fatal shots killing the couple. Within a short while every member the gang of assassins was arrested.

The assassinations called forth a strong a note of protest and a message amounting to an ultimatum from Austria, in which they accused the Serbians of tolerating the machinations of dissident groups ranged against the Austrian-Hungarian monarchy. Although holding itself guiltless, Serbia made wide concessions. However, they could not accede to all ten points listed in the note:

1. *To suppress all publications inciting to hatred of Austria-Hungary and which were directed against her territorial integrity.*

2. *To dissolve forthwith the Narodna Odbrana* ['National Defence' – a propaganda society formed in 1908 to present Serbia's cause to the world]; *and to confiscate all its means of propaganda; to treat similarly all societies engaged in propaganda against Austria-Hungary, and to prevent their revival in some other form.*

3. *To eliminate from the Serbian educational system anything which might foment such propaganda.*

4. *To dismiss all officers or officials guilty of such propaganda, whose names might subsequently communicated by Vienna.*

5. *To accept the 'collaboration in Serbia' of Austria-Hungarian officials in suppressing 'this subversive movement against the monarchy's territorial integrity.*

6. *To open a judicial inquiry into the murders, and to allow delegates of Austria-Hungary to take part in this.*

7. *To arrest without delay Major Tankosic and Milan Ciganovic, implicated by the Sarajevo inquiry.*

8. *To put an effectual stop to Serbian frontier officials sharing in the 'illicit traffic in arms and explosives', and to dismiss certain officials at Sabac and Loznica who had helped the murderers to cross over.*

9. *To give explanations regarding the 'unjustifiable language used by the high Serbian officials after the murder.*

10. *To notify Vienna without delay of the execution of all the above measures.*

Point 6 was a violation of of the Serbian Constitution and their Law of Criminal Procedure and consequently the Serbian government felt unable to comply fully. It did however, agree to the other demands. More than ready to make what reconciliatory moves it could the Serbian government also stressed that it would be prepared to refer the matter to the Hague Court, should the Austro-Hungarian government feel dissatisfied.

The last thing that the government of Serbia wanted was another war, they had just been involved in two and were exhausted. It was generally agreed by the Great Powers that they were unlikely to have done anything so provocative as being a party to murdering the heir to the Hapsburg dynasty – neither instigating it nor desiring it. Even some German diplomats could not see the logic or reason in the Serbian government picking a fight with a more powerful neighbour and saw the reply to the ultimatum as compliance. Not so the Viennese government. A week after the assassination

Franz-Joseph, Emperor of Austria-Hungary, wrote to the Kaiser of Germany:

'According to all the evidence so far brought to light, the Sarajevo affair was not merely the bloody deed of a single individual, but was the result of a well-organized conspiracy, the threads of which can be traced to Belgrade and although it will probably prove impossible to get evidence of the complicity of the Serbian Government, there can be no doubt that its policy, directed towards the unification of all countries under the Serbian flag, is responsible for such crimes, and that a continuation of such a state of affairs constitutes an enduring peril for my house and my possessions.'

As may be judged from the tone of the letter, there was absolutely nothing that the Serbian government could do to placate the Emperor and avoid war. Assurance of support for the Austrian stance came by telegram the following day from German chancellor, Herr von Bethmann-Hollweg who, speaking on behalf of Kaiser Wilhelm, wrote:

Franz-Joseph, Emperor of Austria-Hungary

'His Majesty desires to say that he is not blind to the danger which threatens Austria-Hungary, thus the Triple Alliance as a result of the Russian and Serbian Panslavic agitation. As far as concerns Serbia, His Majesty of course cannot interfere in the dispute now going on between Austria-Hungary and that country, as it is a matter not within his competence. The Emperor Franz-Joseph may, however, rest assured that His Majesty will faithfully stand by Austria-Hungary as is required by the obligations of this alliance and of his ancient friendship.'

Germany would stand by Austria-Hungary in her punitive action against Serbia whatever the consequences. Regarding help and support for Serbia, as it became increasingly obvious that there was no placating the House of Hapsburg, the Tsar of Russia sent a telegram to the prince regent of Serbia on the 24 July:

German chancellor, Herr von Bethmann-Hollweg

'When your Royal Highness applied to me at a time of special stress, you were not mistaken in the sentiments which I entertain for you, or my cordial sympathy with the Serbian people. So long as the slightest hope exists of avoiding bloodshed, all our efforts must be directed to that end; but if in spite of our earnest wish we are not successful, your Highness may rest assured that Russia will in no case disinterest herself in the fate of Serbia.

Russia stated that her forces would be mobilized the moment Austrian troops crossed the Serbian frontier. Immediately, the attitude of Germany stiffened and it became evident that even a partial mobilization of the Russian army would be regarded as a belligerent act.

Nicholas II Czar of Russia

These were grounds for war, not only against Russia but against Russia's ally, France. In vain Russia protested that her partial mobilization was a precautionary undertaking. Secretly, Germany's own preparations for war were well ahead of those of any other European nation, as events would soon prove.

Matters began to move quickly. Four days later, on 28 July at 11 am, Austria-Hungary declared war sending a telegram to that effect to the Serbian town of Nis. They considered it the golden opportunity to settle the matter once and for all – that troublesome hotbed of intrigue and rebellion Serbia would be 'brought to heel'.

The arrival of the declaration that was to launch the biggest slaughter in the history of mankind was remembered by a junior official in the Serbian Ministry of Foreign Affairs, 'I was having lunch in the Hotel Europa in Nis. The dining-hall was crowded with people from Belgrade. Between twelve and one o'clock a postman entered and handed something to Mr Pasic, who was eating about two tables away from me. Pasic read what the postman had handed to him and then stood up. The room fell deadly silent and he announced "Austria has declared war on us. Our cause is just. God will help us!"' An identical telegram was sent from Vienna to the Serbian supreme command.

Doubts about the authenticity of the telegrams arose when at 3 pm Pasic enquired of the German minister only to be told that the German Legation knew nothing about the matter. Immediately Pasic sent cables to the governments in London, Paris and St Petersburg about the strange telegrams asking if it could possibly be true that Austria-Hungary had declared war on Serbia.

Before he got answers to his cables Belgrade authorities informed him that guns were bombarding the Serbian capital. The last hopes that war could be avoided vanished.

True to her word and in support of her Serbian friends, on Friday 31 July, Russia declared war on Austria and the following day Germany retaliated by declaring war on Russia. Because of the German war plan (drawn up by German strategist Count Alfred von Schlieffen) any war with Russia on the eastern frontiers meant an attack, in the first instance, in the west against

The Russian Emperor, Czar Nicholas, received members of the council of the empire and the Duma (Russian parliament) in audience at the Winter Palace, St Petersburg:

'In these days of alarm and anxiety through which Russia is passing, I greet you! Germany, followed by Austria, has declared war on Russia. The enormous enthusiasm, the patriotic sentiments and the love and loyalty to the throne – an enthusiasm that has swept like a hurricane through the country – guarantees for me, as for you, I hope, that Russia will bring to a happy conclusion the war which the Almighty has sent it.

'It is not only the dignity and honour of our country that we are defending, but we are fighting for brother Slavs, co-religionists, blood brothers. I see also with joy the union of the Slavs with Russia progressing strongly and indissolubly.

'I am persuaded that all and each of you will be in your place to assist me to support the test and that all, beginning with myself, will do their duty. Great is the God of the Russian fatherland.'

Germany's traditional enemy, France. The theory was that by the time Russia had effected total mobilization, the enemy on the opposite border would have been annihilated within forty-two days. The national railway system would then transport a major part of the German army eastwards to defeat, in turn, the Russians who would likely have overcome the holding forces and be threatening German territory.

The German plan also called for passage of its main thrusting columns, comprising four armies, through neutral Belgium to get at France. Britain, whose foreign policy had always been to avoid, if at all possible, a super power dominating Europe, particularly the coastline opposite her shores, sought to support Belgium. The German government, on Sunday 2 August, had demanded that Belgium grant its armies free passage or suffer the consequences. At 10 o'clock that night German troops crossed the Belgian frontier from the direction of Aix-la-Chapelle. Simultaneously their forces

entered the independent duchy of Luxemburg en route to the French border. The first shots were fired by the French outposts in the provinces of Alsace and Lorraine. On Monday Albert King of the Belgians telegraphed King George V asking for help:

'Remembering the numerous proofs of Your Majesty's friendship and that of your predecessor, and the friendly attitude of England in 1870 and the proof of friendship you have just given us again, I make a supreme appeal to the diplomatic intervention of Your Majesty's Government to safeguard the integrity of Belgium.'

The British government was officially informed by Belgium on 4 August that German troops had invaded Belgium and that the violation of that country's neutrality had become an accomplished fact.

Albert King of the Belgians.

Immediately, a telegram was sent by British prime minister Mr Asquith to the British ambassador in Berlin, to the following effect:

The King of the Belgians has appealed to His Britannic Majesty's government for diplomatic intervention on behalf of Belgium. The British government is also informed that the German government has delivered to the Belgian government a note proposing friendly neutrality pending a free passage of German troops through Belgium and promising to maintain the independence and integrity of the kingdom and its possessions on the conclusion of peace, threatening in case of refusal to treat Belgium as an enemy.

Sir Edward Grey, the British Foreign Secretary, had requested an answer within twelve hours. The Prime Minister, Mr Asquith, then read a telegram from the German foreign minister, which the German ambassador in London had sent to Sir Edward Grey. The reading was

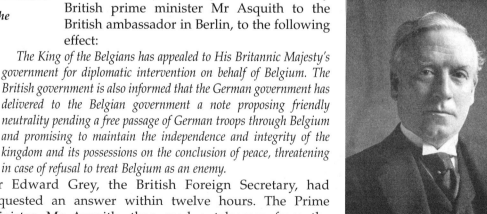

Herbert Henry Asquith, British Prime Minister.

Sir Edward Grey, the British Foreign Secretary

greeted with hoots of laughter in the House of Commons:

Please dispel any distrust that may subsist on the part of the British government with regard to our intentions by repeating most positively the formal assurance that even in case of armed conflict with Belgium, Germany will under no pretensions whatever annex Belgian territory.

Premier Asquith was able to read to the House a telegram from Brussels which informed them that, the German government 'deeply to its regret', would be compelled to carry out by force of arms the measures 'considered indispensible in view of the French menace'.

Excited crowds gathered at Buckingham Palace and in Parliament Square, London, to witness the last seconds of peace ticking away and to greet a popular event. The deadline for Britain's ultimatum to Germany expired at 11 o'clock (midnight in Germany). The striking of that fateful hour by Big Ben was the signal for an almighty, enthusiastic roar. Patriotism, 1914 style, was born. Tuesday 4 August 1914, Britain and Germany were at war.

It had come as no surprise to some. Certainly British Military Intelligence had been predicting an all-out war with Germany since 1907, according to recent research into hitherto unexamined documents originating in the

When it became known on Tuesday afternoon that Britain had issued an ultimatum to Germany and demanded a reply to it before midnight, huge crowds assembled outside Buckingham Palace and continued waiting there until the early hours of the morning. When the news was made known that Britain was on the point of declaring war against Germany 'the enthusiasm of the people knew no bounds, and patriot demonstrations occurred, not only outside Buckingham Palace, but also all over London'.

King George V, the Queen and the Prince of Wales greet the crowd from the balcony of Buckingham Palace.

The Kaiser's address to the people of Berlin from the balcony of his palace in the Unter den Linden:
'A fateful hour has fallen for Germany. Envious people everywhere are compelling us to our just defence. The sword has been forced into our hands. I hope that my efforts in the last hour do succeed in bringing our opponents to see eye to eye with us, and in maintaining peace, we shall with God's help so wield the sword that we shall restore it to its sheath again with honour. War would demand of us enormous sacrifices in property and life, but we should show our enemies what it means to provoke Germany.
'And now I commend you to God. Go to church and kneel before God and pray for His help and for our gallant army.'

Foreign Office and Admiralty. British agents had detected a pro-war faction among the senior offices of the German military who had become convinced that war was essential for the ongoing development and benefit of the German army. That belligerence was aimed mainly at Great Britain and her Empire and was, apparently, fed to the Kaiser as a regular diet of hate. The Kaiser, however, would make his move when he was absolutely convinced of a victory. With the situation in Serbia he felt that the opportunity had arrived. Certainly the masses were ready for it.

There were scenes of patriotic fervour and martial ardor during the first days of August in all the European capitals directly affected by the war. In London, Paris, St Petersburg, Vienna and Berlin enthusiastic crowds filled the streets, singing national anthems and hymns, cheering their respective rulers and national heroes. The 'War of the Ages' had been launched and,

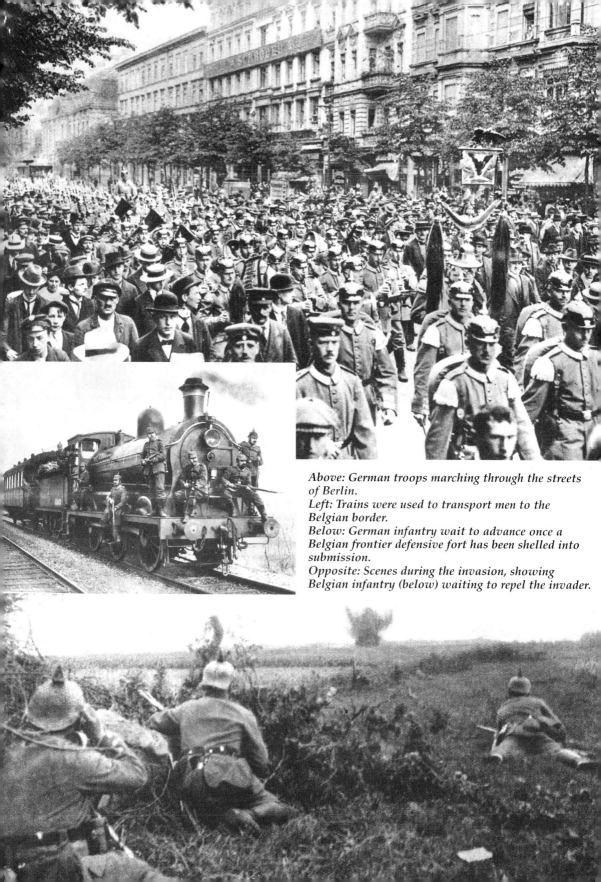

Above: German troops marching through the streets of Berlin.
Left: Trains were used to transport men to the Belgian border.
Below: German infantry wait to advance once a Belgian frontier defensive fort has been shelled into submission.
Opposite: Scenes during the invasion, showing Belgian infantry (below) waiting to repel the invader.

over the coming months, the citizens of those same capitals of Europe would begin to experience heart-rending mourning as husbands, sons and lovers began to fall on the battlefields in such numbers as to surpass all former records of history.

In support of Belgium

In Britain preparations for war had been going on some days prior to the expiration of the deadline. Reservists were called up and the Territorials were brought back from their summer training. Bank Holiday weekend (Bank Holiday Monday was 3 August) was the start date for the annual army camps, however, this time, the unfolding international events were to add excitement and drama to the occasion. No sooner had the trains taken the 'Saturday Night Soldiers' to their seaside locations for their fortnight of military training than they were running them back to their towns and cities. It was no mean feat, the South Midland Division under canvas near Rhyl was estimated to number around 10,000 men. As disgruntled holiday-makers were finding their excursion

Early casualties – blood was beginning to flow.

trains had been cancelled, the territorials were arriving back at their drill halls. As an integral part of the National Mobilization Plan the Territorials were, within days, being transported to pre-planned coastal defence positions.

The first four infantry divisions of the Regular army, comprising two thirds of the British Expeditionary Force, were in France by 12 August shortly to be pushed back by the huge columns of grey-clad invaders. An American correspondent for the *New York World*, Alexander Powell, described the awesome spectacle presented by the invaders:

'It was a sight never to be forgotten. As far as the eye could see stretched solid columns of marching men, pressing westward, ever westward. The army was advancing in three mighty columns along three parallel roads. These dense masses of moving men in their elusive blue-grey uniforms looked for all the world like three monstrous serpents crawling across the countryside.

American flags which fluttered from our windshield

A prophetic anti-war speech

'This will be the greatest war the world has ever seen, and I hope Great Britain will not be drawn into such a crime against civilisation... Why should we be contemplating, at the present moment, a declaration of war to assist France?... The time has come when it should not be in the power of any man or clique of men to say that men should slay each other. It is the people who ought to determine. Don't make any mistake, it is the people who will have to suffer. It is all very well for those who make their money producing armaments – that filthy gang which makes profits by creating jealousies and bad blood between nations. The high prices which will immediately follow will not cause any hardship to the capitalists. The working class have to pay now, and I wonder how long it is going to continue.'

Fred Jowett MP. His speech at a public meeting in Manningham Tide Field, Bradford, 4 August 1914.

BRADFORD PALS, David Raw

proved a passport in themselves and as we approached the closed-locked ranks they parted to let us through.

We passed regiment after regiment, brigade after brigade, of infantry, and after them hussars, Uhlans, cuirassiers, field batteries, more infantry, more field guns, ambulances, then siege guns, each drawn by thirty horses, engineers, telephone corps, pontoon wagons, armoured motor cars, more Uhlans, the sunlight gleaming on their forest of lances, more infantry in spiked helmets, all sweeping by as irresistible as a mighty river, with their faces turned towards France.

Every contingency seems to have been foreseen. Nothing was left to chance or overlooked. Maps of Belgium, with which every soldier is provided, are the finest examples of topography I have ever seen. Every path, every farm building, every clump of trees is shown.

At one place a huge army wagon containing a complete printing press was drawn up beside the road and a morning edition of the Deutsche Krieger Zeitung (German War News) was being printed and distributed to the passing men. It contained accounts of German victories of which I had never heard, but it seemed greatly to cheer the men.

Field kitchens with smoke pouring from their stovepipe funnels rumbled down the lines, serving steaming soup and coffee to the marching men, who held out tin cups and had them filled without once breaking step.

There were wagons filled with army cobblers, sitting cross-legged on the floor, who

Belgians rounded up for execution by the invading Germans. They were deemed to be civilian terrorists who had fired on German troops.

were mending soldiers' shoes just as if they were back in their little shops in the Fatherland. Other wagons, to all appearances ordinary two-wheeled farm carts, hid under their arched canvas covers machine guns which could instantly be brought into action.

The medical corps was as magnificent as it was businesslike. It was as perfectly equipped and as efficient as a great city hospital.

Men on bicycles with a coil of insulated wire slung between them strung a field telephone from tree to tree so the general commanding could converse with any part of the fifty mile long column.

The whole army never sleeps. When half is resting the other half is advancing. The soldiers are treated as if they were valuable machines which must be speeded up to the highest possible efficiency. Therefore they are well fed, well shod, well clothed, and worked as a negro teamster works mules.'

The Germans had expected that Belgium, with its small army would, at most, offer a token resistance. While ineffectual in halting and throwing back the grey hordes surging across their fields and into their towns, they did manage to cause a delay of three valuable weeks. Close to the border were the Belgian towns of Visé and Verviers and they had been the first objectives of attack and Belgian defence. Both were occupied after desperate resistance and the town of Visé was systematically burnt in reprisal, it was claimed, for the firing by civilians on the German invaders.

A vivid description of the march into Belgium and the fighting in front of the fortress-ringed frontier town of Liège was given in a letter by one German officer who was wounded in the battle:

'Our trip towards the Belgian border was a triumphal procession, although it was pouring with rain as we marched through the Ardennes. The towns and villages seemed to us to be deserted. We had no rest and during the night we were fired upon.

On 6 August, at dawn, we reached the Ourthe valley – there were obstacles everywhere. It was an awful march, the roads were frequently blocked by felled trees and rocks, and bridges over rivers had been destroyed. In the afternoon we took up quarters in a village some distance south of Liège.

Seven o' clock in the evening the order was given by the captain to march on Liège. It seemed impossible; we felt that we could go no farther for the forts were thirty-five kilometres away. But, nevertheless, we pressed on.

After thirty minutes the column was fired upon from the surrounding high ground. It was dark and pouring with rain and a thunderstorm was roaring. Then suddenly shots were fired from quite close by and we see some of our men falling. Then we learned that our baggage train, bringing up the rear, had been attacked. Such are the atrocities of the franc-tireurs [guerillas, or civilian snipers]. *The night cleared and and there was bright moonlight. In the distance we could hear the sound of heavy artillery pounding the forts.*

One Company was ordered to turn back to the village that we had just passed through. There, the people were all shot and their houses burned.

Meanwhile we keep marching on, and close to Liège we turned off and took cover behind a wood. Four regiments lay down their knapsacks and 'iron rations' were

The British public were kept up to date on the war through diagrams and maps reproduced in popular magazines. The above appeared in the **The Sphere** *of 22 August 1914.*

consumed. After resting we were then roused and formed up in attack formation. The last exhortations were given.

We charged into a hail of bullets and shells which were being fired in our general direction, but with little accuracy. Along the way we ran past our own artillery with the guns and limbers stuck up to their axles in mud.

Suddenly a hail of bullets came at us from directly ahead. It was our own men who were firing upon us – we had been mistaken for the enemy. Just in time we were identified and the firing ceased. We were then directly in front of the firing line of the forts. There was confusion all around and the password 'Woerth' was given as friend and foe looked alike.'

From the foregoing it is understandable that with hundreds of thousands of soldiers on the march cases of mistaken identity should occur. Today 'Friendly Fire' or 'Blue on Blue' (or, more commonly, 'Home Goal') are terms used to described such incidents. Back in August 1914 wounding and death suffered by the Germans in their advance was attributed to armed civilians, rather than highly nervous and trigger-happy comrades. Similarly, bridges, tunnels and telegraph lines that were blown up had to be the work of civilian saboteurs rather than Belgian military engineers.

Quaffing looted wine in order to quench their thirst during the marches probably contributed to the shooting incidents that were taking place. Again,

Field Marshal Earl Kitchener was appointed Secretary of State for War.

believing such casualties to be the result of the work of Belgian civilians, the German army took reprisals. Time and again the actions of so-called *franc-tireurs* were used as the reason for the bombardment and burning of towns and villages. They were claimed by the Germans to be acts of revenge for hostile acts carried out by non-combatants and intended to prevent their occurrence elsewhere by striking terror into the hearts of the Belgian populace. Whatever the pretext or excuse, the historical fact remains that the result of the German progress toward the Franco-Belgian border constituted a martyrdom for Belgium. It gained the sympathy of the civilized world, put off potential allies to the Central Powers and stiffened Belgian resistance. The German timetable was thrown out enabling the French fully to mobilize and Britain to land its expeditionary force. Consequently, between them, the British and the French forces were able to oppose the German advance on Paris effectively.

It was becoming clear to the discerning leaders in the west that it would take a mighty force to halt and ultimately defeat the powerful war machine that had been fielded by the German High Command. Little wonder that the Kaiser referred to the British Expeditionary Force which numbered in the first weeks a mere 94,000 men, as 'contemptibly little'.

On 5 August the popular hero of Khartoum, Field Marshal Earl Kitchener, was appointed Secretary of State for War. Immediately he began procedures to expand the size of the British Army – he realised that it was going to be a long struggle, despite the popular optimism among the uninitiated who predicted a victory and return to peace by Christmas. In Britain it was estimated that there was potential for bringing 500,000 men to the colours and Kitchener knew that this would have to be achieved if Germany and her allies were to be defeated. A personal appeal in the newspapers for 100,000 men brought a tremendous response. Rather than use the existing Territorial system with its part-time, weekend image replete with purpose-built volunteer drill halls as military centres, Kitchener opted for a new creation, a 'New Army'. New battalions would be based upon and around existing regiments and would exist for three years or the duration of the war. They were to be termed 'Service' battalions that would be disbanded once the need ended and the men would return to their civilian lives. Numbering of the Service battalions would follow on consecutively after the Territorial battalions. The full-time professional 'Regular' battalions usually took the first two numbers, for example: 1st and 2nd Battalions York and

Lancaster Regiment with the 3rd as a reinforcement unit. Four front line Territorial battalions numbered 1/4th (Hallamshire) Sheffield based; and 1/5th Rotherham based . Two further battalions numbered 2/4th and 2/5th were formed after war broke out. Reserve battalions were formed in 1915, 3/4th and 3/5th to provide replacements for battle casualties. Kitchener's New Army men were centred on Pontefract Barracks where volunteers were gathered into six 'Service' battalions numbered 6th, 7th, 8th, 9th, 10th and 11th, approximately 6,000 men. Then came three battalions, two from Barnsley and one from Sheffield. They were numbered '12th' Sheffield, and '13th' and '14th' from Barnsley. These became known as 'Pals' battalions, or in the case of the Sheffield raised men, the 'City' Battalion. The Pals were different in the sense that they were raised and paid for, initially, by the local authorities headed by the mayors of Barnsley and Sheffield and later handed-over as a complete unit to the War Department. In that sense they were different from the other Service battalions in Kitchener's New Army – they 'belonged' to the town. Local interest and pride focused on the 3,000 Pals, eventually to the annoyance of men serving in other battalions of the British Army from the same towns.

Meanwhile, the battles of Mons and Le Cateau had been fought on 23/26 August and it became clear to those who could see through the propaganda reporting of the newspapers that the military situation in Belgium was serious. News that the British Expeditionary Force was being forced back seemed to act as a spur to recruiting and when, on 28 August, Kitchener

The British Army begins arriving in France. A Highland Regiment crosses the Pont Marguet at Boulogne.

called for a further 100,000 men, the daily recruiting figures broke all records. At first the early recruits had come from the unemployed, unskilled and agricultural work force, there still remained the better-educated employed in offices and businesses.

Soldiering, pre-war, held a certain stigma as reflected in the paucity of volunteers for the Territorial Force – they were always under strength. Officers and Non-commissioned officers (NCOs) were forever cajoling and persuading men to join the part-time army, but with little success. All that was to disappear overnight in a wave of war fever. In Barnsley there was no trouble in recruiting men for the local volunteers. The local newspaper carried the headline 'Hundreds of volunteers' and the National Reserve Club was described as being a 'hive of patriotic activity' as reservists rushed back to get into uniform once more.

> C'lerks have been busy for hours daily taking names, and late last night there was no falling off in number of Volunteers. The names of hundreds of men have been taken over and above the numbers required to complete the establishment of the 5th Battalion York and Lancaster Regiment, the 6th West Yorkshire Regiment, the Royal Horse Artillery – Wentworth, and the West Riding Field Ambulance Corps.'

Such was the overwhelming response that the *Barnsley Chronicle* was able to report,

> 'Such a noble response has been made for volunteers to go to the seat of the war that the supply of documents used for this purpose gave out on Wednesday. The recruiting officer and the magistrates of Barnsley have been indunated with applications from willing recruits, and the signing on was temporarily postponed until the arrival of another batch of papers.'

With the ranks of the Territorials swelled to capacity the Barnsley companies of the 5th Battalion (soon to become 1/5th) paraded in town before travelling by train to their Regimental Headquarters at Rotherham where they would join other companies from Wath, Treeton and Rotherham. Civil dignitries gathered on Market Hill and the Mayor, Councillor England, delivered a rousing speech:

> 'Officers, non-commissioned officers and men of the 5th Battalion York and Lancaster Regiment. On behalf of the citizens of this town, and speaking with the full sense of responsibilities which rests upon me, on this momentous occasion, I have come to wish you God speed on the mission you have undertaken.

> 'The cloud which had for forty years been gathering over our heads has suddenly burst and we as a nation are compelled to go into a war that has been forced upon us by the mad caprice of the German Emperor.

> 'The marvellous manner in which the mobilization of the forces has been accomplished, must have been an object lesson to the nations around us, for never in the history of our nation have our naval and military forces been ready at such short notice.

> 'The call has been made and it has instantly and willingly been obeyed. For some years you have played your part as citizens, but now at short notice you are soldiers of the King. See to it that you acquit yourselves like men.

> 'And to quote The Times of the other day, "in this hour of national trial go into it

Thursday 6 August 1914. In front of the Old Corn Exchange on Market Hill, Barnsley's dignitaries turn out to give the 'Terriers' of the 5th Battalion a civic send-off. 'Three cheers!' Mayor, Councillor William Goodworth England, exhorts the men to do their duty and wishing them 'God speed' on their mission, Reverend Richard Huggard placed God's stamp of approval on the proceedings. To the clergyman's right is Joseph Hewitt, who would become the commanding officer of the First Barnsley Pals battalion.

Lieutenant Colonel Fox and more than 200 men of the two Barnsley companies listen to the speeches before marching to Barnsley station for the 3.30 pm Midland train to Rotherham and the Territorial HQ of the York and Lancaster Regiment.

united, calm, resolute, trusting in God" – that is the mood in which our forefathers fought – with the firm hope that in a just and righteous cause, the only Giver of all victory will bless our army.

On behalf of our towns men I sincerely wish you God speed, and a safe and speedy return to your native town.'

The Barnsley Terriers were just one unit among thousands of similiar khaki clad soldiers swelling the transport systems of this country.

Chapter Two

RAISING, EQUIPPING AND TRAINING THE PALS

THE MACHINERY of the peace time recruiting office was not designed to pass thousands of men a day through its system . In one day in August the system processed what it normally would have done in an entire year. In recognition of the problem the Government established offices, not only in the principal centres of all the large towns in England, but in the suburbs and in the villages and small market towns. The numbers of men clamouring for enlistment in the forces were so great that it became almost impossible to cope. There were all the medical examinations to be carried out, the swearing in, organising and billeting of the masses of recruits. As for cladding them in khaki uniforms and webbing and arming them with rifles, that seemed a long way down the line. Improvisation was the order of the day in all the large cities and

Scene in Throgmorton Street at the outbreak of war. London Stock Exchange ceased trading and stockbrokers became unemployed. Sir Henry Rawlinson suggested forming a battalion exclusively for office workers. The idea of 'Pals' serving together was born.

towns from London to the industrialised centres of the Midlands and the north of England, and on to Scotland.

Incredibly, Britain was seeking to acquire an army numbering one million. Within days of the announcement from Parliament that the British Army was to be so enlarged, there appeared on every public form of transport in London, followed by the rest of the country, posters appealing for even more volunteers. That appeal hit the eye at every turn, so that it became impossible to avoid it: in newspapers, flashed on the cinema screens, printed on tram tickets, pasted on the windows of private houses; it was preached from the pulpits, there was no escaping it – 'Your King and Country Need You', with the words left unsaid, 'so what are you going to do about it?' Some newspapers not only echoed the national appeal but added their own voice to the call for men, even adding monetary incentives: the *Daily Sketch* of 29 August 1914 carried the editorial statement:

> *We think that every able-bodied man between the ages of 20 and 30 should enlist. We are prepared to give to any of our employees who do so a minimum of four weeks' full wages from the date of his leaving his work.*
>
> *Married men will, at the end of four weeks, receive half-pay during the whole time they are on duty; single men who have relations dependent on them will have special arrangements made for them.*
>
> *All who enlist will be given, after the war, three weeks' holiday on full pay, providing that two weeks are spent in camp.*
>
> *All men will be re-engaged when the war is over.*

This was an extremely generous gesture and a powerful incentive. Most likely propounded by the proprietors, Messers. E Hulton and Co. Ltd,

Whitehall Recruiting Depot besieged by hundreds of eager young men responding to Lord Kitchener's appeal.

unreservedly in the euphoric atmosphere of the times. The mention of three weeks holiday on full pay 'providing that two weeks are spent in camp' is probably a reference to post war reservist service in the Territorial Force. Obviously, the incentives were made on the assumption that the war would be over in approximately four months. The same edition carried the suggestion that entire football teams should enlist: 'If our footballers enlisted tens of thousands of their admirers would follow.'

If Waterloo was won on the playing fields of Eton, could not Germany be defeated on the football fields of England? It is pointed out that if the 7,000 trained athletes were to enlist and charge the Germans instead, they would be heroes of the day. And most important of all tens of thousands of football enthusiasts would follow their example.

It is also suggested that football grounds should be turned into drilling grounds and recruiting centres. The Council of the Football Association are to consider the idea on Monday.

The battalions, if formed, will be known as the Footballers' Battalions. Names of football clubs might be immortalised as regiments.

The result of whole scale enlistment was that businesses were suddenly denuded of managers, clerks, skilled workers and other key employees. Then the more patriotic employer offered compensation to the families of those who enlisted convinced, no doubt, that the critical situation was short-term. It has to be said that the women of the nation made it all possible by their whole-hearted support and belligerent urging of the young men:

They should be compelled to take up arms in our defence. It is far better and easier to grieve over an honest lost one than it is to find our breath quicken, our teeth clench, and our face blush with shame for anyone dear to us. If it comes to the point that all men are forced to go to war and scarce any are left, as in plucky Belgium, then I am willing to drill and fight than harm shall come to older women or children than myself. My own children I would willingly leave in God's care. I would sooner do this than let them be undefended.

...Perhaps the young people do not realise to the full their responsibility to their country.

Those passionate words, which appeared in the press, of a young housewife named Rose Green Barry, serves as a typical example of feminine support being generated in 1914. This nationalistic fervour was not an isolated case as women throughout Europe sent their men to war without flinching.

After taking the oath and the King's Shilling the new recruit was marched off, after a fashion, with fifty or sixty other men to the railway station where a train would take him to a regimental depot. Those who had no

Signing up for three years military service or the duration of the war.

preference for any particular regiment were assigned by the recruiting office where he had enlisted. Crowded trains left Waterloo station regularly for the great army camps of Aldershot, Devizes, Salisbury Plain, Winchester and the great artillery camps at Okehampton. In so many instances the new recruit would find, upon arriving at the depot, that there was no place for him to lay his head. A discouraging experience for the young patriot fired with a zeal to serve his country. Usually two blankets were issued to him with the instruction to find himself somewhere to curl up for the night. As it happened, the late summer nights of 1914 were warm and sleeping under the stars proved little hardship, even for the ones experiencing outdoor life for the first time. There was far worse to come in the experience of sleeping under the stars in the months ahead.

Tent towns began to spring up in the open fields under the watchful eye of batches of 'dug-out' NCOs. Later in the month lorries would arrive loaded with timber and the familiar army huts were constructed often by the men themselves. The sprinkling of officers in the new battalions that were springing up were keeping a sharp lookout for any man showing initiative, and promotions to the rank of lance corporal and corporal were numerous and quick in coming.

Meanwhile, all around London, open spaces including parks, school playgrounds and even churchyards, became filled with young men being drilled to the scream and bark of instructors. Dressed in their civilian clothes, often in shirt sleeves, the young men formed up and wheeled about, advanced and retired, formed two ranks then four. All this with heads erect, shoulders back and with serious determined faces, as they concentrated on the unfamiliar manouevres required for those who were members of the British Army. Here, perhaps for the very first time on this scale, was the mingling of the social classes. Men who had grown up in the big landowner's house cared for by a nanny, found himself sleeping and eating alongside the son of a servant or a field labourer.

'Repeat after me: "I swear, to serve His Majesty the King... His heirs and successors... And the generals and officers set over me... So help me God".' Swearing on the Bible ceremony.

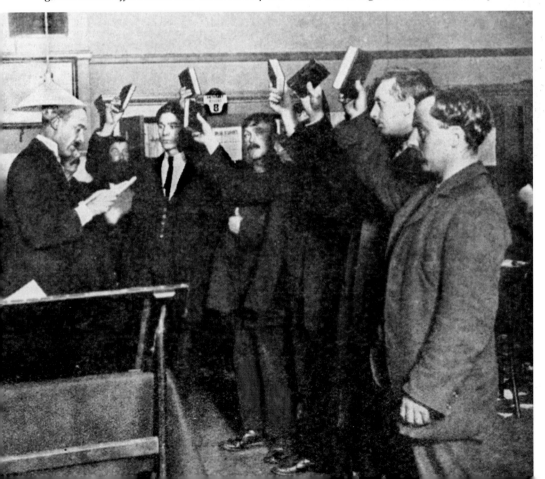

All the increase that was taking place, as Kitchener's New Army blossomed, was made possible because of the organisation that was in place during peacetime. The United Kingdom and Ireland were divided into 'commands' that could cope with a sudden influx of men.

London (district) Command included the County of London and Windsor.

Aldershot Command included part of Hampshire and Brooklands in Surrey where the Royal Flying Corps was stationed.

Eastern Command had Northamptonshire, Cambridgeshire, Norfolk, Suffolk, Essex, Huntingdonshire, Bedfordshire, Hertfordshire, Middlesex, Kent, Surrey, Sussex and Woolwich.

Northern Command took in Northumberland, Durham, Yorkshire, Lincolnshire, Nottinghamshire, Derbyshire, Staffordshire, Leicestershire and Rutland.

Southern Command consisted of Warwickshire, Worcestershire, Gloucestershire, Oxfordshire, Buckinghamshire, Berkshire, Cornwall, Devonshire, Somersetshire, Dorsetshire, Wiltshire and Hampshire.

Western Command took in Wales and the counties of Cheshire, Shropshire, Herefordshire, Monmouthshire, Lancashire, Cumberland, Westmoreland and the Isle of Man.

Then there were Scottish and Irish Commands.

With the advent of the twentieth century, within each command, there were the regimental depots – in Britain and Ireland sixty-eight of them. Recruiting for the Regular Army was centred on those regimental depots. Within that system was the amazing mechanism to enable the creation of six new volunteer armies in a matter of months.

Officers
At the beginning of the war, with the rapid expansion taking place, two thousand officers were called for, and around 20,000 applied to fill the places. That demand would grow until 50,000 new officers were absorbed into the Army. That number would continue to increase to double that figure as casualties called for replacement officers – always subalterns. Whilst the war was in progress several systems of officer training were running at the same time. First was, of course, the regular system that was in operation at Sandhurst and Woolwich where applicants continued to be processed in the well tried way, almost as if there was no emergency. The second system which rapidly filled the officer ranks was through the public schools, grammar schools and universities where the Officers' Training Corps arrangement was in operation. In 1914 and 1915 every effort was made to preserve the gentleman officer distinction and recruits to officer ranks were drawn from the 'correct' social stratum. 'What school did you attend?' was the standard question.

The OTCs provided the basic training that every private infantryman in the British Army underwent, including the use of the standard issue rifle. In addition there were lectures on command and tactical movement of men in the field, which invariably included consideration of the standard work *The Defence of Duffer's Drift* by the then Captain Swinton DSO, RE. However, the text book was based on fighting the Boers in South Africa, hardly a preparation for the fighting then taking place across the Channel.

Then there was the matter of adopting correct and proper aloofness from the men. Woe betide the officer who had it in mind to change the established and accepted ways. In 1915 the novelist Edgar Wallace reported on a lecture for new officers that he attended:

I want you to understand that if you go into the Army with the idea of introducing some new method or some new system for improving its character, you are going to have a very unpleasant time. If you go to work ostentatiously to gain the confidence of your men, you will merely arouse their suspicion or their contempt. British soldiers do not want mothering, they want leading; and to be led properly they must have complete confidence in their leader.

All soldiers have grievances: it is their legitimate possession. And if you wander round looking for grievances you will find six in every tent, providing that there are six people sleeping there. The more people sleeping in the tent the more grievances you will find. It is, in effect, an Army saying that to 'grouse' is the soldier's privilege.

Furthermore, you must be careful in dealing with a non-commissioned officer. Remember that he knows a great deal more about soldiering than you do,

The Inns of Court Officers' Training Corps, in training at Lincoln's Inn and Berkhamstead. By early 1915 this training corps was producing forty officers a week. Top left would-be officers are taught how to perform the slow march. Resting between drill; being instructed in musketry; and bayonet fighting.

or will do, for a very long time. He will salute you and pay you every mark of respect, but for quite a while his mental attitude towards you will be one of derision and pity. A bit of advice: should you catch a non-commissioned officer out in any slip – then keep it to yourself. For should you give in to the joyous impulse to correct the NCO in front of his men, then rest assured, at some future occasion he will correct you by inference. This is because, for every mistake he makes, you will make twenty. Do not be familiar with the non-commissioned officer in an attempt to gain his approval, because the result will be the reverse to what you desire.

Remember, that it is your business to maintain the discipline of the regiment, and the best disciplined regiments are invariably the best fighting regiments. You have to set your mind on arriving in the trenches so firmly established in their esteem and regard, that if you were suddenly reduced to the ranks and the men were called upon to elect their officers, you would be among those elected. soldiers do not want you for your geniality, and they will not prize you for your graciousness. They recognise that it is your business to lead, and to show then the way in and the way out whenever circumstances call upon you for the exercise of your judgement. If you fail them in their hour of need, or show weakness at a moment when strength is required of you, you are finished and done with.

Also remember this, that the soldier's highest term of praise is: "Mr So-and-so is a gentleman" and let that always be on your mind in all situations whether travelling or on leave and you meet soldiers in the street. When a soldier salutes you, will you please remember that he is not saluting Mr Johnson or Mr Brown, nor is he saluting the well-cut uniform that you wear, but he is saluting the King's commission which, in theory, is neatly folded up in your breast-pocket. The salute to the officer is a salute to the King, and if you fail to acknowledge that salute, or take it as being directed at yourself, then you are acting carelessly towards the King whose commission you carry.

The officer delivering the words of wisdom to the new intake went on to discuss their behaviour under fire: that although they would be expected to conduct themselves bravely, they were not to risk their lives unnecessarily, that the government had gone to great trouble and expense that they might carry out certain duties, vain heroics were to be dismissed from their minds. The speaker concluded with the words of a French general of the Napoleonic war who, when referring to a fellow officer who had lost his life in a particularly foolish expedition, declared that the officer had 'deserted to Heaven'. He then added that he wanted them all to keep that accusation in their minds.

As a direct result of Kitchener's recruiting campaign far too many men who were deemed of being potential officer material were ending up as private soldiers. Public School battalions were denuded as their 'other ranks' were 'gazetted' (their names announcing their commission appearing in the *London Gazette*).

It was not just the Public Schools that lost men in this way: the 14th Royal Warwickshire Regiment (1st Birmingham Battalion [Pals]), by the end of 1915 had given up 302 men; well over 400 men of the Leeds Pals (15th West Yorkshire Regiment) were commissioned and reassigned prior to the battalion sailing for Egypt. The near despair of the colonels commanding the battalions can only be imagined as they suffered the loss of their very best members of the rank-and-file.

The Pals phenomenon

In the Liverpool newspapers on 27 August 1914, there appeared an article by the Rt. Hon. The Earl of Derby in which he suggested that businessmen who were interested in serving their country might wish to join a battalion of comrades. A meeting was advertised for the following evening to be held at the Territorial drill hall of the 5th Battalion The King's (Liverpool Regiment). He personally wrote to the proprietors of

The Rt. Hon. The Earl of Derby.

the large businesses in and around Liverpool explaining the national situation and suggesting that they encourage those among their work force, so inclined, to enlist immediately.

He, like so many others, believed, that the war with Germany would be over in a matter of months and that the men would be able to return to their previous employment after a brief military sabbatical.

In *Liverpool Pals* Graham Maddocks describes for us that historic meeting which took place on a warm August Sunday evening:

> Long before 7.30, on the evening of August 28th, St Annes's Street was crowded with eager young men trying to get into the drill hall. Those inside found that the hall was packed to capacity, and men were standing in the aisles, the doorways and even the stairs. So great was the crush, that another room below also had to be opened to take all those who wanted to enlist. When Lord Derby arrived and stepped onto the platform to address the multitude, his welcome was tumultuous, and this was only matched by the cheering and throwing of hats in the air which accompanied the news that Derby's brother Ferdinand was to command the new battalion when it was formed. It was obvious to Lord Derby even then, that there were more than enough men present to form one battalion.

In his speech Lord Derby said that he would be sending Lord Kitchener that very night a telegram to say that, not one but two battalions had been formed. 'We have got to see this through to the bitter end and dictate our terms of peace in Berlin, if it takes every man and every penny in this country.' It was during that stirring speech that he referred to 'Pals', battalions comprising around 1,000 men, where friends from the same office would fight shoulder to shoulder. In his emotional conclusion Lord Derby went on to say to the packed crowd:

'I thank you for from the bottom of my heart for coming here tonight and showing what is the spirit of Liverpool, a spirit that ought to spread through every city and every town in the kingdom. You have set a noble example in thus coming forward. You are certain to give a noble example on the field of battle.'

The example had indeed been set and idea of Pals took off swelling further the Kitchener New Army ranks.

The following morning massive queues of men formed up outside St George's Hall. In acknowledgement, and anticipation of the whole Pals concept, and in response to Lord Derby's direct appeal to businesses and organisations, separate tables had been placed for each of the main areas of commerce in the city. Thus, for example, office employees of the shipping lines, Cunard and White Star, could be sure of staying together as the battalions were formed. There were tables for men working at the Corn Trade Association, General Brokers, Cotton Association, The Seed Oil and Cake Trade Association, Fruit and Wool Brokers, The Law Society and Chartered Accountants and Bank and Insurance Offices. The Stock Exchange employees actually formed up in ranks of four and were marched to be attested.

Once inside St George's Hall each man gave his personal details to one of the clerks at the tables. Then small

Lord Derby's direct appeal to businessmen proved to be an overwhelming success. Dale Street, Liverpool, 31 August 1914, men waiting their turn to enlist at St George's Hall.
GRAHAM MADDOCKS

groups of men moved to another table where magistrates swore them in, each man holding up a copy of the Bible. From there they lined up outside nearby rooms where medical examinations were carried out.

All the activity was overseen by Lord Derby himself and he noted the numbers of men who had been recruited and, with the medical examinations taking up the time, when the number reached 1,050 men he halted the proceedings. He had his first battalion made up of groups of friends, chums or pals. Those waiting outside were told to return in two days' time. By the following Monday, in just over a week, over 3,000 men had been recruited, sufficient for three battalions. It was remarkable in that men had already been taken into other Service battalions, as well as the Royal Navy and Mercantile Marine. A fourth Liverpool Pals battalion was formed within eight weeks with sufficient men for two reserve battalions. The six battalions were in the King's (Liverpool Regiment) and were numbered 17th, 18th, 19th, 20th, 21st and 22nd. The first four became front-line battalions and the last two never went abroad and were used as feeder and training units for the others. (Four battalions went to make up a brigade; three brigades, a division and two to four divisions, depending on circumstances, were grouped into an Army Corps.)

Middle-class and professional class volunteers

News of the recruiting success at Liverpool was reported in the national and regional newspapers. That in turn prompted 'letters to the editor' and editorial features clamouring for similar formations to be raised in their own city or town. For example the *Birmingham Daily Post* of 28 August 1914, ran the following editorial:

> Roughly...it may be fair to estimate that Birmingham has already contributed some 25,000 men to the defence of the national honour. Even if it be assumed, which it cannot, that all these are under thirty there would still remain 115,000 men eligible by age to join the colours. Of these, probably rather less than half, at least 50,000 are unmarried.

> What are these 50,000 men, nearly all without dependents, doing that they have not presented themselves for the service of their country? Have they realised that upon them rests the first responsibility; that whatever may be said of the duty of our married manhood there can be no question that patriotism insists that the unmarried shall offer themselves without thought or hesitation?

> Something might be done if the authorities would facilitate the raising of a battalion of non-manual workers. Splendid material is available, and we do not doubt that such a battalion, if associated some way with the name of the city, would fill rapidly. We think the suggestion, which has reached us from more than one quarter, is well worth consideration by the War Office.

Coat of Arms of Lord Derby became the cap badge of the Liverpool Pals. They were numbered to the King's (Liverpool Regiment).

Birmingham's non-manual workers in the city's commercial district were a-buzz with the possibility that a special battalion, just for them, might be raised. The Deputy Lord Mayor, prompted by the public response to the idea, sought advice from Birmingham's most senior Territorial officers as to how it could best be achieved. Later, in a press interview, he explained

Birmingham Municipal Technical School – the centre for recruiting in 1914.
TERRY CARTER

that the middle-class men, obviously of officer material, were too numerous for the relatively limited number of commissions available in the Army. It was his considered opinion that this fact was causing them to hold back from joining the colours. However, he went on to explain that should a battalion be formed where men could serve together as private soldiers in companies, among those of their own class, then there would be an immediate response.

One of the senior Territorial officers, Lieutenant-Colonel Ludlow, agreed with the Deputy Lord Mayor that, 'the class from which the men should be drawn would include school teachers, clerks, articled pupils, shop assistants, warehousemen, farmers, corporation officials and others'. He added that each profession and trade would find its own special quota, and that Birmingham University and Old Boys could also serve together in the same company within such a special battalion.

It had become noticeable that the middle-class men were not coming forward and one stinging letter was published in the *Birmingham Daily*

Mail that summed the situation up:

> To anyone who has seen the recruiting parades through the city during the last few days the question, "do we deserve to win?" surely has occurred. The recruits with one or two exceptions, have been composed entirely of the so-called working classes, while the streets have been lined with young fellows wearing good clothes, looking superciliously on. Will these 'knuts' never realise that for the men whom they refuse to mix with, they would have to learn to shout "Hoch! Hoch!" and the flappers and the barmaids, whom their life's work seems to be to fascinate, will be treated as the Belgian women have been treated by the Germans.

Birmingham City battalions wore the Royal Warwickshire badge with an extra scroll identifying each of the three battalions.

There would have been a natural reluctance by some to mix with men of a different and lower social class – it was all a matter of upbringing and status. But another letter which appeared in the press from a member of that middle-class suggested that it was a barrier that could be overcome:

> ...In this most serious period of our nation's history, snobbishness is quite out of all our minds. We young men feel that we ought to be "up and doing," each his level best in defence of our great Empire. At the same time there are those of us who would more gladly join such a company as this than any other at present in existence.

Terry Carter, author of *Birmingham Pals*, informs us that the writer of the above, Harry Gibbons, did within the following weeks become a private in the Second Birmingham Battalion. Two years later he was killed during an attack on a German position.

Following the phenomenal success at Liverpool, two students at Sheffield University approached the University Vice-Chancellor, Mr H A L Fisher, with a suggestion for a Sheffield University battalion. Fisher readily supported the idea and at the conclusion of one of his war lectures held at the Victoria Hall, Sheffield on 1 September, 1914, he announced that a special committee had secured permission from the War Office to raise a Service Battalion which would be numbered to the York and Lancaster Regiment. It would be called 'The Sheffield University and City Special Battalion' (later to become simply the 'City Battalion'). Volunteers were sought from the professional classes, especially those from the university, ex-public school men, lawyers, clerks and journalists. Among them were those men who had tried to obtain commissions, but had not been successful. An advert in the *Sheffield Daily Telegraph* for recruits to the 'Sheffield University and City Special Battalion' announced to would-be volunteers: 'Intended primarily for Professional and Business Men and their Office Staffs'. It stopped short of carrying the words 'others need not apply'. In the event there were some notable exceptions when, somehow or other, some railway workers and miners, mainly from the nearby town of

Penistone, ended up being accepted into the Sheffield City Battalion.

The City of Leeds, likewise, was roused to form a Pals battalion from its middle-class. In the *Yorkshire Observer* on 31 August 1914, a correspondent wrote a letter to the editor:

> *Sir, is there no influential citizen of Leeds who will come forward and call a meeting re the Earl of Derby's scheme for a battalion of 'pals' for this district? The amazing success of the Liverpool meeting is most gratifying, and there must be a great number of young men to whom the scheme appeals. Surely the sooner the matter is put on a definite footing the more use the battalion will be.*

The *Yorkshire Evening Post*, in an editorial of the same day, reported on the raising of the Liverpool Pals and suggested a similar 'Friends Battalion' for Leeds, 'perhaps composed of the vast and as yet, untapped recruiting ground of the middle class population engaged in commercial pursuits'. The matter was already in hand. Lieutenant-Colonel J Walter Stead, a Leeds solicitor and former commanding officer of the 7th Battalion (Leeds Rifles), The Prince of Wales's Own (West Yorkshire Regiment), TF, had already set the raising of a Pals battalion in motion. A recruiting poster invited, 'Businessmen show your patriotism' and they were reminded that 'your country needs you, her peril is great'. Banners appeared spanning the streets and appealing to the middle-classes with the words 'Businessmen of Leeds. Your King and Country Need You. Join the Leeds City Battalion'.

The committee of prominent dignitaries formed to administer the raising of the 'Leeds City Battalion' included leading clergymen, The Vicar of Leeds, Dr Bickersteth; The Bishop of Leeds, Dr Cowgill and President of the Leeds Free Church Council, the Rev. John Anderson.

Lieutenant Colonel J Walter Stead. Leeds solicitor and former commanding officer of the 7th Battalion (Leeds Rifles), The Prince of Wales's Own (West Yorkshire Regiment), TF, set the raising of a Pals battalion in the city of Leeds in motion.
LAURIE MILNER

In Manchester the appeal to the middle class was also unashamedly direct. At a meeting of the Manchester Home Trade Association held on Monday 24 August 1914 it was agreed that recruiting should be directed towards the clerks and warehousemen employed in the numerous commercial businesses in the city. The new War Service battalion would be known as the Manchester Clerks' and Warehousemen's Battalion. An organising committee was formed and a fund set up to finance the provision of uniforms and equipment. The dignatries and businessmen present pledged a sum of £15,000. A telegram was immediately sent to the War Office offering to raise and finance a battalion of local men at the expense of the city.

Within three days the Manchester battalion received official blessing:

Your telegram just received. Hope you will be able to raise a battalion in Manchester and thus give your signal help to the armed forces of the Crown. Any man joining the battalion will be doing a patriotic deed, and I shall hope to welcome them in the army, where their comrades await them. Will give you every assistance.

Let me know how you succeed. Kitchener.

Leeds Coat of Arms was used as the cap badge for the Leeds Pals. They were numbered to the West Yorkshire Regiment. Bradford Pals wore the cap badge to the West Yorkshire Regiment.

As soon as the news became public through the pages of the *Manchester Guardian* men flocked to the designated recruiting office at the Artillery HQ in the city. In order to identify genuine clerks and warehouse men, and so ensure their being given first place, enlistment tickets were issued through the relevant firms. The response was so overwhelming that the personnel at the Drill Hall, including the two doctors carrying out the medical examinations, were unable to cope.

The forming of Pals battalions was deemed to be the answer to a problem that was being recognised everywhere. Nationally, recruiting was going well but in Hull, as in Leeds, Sheffield, Birmingham, Bradford and other cities, it was not as good as the authorities had hoped. Letters to the local papers suggested solutions. One correspondent, who went under the pseudonym 'Middle Class', wrote to the *Hull Daily Mail* that many men were not joining the colours because they did not like the idea of having to herd with all types of men now being enlisted,

Instead of some of the larger employers of labour in Hull giving big donations of money they should use their influence to organise Corps of the middle class young men – clerks, tailors, drapers' assistants, grocers' assistants, warehousemen and artisans. Then we should see men living, sleeping and training in company of others of their own class.

The Lord Lieutenant of the East Riding of Yorkshire, Lord Nunburnholme, met with Lord Kitchener and it was agreed that Hull would raise a battalion for the East Yorkshire Regiment called the 'Commercial Battalion' or, officially, the 7th (Hull) Battalion. In its editorial of 2 September the *Hull Daily Mail* commented:

Today has seen the commencement of the recruiting for the middle-class, clerks, and professional men, or the "Black-coated Battalion". It must not be thought there is a desire for class distinction but just as the docker will feel more at home amongst his everyday mates, so the wielder of the pen and drawing pencil will be better as friends together.

Hull Pals wore the cap badge of the East Yorkshire Regiment.

In the first day of recruiting for the 'Commercial' battalion 695 men were attested. Within a week the battalion was at full complement. The idea was working and a further battalion was got under way designated 'Tradesmen' and in three days had reached full strength. Following the Second Hull Battalion came the 'Sportsmen' battalion and by October it too had reached over a thousand. And still they came. Lord Kitchener gave permission to raise a fourth. The Fourth Hull Battalion was known as "T'Others' because it took any fit man regardless of their class or trade.

Because of the way in which the Hull battalions had been recruited there were bound to be incidents – or accusations – of snobbery. One private soldier in the 'Tradesmen' battalion commented at the time that the men in the Second, Third, and Fourth battalions felt that the First Battalion 'Commercials' considered themselves a cut above the others. It was referred to as a 'nobs' battalion. 'The Commercials used to snob you a bit, they was all clerks and teachers.'

Lower working class

In the mining town of Barnsley, news of the raising of Pals battalions in Liverpool prompted civic leaders to attempt something similar. The usual procedure was followed: a telegram to Lord Kitchener offering to raise a battalion of 1,000 plus men. The formal reply from the War Office served as the impetus to 'get the ball rolling'. In Barnsley's case they did not wait for official blessing but surged ahead without waiting for a reply. The first public meeting took place at the Staincross Picture Palace on 1 September 1914. A crowd packed into the building to hear the three principal speakers: Mayor, Councillor England; Mr Joseph Hewitt, local solicitor; and J W F Peckett, county councillor. The mayor reminded the audience, made up mainly of miners from the local collieries:

> In an eight or nine hours journey they could meet the most formidable foe of modern times. They should look to their laurels to try and preserve the integrity of the Empire they so loved.

Peckett evoked a cheered acknowledgement in his stirring speech:

> I am convinced that it is the duty of every Englishman to do his individual part in the life and death struggle. The Government has asked for 500,000 men. In this country there are nine million men between the ages of twenty-five and forty-five, and the portion asked for was only 50 in every 1,000. Would they give them?

A roar of 'Yes' went up from the audience.

In Little Houghton, another pit village in the Barnsley coal field, men completing the day shift flocked to the recreation ground to hear their

This poster appeals to patriotism and those men who would seek glory.

local branch representative of the Yorkshire Miners' Association address them:

> I put my weight behind Lord Kitchener's recruiting drive and I hope that miners will respond to the call. Colonel Hewitt has just told me that if at Houghton we get a company's strength, or two companies, that our men will be kept together. He assures me that just as you have worked together in the pit, you will be able to work together as soldiers.

After singing the National Anthem the men surged to the colliery offices and upwards of 200 handed in their names. The following morning they were taken by motor coaches to the outskirts of Barnsley. There, they were formed up into four ranks and marched, as best they could, to the Public Hall in town to join other volunteers already gathered there. Along the way they sang with great gusto 'It's a Long Way to Tipperary'. They were of course in their best civilian suits – mostly navy blue serge – and just about every man wore the popular style head gear of the day, a large floppy flat cap, consequently uniformity of a type was achieved.

The York and Lancaster Regimental badge was worn by men of the Sheffield City Battalion and the Barnsley Pals.

Meanwhile, over the Pennines, desperate circumstances added impetus to the recruiting drive. In the summer of 1914 East Lancashire suffered a recession in the cotton industry. In the town of Accrington one of the largest employers, Howard and Bulloughs, was still closed after a dispute which had lasted ten weeks. Even the war, with its insatiable demand for raw materials, had not brought about a settlement. This company alone had employed 4,500 men and their families. They were having to exist on lockout pay of £1 a week, or in some instances, ten shillings. In total more than 7,000 cotton workers were unemployed or working part time in the town of Accrington. Six hundred families were on relief and each day 700 children received a hot meal at Accrington Town Hall under the 1906 Necessitous Children's (Provision of Meals) Act.

In that situation poverty was added to that of patriotism, providing a powerful incentive to join the colours. For a man to be a soldier in the company of his friends and to be paid £1. 1s. a week (this included billeting allowance) to stay at home with his family, proved irresistible. Everyone was saying that the war would be over by Christmas and joining the Accrington battalion was for just as long as the war lasted. It all seemed too good to miss – a temporary respite from poverty with a paid adventure thrown in.

The procedure at the attestation centres at Willow Street Sunday School and Cannon Street Baptist Church Sunday School, Accrington, followed the same system in operation in countless other centres throughout the country. First, each man (in some cases, a boy as young as fifteen or sixteen) was given a brief medical examination which included him being weighed and his height measured. A doctor checked his heart and lungs and took his chest measurements. Eyesight was tested, teeth were examined and a 'once-over' made for varicose veins, signs of rickets and other infirmities. Details were entered on the individual's attestation form and it was signed by the doctor. Next was the swearing-in ceremony where half a dozen at a time were dealt with. Each recruit was given a New Testament to hold up and he was told to repeat loudly, line by line after the officer, the oath in the following manner:

> *I swear,*
> *To serve His Majesty the King*
> *His heirs and successors*
> *And the generals and officers set over me*
> *So help me God.*

In some instances the officer swearing them in would instruct the recruits to kiss the Bible. That was done at Accrington and from the attestation centres the new recruits were ordered to proceed immediately to the Town Hall to collect their first day's service pay of

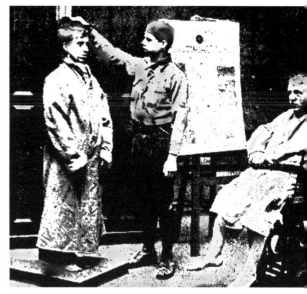

Recruits in Burnley undergoing the army medical. One man's height is being checked by a Boy Scout acting as a medical orderly.
WILLIAM TURNER

one shilling and nine pence – all in pennies. The following day they were ordered to turn up at the Territorial Drill Hall to learn the rudiments of military drill. All, of course, without a single item of equipment; no uniforms, army boots or the main arm of the British infantryman, the Lee-Enfield rifle. All these necessary soldierly things would appear in dribs and drabs over the coming months.

The Accrington Pals wore the badge of the Ea Lancashire Regiment.

With Manchester shortly to raise its fourth Pals battalion, in the adjacent district of Salford, men tired of waiting for a battalion where they could serve together with their friends were beginning to drift towards the city in response to its continued hollering for more volunteers. If Salford failed to act soon, it was reasoned, the chance to raise its own battalion would be gone and with it local civic pride. The dignatries of Salford called a meeting to be held at the Salford Hippodrome on the evening of 3 September 1914. Every seat was taken and the aisles were packed by an enthusiastic crowd. Thousands unable to get in crammed into the Unitarian School across the road and, when that filled, crowds remained in the street between the two buildings. The Mayor of Salford, Alderman Dequesnes, aimed the opening speech directly at the unemployed in the Salford area:

> *...We are fighting for our wives, for our children, for everything that is dear to us. We are fighting for our shores, the liberty of our country, for our hearth and homes. Let us not forget that. I said, "we are fighting", perhaps I ought to say that others are doing the fighting and that we, many of us, are sitting comfortably at home. It is quite true that we cannot all go to the war, but many*

of us who have not gone could.

I want to speak to those young men of Salford who are young and able-bodied and I want to say to them that we have no room for the unemployed with their opportunities. There is now employment for all. Those able-bodied men who are at home who have no work to do can find work of a noble kind elsewhere.

Thus it was that the Mayor targeted the out-of-work young men.

If any present wondered about Christian morality, the taking up of arms and Britain's position in the eyes of the Almighty, that issue was taken care of by the Bishop of the Manchester Diocese, Bishop Welldon. He informed his audience that one hundred clergy had already volunteered and that he had even offered to go himself. He described the German position as diabolical and that the German nation had placed itself in the very mouth of the Devil himself. The stamp of ecclesiastical authority was thereby imprinted upon the recruiting drive. Michael Stedman in his book *Salford Pals* comments that Bishop Whelldon's sermons set the tone for many local clergy who provided constant support to the area's recruitment and its local battalions.

Local MP Sir George Agnew took the political line in his speech and presented 'evidence of justification' for declaring war on Germany.

Chairman of the All-Party Parliamentary Recruiting Committee, Mr Montague Barlow, roused the audience with a bitter attack and wild tirade against German atrocities. He referred to the use of civilians as cover, driving Belgian women and children in front of their advancing armies; the bricking up of coal mine shafts entombing Belgian miners; the ill-treatment of captured, wounded British soldiers; the shelling and wanton despoiling of historic towns. As far as he was concerned, there could be no question as to the truthfulness of the allegations that were being reported upon in the press and popular magazines such as the *Illustrated London News*, *The Graphic, Sphere* and the numerous magazines beginning to appear dedicated to covering the Great War in weekly instalments. Having roused the blood of his audience, Barlow concluded in melodramatic style:

A Hun officer 'eyes up' a Belgian women with obvious intent. Front cover of the **Sphere** *magazine, August 1914. All helped to rouse indignation and hatred against the barbaric 'Hun' and assist recruitment.*

Some of the last recruits to the First Battalion Salford Pals before drilling, training and uniforms had transformed them.
MICHAEL STEDMAN

Salford Pals wo the cap badge of the Lancashire Fusiliers.

> *Who is for the King? I am going to make the same appeal to you tonight. Who is going to hold his hand up and volunteer to go from this magnificent meeting to fight for his King and Country?*

The response of the Salford men was as to be expected and Barlow could write to the War Office offering to 'raise, clothe, feed and house a battalion provided at least 1,100 recruits come forward'. Confirmation was quick in coming and on Wednesday, 9 September, 1914, the Salford Pals Battalion was established. Over the weeks the full complement was reached and the men drilled at the local recreation ground, no longer in their best suits in which they had enlisted, but in their rough working clothes, indicating to all onlookers their working class origins. After each day's drill the men returned to their homes in Ordsal, Lower Broughton and Pendleton.

There was a competitive spirit between the large cities as to how many men had been raised in response to Kitchener's appeal. The *Manchester Guardian*, dated 10 September, ran a lengthy editorial feature which included a comparison:

> *London has furnished about 57,000 recruits. Manchester's total thus far is*

*Manchester Pals
cap badge was
that of the
Manchester
Regiment, which
was the Coat of
Arms of the City.*

estimated at over 25,000. In Glasgow 22,000 recruits have been enlisted. Liverpool and the immediate district has contributed 20,000 for foreign service. Birmingham has supplied 23,000 and Sheffield 20,000.

No mention of the north east where not battalions but two brigades, of Pals were raised from among the large population crowded around the Rivers Tyne and Weir. Coal mines, iron and steel works and ship building yards meant that there was a large immigrant community originating from Scotland and Ireland. However, with the raising of the Tyneside Irish and the Tyneside Scottish things did not, at first, run smoothly.

Recruiting for the Tyneside Scottish as a Pals battalion went ahead without official sanction. The first knock back came when it became known that the War Office would not permit the unit to wear the kilt. One correspondent to the local press expressed total disbelief, pointing out that the London Scottish and the Liverpool Scottish could don the kilt, why then not the Tyneside Scottish? He pointed out that it would bring in a better class of recruit 'Only a Scotsman knows the feeling of national pride awakened by the sight of a kilt'. But worse was to come, a letter from the war Office dated 18 September 1914 read:

With reference to your application to raise a battalion in Newcastle upon Tyne, I am commanded by the Army Council to inform you that owing to the number of local battalions already authorised they have decided that no more such battalions can be authorised. I am to express to you the sincere thanks of the Army Council and to say that whilst they appreciate the patriotic spirit which has prompted your proposal they much regret that they are unable to accept it.

During the Boer War, in the year 1900, attempts had been made to raise a Scottish Volunteer Corps and it too had been turned down. Now, in an even greater national emergency, the decision was still 'no'. The story was the same for the raises of the Tyneside Irish – an official refusal. However, a change of heart by the War Office towards Newcastle-upon-Tyne was prompted by the falling off of volunteers during October 1914.

The Lord Chancellor, Lord Haldane, visited Newcastle on 10 October 1914 and included in his itinerary an address to a crowd of around 8,000 at the Tyne and Pavilion Theatres. During his speech he made a dramatic announcement:

I bring to the city of Newcastle a message from Lord Kitchener. He is asking you to say that you will raise two more battalions in Newcastle, two good Tyneside battalions, and one of them, I think, might consist of the Scots who are my own countrymen [it was at that point that some wag in the audience shouted out "make it three,

*The Lord Chancellor, Lord
Haldane.*

Englishmen, Irishmen and Scotsmen."]

Undeterred, Lord Haldane responded,

> *That is what we are going to do. We are going to give you a Scottish battalion here. We are giving every encourage ment to the Irish, who are a splendid fighting race, to make their battalions together. As for the English – they will have no difficulty – there are lots of famous North Country regiments. We can provide for those who have national or clannish feelings to be together.*

The Scottish bad was designed specifically for t Tyneside Scottis battalions. The f battalions were numbered to the Northumberland Fusiliers Regime

It would be as well to point out here the conditions that had to be met before a Pals battalion could be formed. First stipulation was that each recruit should meet the minimum height requirement for the British Tommy at that period, which was five foot five inches tall. The chest dimension, expanded, had to be at least thirty-four and a half inches. Age was to fall on and between nineteen and forty-five years. The War Office also required that 1,100 men to be the full complement of a battalion after medical examination – this allowed for 10% rejection, for various reasons, after the battalion was formed.

Recruiting for the Tyneside Scottish covered Berwick, Alston, Sunderland and Stockton. Although the kilt would not be worn a distinctive headdress and cap badge would be permitted. This, despite the fact that the battalion would be numbered to the Northumberland Fusiliers. In less than a week 833 men had been recruited. By the end of October it became clear that enough were coming forward to consider a second battalion of Scottish. The motto of the Tyneside Scottish was advertised as being 'Harder than Hammers'. And it was claimed that the battalion was being filled with the 'Toughest, Hardest and Best Tyneside Fighting Men'. It was made known that the War Office had approved the wearing of the glengarry cap along with a specially designed badge, left to the discretion of the Raising Committee. Immediately, the battalion would be kitted out in khaki instead of the widely available navy-blue serge being issued to other Pals battalions. Factors which encouraged men to sign up at an ever increasing rate for the Tyneside Scottish.

It was recruiting to the 3rd Tyneside Scottish that was to set a record that was, and remains to this day, unsurpassed in the annals of recruiting to the British Army. In just over twenty-four hours from the directive to begin recruiting it was proudly announced that the battalion had reached 1,169 men and so was full. Four battalions constitute a brigade and still men were clamouring to join the Scottish. It was rumoured that the War Office would never sanction more than four, or brigade strength. As a consequence those who were considering joining the Scottish should get a move on before it was too late. Graham Stewart and John Sheen, authors of *Tyneside Scottish*, record that on 12 November a wire was received from Mr Wilkie MP, who was in London at the War Office, acting as an agent for the committee. His wire was brief and to the point,

> SEEN UNDER SECRETARY STOP HE IS FAVOURABLE TO A FOURTH BATTALION STOP

The incredible had happened. A Tyneside Scottish Brigade would take its

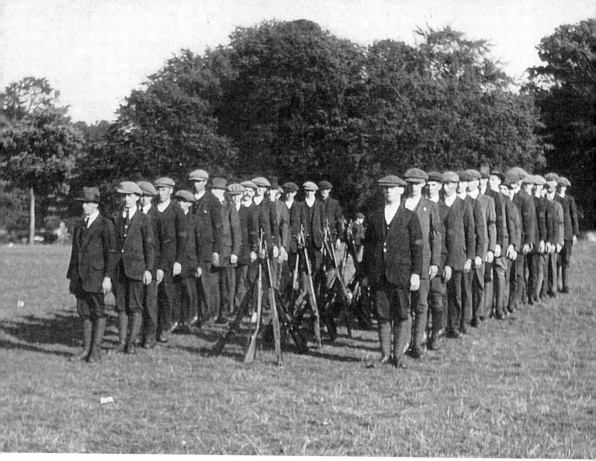

Northumberland Fusiliers wearing armbands and with some wearing puttees.
GRAHAM STEWART & JOHN SHEEN

place in the British Army Order of Battle.

The Tyneside Irish took longer to get under way, but was however, fortunate in having a number of ex-regular soldiers join at the start. They were men who had served with the Connaught Rangers and the Royal Irish, and had seen action in the Sudan and against the Boers in South Africa. Their experience was invaluable in the training of raw recruits. The commander of C Company, Captain Jack Arnold recognised their value and he was especially full of praise for his Company Sergeant Major, Jack Erett, who he described as a man 'from whom I learned more than I could ever repay... he made an ideal sergeant major, keen, intelligent even tempered and strictly temperate. I liked him from the beginning and we worked together to make the company as good as it could be'. Captain Arnold's heartfelt praise of his CSM can be better appreciated in the light of his impressions of the rank and file that he was to command. The realisation of the tremendous amount of work in store for the officers and NCOs can be gleaned from his written observations when he first cast eyes on the raw material of the First Tyneside Irish Battalion:

I found a motley throng very reminiscent of the types that used to file along the roads to annual militia musters in Ireland. They had no uniforms, no collars, boots that had toes peeping through them and trousers that were more patch than piece; there were old and young, some born in Ireland, some in England of Irish parentage, some having no connection with Ireland beyond the same church or the fact that they worked in the same pit as an Irishman. An unusual high number were illiterate. The married ones hardly knew how many children they had got and the single ones were not sure if they were married or not, and it was evident that they had one characteristic in common, many were no stranger to an empty belly.

In absence of uniforms, initially, the men were supplied with coloured arm bands: the Tyneside Irish wore green and the Tyneside Scottish a tartan one. The Newcastle Commercials wore a red lanyard.

Recruiting to the Tyneside Irish carried on apace and by December it was looking like a third battalion would be viable. After Christmas members of the raising committee travelled to London to seek permission for a fourth battalion. Like Manchester (two City brigades), Salford, Hull and the Tyneside Scottish, Tyneside Irish would produce an entire brigade consisting of four battalions for Lord Kitchener.

At the outset there were problems of a religious nature in connection with the Tyneside Irish.

Billets, equiping and training

Billets and accommodation had been set up at a skating rink for the Tyneside Irish until huts could be constructed. Welcoming committees had been formed by the various faiths to care for the social and spiritual well-being of the men and immediately there were disagreements between the committees. A large percentage, sixty-two in every hundred, of the men in the First Battalion were Roman Catholic. Father Morrell, heading the RCs, was having a problem with the idea of a joint committee working with representatives of the other three faiths, Church of England, Primitive Methodist, and Wesleyan. It was regretted by the chairman who stated, 'it is deplorable that these petty local matters should be allowed to interfere or to enter into this great question'. They finally agreed to act independently and to open their respective meeting places for recreational purposes. In March the hutted camp at Alnwick was completed and effective military training could really begin for the Tynesiders.

The Tyneside Irish had a distinctive collar badge and shoulder title. However, the cap badge was that of the Northumberland Fusiliers.

Throughout the north, army camps were being constructed to accommodate Kitchener's battalions. Usually, land was either Corporation owned or donated by landowners and situated in moorland areas. Within a matter of weeks roads, water and gas were laid on. Concerning the Service battalions of the West Yorkshire Regiment, the Bradford Pals, the *Bradford Weekly Telegraph*, of 6 November 1914, commented on the location for the construction of hutments,

It would have been difficult to find a more suitable site in the Craven District. It is well elevated, and there is an excellent water supply. The camp will consist of wooden huts, each hut being a barrack room 60ft. by 20ft., and

Interdenominational problems arose in connection with recreational facilities for the Tyneside Irish. Rather than working jointly to provide the means for the soldiers to enjoy their leisure time, after much debate the different churches finally agreed to act independently. The Roman Catholic Institute at Washington with some visiting soldiers on leave. JOHN SHEEN

> *good accommodation for horses etc. Water and gas will be laid on, and the necessary drainage is to receive the most careful consideration. The work of construction will commence at once, and it is expected that 1,200 men will be in residence in about four or five weeks.*

Another battalion of the West Yorkshire Regiment, the City of Leeds Battalion, had a ready-made camp, (almost) at Colsterdale where huts recently used to house navvies employed on reservoir construction provided a base. Consequently, the battalion was in proper hutted accommodation by the end of September, months ahead of other Kitchener's Pals battalions. D Company was allotted the huts and the other Companies went under canvas until the camp could be completed.

At Liverpool, where the Pals concept originated, the four battalions were spread around the district, training at various locations, sports grounds and parks, the men returning to their homes each day. Apart from the First Pals which was billetted in an old watch factory. Lord Derby decided to use his property at Knowsley Park to house the brigade and plans were drawn up. By the end of January all four battalions of the King's (Liverpool Regiment) were in hutted camp together.

Redmires Camp gateway always attracted inquisitive crowds.
PAUL OLDFIELD & RALPH GIBSON

To the west of Sheffield, in the foothills of the Pennines, an area was chosen as the location for the camp to house the City Battalion, 12th Service Battalion York and Lancaster Regiment. The surrounding moors, it was reasoned, would prove to be a handy training ground for a British infantry battalion. The land at the head of Rivelin valley had been used pre war by the Territorial Army as an artillery range. In the 1939-1945 conflict, a prisoner of war camp would be set up in the vicinity and contain some hard-core Nazis as inmates. Council contractors constructed the City Battalion camp at Redmires and before it was fully completed the battalion marched out in pouring rain to take up residence on Saturday 5 December 1914. They had recently received delivery of 600 obselete rifles, enough to make a reasonable impression on the crowds who gathered along the route. Meanwhile, the neighbouring Pals battalion, the First Barnsleys, had still to make do with broom handles for practising arms drill.

A pleasant, wooded slope on the outskirts of the village of Silkstone had been acquired as the site for the 13th Service Battalion York and Lancaster Regiment. At 11 o'clock on Sunday morning, 20 December, the First Barnsley Pals marched from their temporary billets at the Public Hall in town to Newhall Camp, Silkstone. Once there they were addressed by their commander, Lieutenant Colonel Hewitt,

The most important aspect of your training here at Silkstone will be musketry along with Company manoeuvres. The sooner that is completed, the quicker the battalion will be despatched to the front.

Newhall Camp was separated from the village of Silkstone by a natural dry 'moat'. It meant a long walk for the soldiers who were keen to reach the pubs and shops in the village. The problem was solved by the men themselves,

> Our pioneers built a rough wooden bridge across a ravine. It was built of rough cut trees and must have been seventy to eighty yards long. It saved all that walk into Silkstone village. When you got over the bridge you were 200 yards from camp. When we marched across we had to break step. I've seen one or two officers go over on motorbikes, I bet they got a rough ride over there.
>
> **Tommy Oughton 13th York and Lancaster Regiment**

Although living conditions at the camp were rough, for many of the ex-

First Battalion Barnsley Pals officers and men at Newhall Camp.

Short cut from Newhall Camp into Silkstone village constructed by men of the First Barnsley Pal.

miners there were some advantages over civilian life. Tommy Oughton, former miner from Wombwell, in a taped interview in the 1980s, described life at Newhall camp, with its muddy tracks between the huts,

> We had three flat boards on trestles and mattresses full of straw. As a rule two of you used to get down together to make like a double. You each had two blankets, so when you got together you'd put one underneath and three on top. Me and Tom Bradbury kipped like that. We had a proper hut for meals and a cookhouse. Of course when we first got there the Barnsley British Co-operative Society was still feeding us. I expect that it all came out of the Government later on, but they catered for us. You could see the big vans coming from Barnsley every day. I heard many men say, men older than me who were married, that they were better fed than in civilian life.

Another step forward with the move to Silkstone was the gradual appearance of rifles. However, because of the defects, (usually loose bolts, damaged sights and rusty barrels) the letters 'DP' were stamped on the wooden butt and onto the metal over the breech of each rifle by the Royal Armoury. This indicated that it was to be used for drill purposes only – it was not to be fired. Because the rifles being issued, mainly Lee Metfords, were obsolete and nationwide there was an ammunition shortage, the use of the bayonet received a great deal of emphasis in most of the poorly armed Kitchener battalions.

> It is a weapon always popular with our men. The War Office knows what it is about when it directs that every encouragement should be given to the recruits to practise bayonet fighting. Not until they are thoroughly skilled in the use of this weapon can the men be sent on active service.

That was the perceived wisdom of the day as expressed through the pages of the *Barnsley Chronicle* by one who called himself 'Old Volunteer'. The commanding officer of the First Barnsleys, Lieutenant Colonel Hewitt, was most emphatic on the use of the bayonet, referring to it as 'the ultimate weapon'. Where did that received wisdom come from? Upon what experience of fighting was it based? The last major land action engaged in by British forces had been against Dutch settlers in South Africa at the turn of the century. The bayonet had been of little use against the tactics employed by Boer marksmen, operating charger-loading Mauser rifles from concealed positions, or the hit and run tactics of the commandos. There may have been isolated incidents during the Zulu War when bayonet charges would have worked, but certainly not at the well-known actions at Isandlwana and Rorke's Drift. But even then, unlike the Germans, the Zulus did not employ barbed wire and use Maxim machine guns. Furthermore, the training involving the movement of infantry in attack and defence would be of little use in the static fighting in France and Belgium. Apart from some instances during the opening moves of 1914, when the fighting between the massed armies flowed across open country in the time honoured way, there would be little opportunity for massed bayonet charges. However, it did serve to instil the offensive spirit in recruits.

First Barnsley Pals being instucted in the art of bayonet fighting at Newhall Camp, Silkstone. There would be little opportunity to employ these gruesome skills when they went 'over the top' for the first time in July 1916.

In the North Eastern Railway Magazine in June 1915 the following comment on bayonet fighting appeared:
'British superiority in this method of close fighting is playing a predominant part in the pesent campaign.' DAVID BILTON

Leeds Pals on the march, led by drummer boys.
LAURIE MILNER

Above: Men of the Birmingham City Battalion in the Mess Hall at Moseley dine under the watchful eye of the Orderley Officer.
TERRY CARTER

Right: Cookhouse at Redmires. Men of the Sheffield City Battalion getting used to cooking for hundreds at a time.
RALPH GIBSON & PAUL OLDFIELD

At camps dotted throughout the country the daily routine was much the same: reveille was at 6 am, when the men received a hot drink and biscuits. Physical jerks (Swedish drill) followed; in the case of the Barnsley Pals, overseen by a physical training expert supplied by the War Office. Some days the physical training took the form of a cross-country run. Breakfast was at 8 am, followed by training at company strength, which involved launching an attack at a pre-designated objective. Then there would be much larger manoeuvres carried out at battalion strength, involving 800 to 900 men. The tactical procedures were in keeping with those used in the South Africa campaign, and were inapropriate for the war being waged in Europe against a well dug in enemy. Lunch was at 12.45 pm and could consist of roast beef, potatoes and beans followed by rice and bread pudding. Afternoon parade and more drill until 4.45 pm, when the bugle was blown for tea which amounted to jam or marmalade, bread and butter and stewed fruit. The men could have the evening to themselves, unless selected for special duties, and could obtain a pass out of camp – return by 10.00 pm, when a roll call was taken. Lights out was sounded by bugle at 10.15 pm.

The unimaginative, outdated techniques being instilled with dedicated conscientiousness by the instructors is best seen in the training of battalion signallers. In order to carry out the signalling procedure the signaller had to be seen clearly by those with whom he was communicating. In every instance it meant him standing in full view on the battlefield waving his arms about as he spelt out his message. German snipers were, by that time, picking off any man who showed himself by as much as an inch above the trench parapet.

As rifles were in such short supply, so were machine guns and yet

Four Signallers of the First Tyneside Scottish. The two men at the end are the Raisbeck twins. Both would be killed by a single shell hours before the Big Push got underway.
GRAHAM STEWART & JOHN SHEEN

Orderly room of the 13th Battalion, East Yorkshire Regiment, Hull Pals (T'Others), May 1915.

machine-gun sections were being formed, encouraged by the General Staff due to the skilled use of the weapon by the Germans. Supply of the automatic weapon would eventually come from the War Office but, in the meantime, the men would have to make do with mock-ups. Strange then the report in the *Barnsley Chronicle* regarding an offer made by a Reverend

Battalion en masse. 19th Battalion Manchester Regiment, Fourth City, parade at Belle View.
MICHAEL STEDMAN

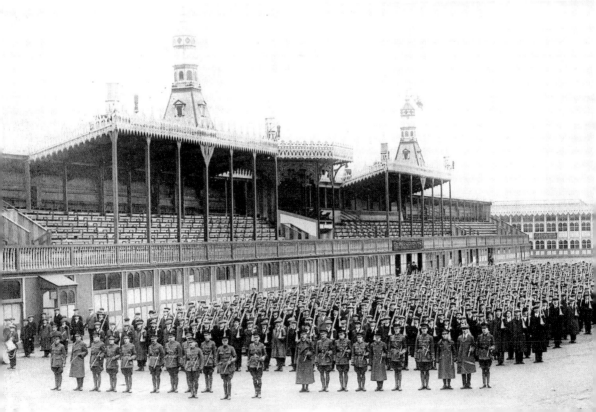

Above: Manchester Pals officers enjoying revolver practice at Heaton Park, Manchester.   MICHAEL STEDMAN

Right: Birmingham men try to get into the spirit of things with a broken German machine gun. The weapon's firing was simulated by a hand-turned rattle.

TERRY CARTER

W H Elmhirst of Pinder Oaks, to sell the First Barnsley Pals Battalion a machine gun. Apparently £102 was raised to complete the purchase. There is no record that the sale went ahead – but where the vicar got his hands privately on a machine gun when they were like gold dust is a mystery.

Part of the training included regular route marches of twenty to thirty

Durham Pals guard detail.
JOHN SHEEN

miles. Footwear has always been a vital item of equipment for the infantryman and with the huge demand for boots in the late summer of 1914, the suppliers were sure of large orders (each soldier had two pairs issued). Competition between manufacturers was keen and corners were cut in order to bring the price down and obtain the business. In the case of the Leeds Pals, their first consignment of boots proved to be worse than useless. They were returned and a more sturdy boot supplied at a slightly higher price. The commanding officer, Lieutenant Colonel Walter Stead, went to another supplier for the second set.

Durham Pals we the cap badge of the Durham Ligh Infantry.

East Coast raiders

On the morning of 16 December 1914, a group of six German battle-cruisers under the command of Admiral von Hipper sailed off the east coast resorts of Scarborough, Whitby and Hartlepool and unleashed a hail of fire on the virtually undefended towns. It was during the raid that a Pals battalion was the first to experience coming under fire from the enemy.

It was 8 am when the *Derfflinger, Von der Tann* and *Kolberg* sailed off into a position just off Scarborough's North Bay and opened fire, before rounding the headland into the South Bay to lay down fire on the sea front. The cruisers turned about and delivered a second salvo, landing high explosive shells further inland. The bombardment lasted less than

Birmingham Pals learning the art of trench construction. TERRY CARTER

The band of the Tyneside Scottish marching through Alnwick, pipers leading. The soldiers watching would likely be Newcastle Commercials or Tyneside Irish.
GRAHAM STEWART & JOHN SHEEN

thirty minutes and killed eighteen people. It was estimated that around 500 shells had smashed into the town. The raiders then laid over 100 mines to prevent the pursuit of any British warships. The *Blücher, Seydlitz* and *Moltke*, under the command of von Hipper, attacked Whitby and Hartlepool killing ninety-three civilians; men, women and children. However, there were those on the east coast who could be described as 'legitimate targets'. Two companies of the 18th (Service) Battalion (1st County) Durham Light Infantry were manning the trenches of the Tyne and Tees defences during the attack on Hartlepool. Author John Sheen described the raid when, for the first time, a Pals battalion of Kitchener's New Army came under fire and lost six men killed. The Durhams were the first men of a New Army division to be killed in action.

A part of the German High Seas Fleet had successfully slipped through British defences and

Right: **Blucher**
Centre: **Seydlitz**
Below: **Moltke**

Opposite Top: **Derflinger**
Centre: **Kolberg**
Below: **Von Der Tann**

Five unexploded shells discovered in Hartlepool and collected after the raid.

delivered a warning, if one was needed, that the world war that was raging would be a 'no holds barred' contest – every Briton was considered to be a legitimate target. Hence the saying, 'a Scarborough warning' entered the vernacular of the British people from that day on. Zeppelin and Gotha bomber raids on England in the months to come would underline that policy.

The 10th (Service) Battalion East Yorkshire Regiment, the Hull Commercials, had been moved to the east coast a matter of weeks before the attack and from the positions they occupied at Hornsea, they could hear the barrage to the north. They had been moved to Coastal Defence because of the invasion scare. The German High Fleet's bombardment served to heighten the tension among the defenders and the Commercials were suddenly equipped with Long Lee Enfield rifles – a weapon usually associated with the Territorials. Ammunition was also made available along with orders that it was only to be used in case of an enemy landing. The 10th's commanding officer, Lieutenant Colonel Richardson, was not impressed either with the restriction on the ammuntion's use, or the rifles just issued. The men needed live ammunition firing experience and he sent a telegram requesting permission. The War Office asked him to report on the condition of the Long Lee Enfields. The Colonel's reply was brief and to the point, 'Reference your telegram Stop, Rifles will certainly go off Stop, Doubtful which end Stop'.

In the March 1915 edition of the *North Eastern Railway Magazine* a letter was published from a serving Hull Commercial which mentions life at the east coast camp. In describing the daily routine he mentions 'musketry and shooting practice' which suggests that the problem of effective weaponry and live ammunition training had been resolved.

Brigades and Divisions

In some instances, where men were billeted over a wide area, training had been difficult at battalion strength. One estimate suggests over 800,000

10th Battalion East Yorkshire Regiment (Hull Commercials) marching to Ripon.
DAVID BILTON

men were housed in hired buildings, church halls and private homes, (War Office regulations stipulated that men should not be billeted on licensed premises). Because of the diaspora, larger formation training would have proved nigh impossible. Consequently, hutted camps were thrown up throughout the British Isles, each one capable of housing an entire British Army division, over 18,000 men. Battalions that had not trained together with fellow battalions in the same brigade were inspected by a brigade commander, a brigadier general, and passed as ready for the next phase of training.

In the case of 94 Brigade, a newly constructed camp on Cannock Chase in Staffordshire would be the meeting up camp for two battalions of Barnsley Pals, the Sheffield City battalion and the Accrington Pals. Inevitably, men were moving into hutments that were half built. It was the month of May, 1915, when soldiers began arriving at Rugeley railway station. It was a four and a half mile march to the hutments on Cannock Chase. Both the Lancashire and Yorkshire men of 94 Brigade remembered the march to the camp. Recalled Ernest Bell of the First Barnsleys:

When we arrived at Rugeley it was throwing it down. We had to march up hill from Rugeley to Penkridge Bank Camp. We were wet through when we got there and we had to go straight to the huts, no change of clothing.

Another observed,

> *As you marched from Rugeley up to the camp our huts were the first lot on your right. Marching up we passed a notice board which said "site for cinema". That was all very well but some of our huts had no roofs on.*

In many instances there were no lights in the huts and no running water within half a mile. At least the Accrington battalion had sent some men ahead and they had helped the civilian workers get roofs on the huts that had been allotted to the 11th East Lancashire Regiment. When the men arrived there were lit coke-stoves bidding them welcome, but no cookhouse arrangements. Their only meal that day was corned beef sandwiches washed down with neat tea – there was no milk or sugar. Over the following days the men were organised into specialist groups, regimental police, transport, medical and sanitary sections. In the case of the Accrington battalion the cookhouse personnel had to be formed from scratch and, as the men were learning to cook for hundreds of men for the very first time in their lives, the results can only be imagined,

> *Things were badly organised. Trouble started one day when we were very short of food. some of us in Z Company refused to parade at dinner time in protest. We were then given a good meal, after which we were paraded and given a long lecture by the Commanding Officer. He told us that we could have been shot for disobeying orders. A voice from the rear ranks called out, "Tha couldn't do that, thad shoot all thi best soldiers!" With that the matter ended.*
>
> Private Marshall, Accrington Pals

It was whilst at Rugeley that the 'tools of their trade' arrived in the form of usable Lee Metford rifles. The serious matter of getting off fifteen

Commander of 94 Brigade, Brigadier General Bowles with his Brigade officers. Military police from each of the four Pals battalions, Accrington, Sheffield and two from Barnsley, provide excort.

aimed rounds a minute could be instilled. Training in the tactics of Brigade formation and movement could go ahead, with the four battalions learning to cooperate together. But it was later recognised by some that the training would do them little good, apart from getting used to obeying shouted commands without thinking about it,

> *On Cannock Chase we used to do a lot of route marching and manoeuvring in the formations of the old type of South African campaigning, with wings of scouts out to the side. We were practising open warfare. It was a burning summer in 1915 and we knew about it when we were marching. They used to fill our water bottles and we had to show them at the end of the march – still full. You were not allowed to drink on the march. We were fit, after a route march we could have still run a full mile with a full pack on without being out of breath at the end of it. That was training.*

> **Frank Lindley, Second Barnsley**

The time arrived at the end of the month of May 1915 when the battalions comprising 94 Brigade were officially handed over to the War Office. Author Bill Turner reported on the ceremony:

> *On 31 May every available man paraded for the acceptance of the battalion by the War Office. The Army Ordnance Department first closely inspected the camp, equipment, clothing, stores etc. of the battalion. The "camp correspondent" of the* Accrington Gazette *later described the acceptance ceremony: "All the officers and men were on parade, and after expressing his satisfaction in all he had seen, and with the smart appearance and bearing of the men, the War Office representative ceremoniously walked down the lines and touched one man in each platoon on the shoulder, thus formerly claiming them as soldiers of the King".*

Accrington Pals practice aiming long Lee Enfield rifles for the camera man on the rifle range at Wormold Green. The range can be seen in the background. WILLIAM TURNER

From that day on, the local authorities of Accrington, Sheffield and Barnsley were free from the responsibilities associated with those four battalions. However, in the case of the main mover in the raising of the Accrington Pals, John Harwood, the War Office expected that he continue to find men for the British Army, as can be seen in the following letter, dated 18 July 1916:

> Sir, I am commanded by the Army Council to offer you their sincere thanks for having raised the 11th Service Battalion East Lancashire Regiment (Accrington) of which the administration has now been taken over by the military authorities. The Council much appreciate the spirit which prompted your assistance and they are gratified at the successful results which added to the Armed Forces of the Crown – the services of such a fine body of men. I am to add that the battalion's success on active service will largely depend on your efforts to keep the depot companies up to establishment.

Because of the hot summer of 1915 the heathland was constantly catching fire and the soldiers were often engaged in fire fighting. Also the chase was alive with wildlife and that gave some of the men the opportunity to employ a former skill, that of poacher. According to those interviewed for the Pals series, gambling was rife among the men. Not only playing cards but a game known as 'Crown and Anchor' was endemic throughout the British Army. Attempts to stop the game proved futile. When General Sir Douglas Haig took overall command of the British Expeditionary Force in December 1915 he made it a penal offence to be caught playing 'Crown and Anchor'. He ruled that after three convictions a man would face a court martial. Being a devout man the General's concern, added to the moral aspect, was the possibilty of trouble in the ranks accruing from men losing their wages, leading to breakdowns in discipline. The law was unenforcable and policing it would have incited indiscipline. The game persisted to the end of the war.

> I used to draw my 'bob' [shilling] walk out and go straight to the hut where they were gambling and stick it on a card. If it came up it was all right and I'd carry on and make myself a little poke... Crown and Anchor men carried a piece of linen with squares on it, and they had a dice marked with crowns and anchors. When they chucked it, if a crown came up and your money was on the crown, you drew it off. There were some crazy blokes, they would always have a Crown and Anchor roll in their pocket and, no matter where they would be, it would be a case of "Come on lads" and out it would come. They made their cash like that. Wherever you stopped, even in the trenches, you had a gamble.
>
> Frank Lindley, 14th Battalion Y & L

At the end of July 1915 the order came for the battalions of 94 Brigade to move to the Fourth Army Training Centre at Ripon in North Yorkshire. The whole area around Ripon was congested with troops of Kitchener's Army.

Three Brigades were brought together to make up the 31st Division. It truly was a Pals Division consisting of:

92 Brigade, with four battalions of the East Yorkshire Regiment and

Accrington Pals have tea in the open air at South Camp, Ripon. WILLIAM TURNER

were 10th (Hull, Commercials), 11th (Hull, Tradesmen), 12th (Hull, Sportsmen), 13th (Hull, T'others).

93 Brigade with three battalions of the West Yorkshire Regiment and were 15th (Leeds Pals), 16th (First Bradford), 18th (Second Bradford), and one battalion of the Durham Light Infantry, (18th Durham Pals).

94 Brigade with one battalion of the East Lancashire Regiment (11th Accrington Pals) and three battalions of the York and Lancaster Regiment, 12th (Sheffield City), 13th (First Barnsley Pals), 14th (Second Barnsley Pals).

The Divisional Pioneer battalion was the 12th King's Own Yorkshire Light Infantry.

A series of inspections by various generals followed ending in one by the new commander of the division, Major General Wanless O'Gowan, who would remain with the division to the end of the war. Battalion commanders, on the other hand, would be replaced by younger men as active service loomed closer with the move of the 31st Division to Salisbury Plain. In its issue of 2 October 1915 the *Barnsley Chronicle* carried a letter from an unnamed soldier of the First Barnsleys in which he summed up his experience of military life:

> *We are at last on Salisbury Plain and there is a feeling of subdued*
> *excitement, a subconscious thrill passing over the Barnsley lads during this*

period, probably the eve of their departure to the Front. It is a feeling that the task they originally volunteered to do, when they gave up their work to join the New Army, is about to commence; the task of actually doing their bit for King and Country.

The year that has gone (for the premier Battalion is now a year old) has been lived every moment of it. We never thought, a year ago, that we should be here now. A great deal has been accomplished; our lads are no longer collier lads, but part of a great New Army of fighting men, trained and skilled in the new and latest devices of modern warfare.

We look back with pleasant memories upon the several camps we have been in. Each camp had its outstanding feature, and by its outstanding feature we think of it. We remember Silkstone for its mud. It was essentially the "Mud Camp". We walked in mud; we sometimes tumbled in it; we lived in it; we did our work in it; we learnt to be soldiers in it – and we look back upon that mud with a certain affection. We loved the Silkstone Camp, and the mud, and its days are full of happy memories.

Then came Penkridge – the camp of fire and smoke, then we were christened the "Fire Brigade". How well we remember the bugle sound of the "fire alarm". On the first note we ran like hares or indians, hatless, coatless with hatchets in hand – like little devils runnning to the mouth of Hell. We attacked the fires, fierce and solemn and in deadly earnest we went to those fires.

Next came Ripon, the most featureless of all camps, from our point of view, unless you can call "red hats" a feature. There was a feeling that we were being watched by those red hats, who watched to see if we were fit, if we had learnt the real thing, if we had stamina and grit in us, if we were real soldiers. Soon we were moved to Salisbury Plain, the great playground of the British Army; the finishing school of the country's trained troops.

Not much can be said of our new camp at Salisbury Plain, as yet, for we have only just arrived. It is the most perfect camp we have ever been in, almost surrounded by gentle slopes of a ridge of a hill (which the men have already christened "Hill 120"). It offers ample room for movement.

The training received on Salisbury Plain was more in keeping with the realities of trench fighting taking place across the Channel. The Lewis gun was supplied to the battalions and gun teams, each consisting of six men, were formed to operate them. The men were introduced to the Mills bomb, a hand grenade with a four-second fuse is a weapon which was proving invaluable in the trench fighting on the Western Front. Another feature of twentieth century fighting was barbed wire; experience in the handling and construction of barbed wire defences was given.

By the month of November 1915 rumour of a move abroad began to circulate throughout 31st Division, and the issue of pith helmets served to reinforce the rumour. Author David Bilton in his work on the *Hull Pals* highlights the last minute change of decisions by the High Command. Quoting a private in the 10th Battalion, Hull Commercials, he says that the soldier, later to become an officer, wrote in his diary:

December 4th: equipment for France issued.

December 6th: equipment for France withdrawn. Pith helmets and puggarees were handed out and it was rumoured that camel humps would be issued. Everyone was certain that the battalion was going to India, or Mesopotamia, or Arabia, or Egypt or somewhere else.

The history of the 11th Battalion, Hull Tradesmen, records a similiar story when it reports that gas helmets were issued in preparation for service in France only for them to be suddenly withdrawn and replaced by 1,025 sun helmets. It would seem that many men in the division recalled marching to the trains that would take them to the departure ports in pouring rain – wearing their recently issued pith helmets.

During the month of December the battalions of 31st Division were on their way to Egypt to defend the Suez Canal from the Turks. Frank

Tyneside Irish on manoeuvres; the brigade is ready to take its place on the Western Front.
JOHN SHEEN

The huts on Salisbury Plain, the final camp for many before being transported to the battle fronts. For the 31st Division it was to be Egypt. DAVID BILTON

Life jacket drill on board the **Nestor** *prior to sailing from Devonport with battalions of the 31st Division bound for Suez.* PAUL OLDFIELD & RALPH GIBSON

Lindley recalled the departure of the Second Barnsleys:

> We went down the Sound at the side of the Hoe and there were some folks there who had got the whiff that we were going. They were waving their handkerchiefs at us. We all waved our pith helmets. If you'd have seen that ship, full of these pith helmets all going round. You couldn't see anything on that ship but pith helmets all over it. It was a sight to be seen. And then it started, someone began singing the song "Homeland" and it was ringing and echoing from the Hoe. And there weren't many of us came back.

Other Pals divisions were already facing the enemy having crossed to France in October and November. The 34th Division, which consisted of four battalions of Tyneside Irish, four battalions of Tyneside Scottish, two battalions of Edinburgh City, the Cambridge Battalion and the Grimsby Chums, sailed for France in January 1916. However the first across the Channel were the Manchester and Liverpool Pals.

35th (Bantam) Division

With recruiting in full swing on Merseyside in September 1914, a sturdy little man tried to enlist at the Birkenhead Recruiting Office. He became furious when he was turned down because he was an inch too short. It was his fifth attempt at joining up, but none of the recruiting sergeants would accept him. A civilian, Mr Alfred Mansfield, had a heart to heart talk with the man and became convinced that the nation was losing some of the finest material by failing small men. Mansfield went off and spoke to Mr Alfred Bigland M.P., who was chairman of the Birkenhead

A Bantam platoon belonging to the 18th Lancashire Fusiliers. MICHAEL STEDMAN

Recruiting Committee. Bigland agreed that something ought to be done to get these men into the army. He took the matter up with the War Office the very next day, asking permission to form a 'Bantam Battalion' at Birkenhead.

Three days after recruiting began; men from Scotland, Ireland and Wales travelled in and well over 2,000 recruits were attested. In height they were not less than five feet nor more than five feet three inches. Soon other authorities began recruiting Bantam battalions until there were sufficient numbers to form an entire division. The original Bantams were fine bodied men, who made up in chest measurement and physical fitness what they lacked in height. However, it became apparent that it was not possible to continually support a Bantam division with such narrow confines of requirements. Many who joined later as replacements were physically immature or weaklings who would never have stood the strain of active service with all its privations. The Bantams lasted until losses in battle had decimated their ranks, and it became obvious that there was not a sufficient number of small men in Britain to supply so large a formation.

In the spring of 1917 the 35th Bantam Division, a unique Pals formation, passed away when the word 'Bantam' was dropped and it became simply the 35th Division.

Chapter Three

FACING THE ENEMY

HONORARY COLONEL of the Manchester Pals, Lord Derby, had inspected the two Manchester brigades for the last time at the beginning of November 1915. A short passage across the Channel two days later and the 30th Division was landing in Boulogne by way of a steady stream of transports. Men's recorded memories of landing in France all mention the steady downpour of rain which soaked them through as they marched to the transit camps high on the hills above the port of Boulogne. Observations concerning the local people's reactions to the foreigners among them changed as the weeks passed and as the novelty of British Tommies marching through the cobbled streets became common place. In November, Private Stubbs of the 18th Battalion, Liverpool Pals could say,

> When we arrived at Boulogne the French people made a heck of a fuss of us, giving us all sorts of things, flowers, sweets and all sorts, and the children as well made a heck of a fuss. then we had to climb a huge hill to get to our rest camp. I didn't know the name of it until a number of years afterwards, and this friend of mine told me it was called 'Blanket Hill' by the troops.

Cross Channel ferry boats in war paint schemes transport thousands of men to the fighting taking place on the Western Front.

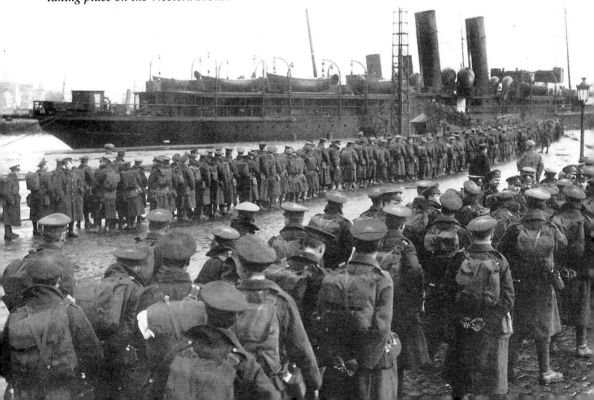

Two months later and observations concerning the reception of the people of Boulogne to British troops disembarking among them was somewhat different. Lieutenant Alan Furse of the 14th (Service) Battalion Royal Warwickshire Regiment, First Birmingham City Battalion, remembered,

> On our first march on French soil the pavé roadway was very difficult at first, especially for those with well nailed boots. We marched away from the docks through the streets and the first thing that astounded us was the apathy of the French inhabitants. They had evidently got used to the sight of our troops that they rarely looked twice at us. This was very disconcerting to us, just landed in France all filled with the idea that the war would soon be over, now that we had arrived and, incidentally, feeling that a better battalion had never crossed over... We marched from the docks up a very narrow street, straight up a hill at the back of the town. It was a very steep incline and progress was quite slow. After about a mile and a half of this we fell out for ten minutes. There were very small cottages on the side of the street and the men were soon on good terms with the inhabitants, accepting water and apples which were offered freely. Our big drummer, Latham, created much fun by nursing a small baby whilst the mother looked on apprehensively. After about a another mile of this steep hill we arrived at the camp at the top.

It was tented accommodation with twelve men allocated to each tent. There was no bedding and just a single blanket per man to keep out the icy cold. It hardly served to dampen the zeal for the job in hand – the majority were eager to get grips with the Germans before a decisive battle that brought victory for the Allies was fought.

From the transit camps the men were shunted by cattle truck closer to the Front line. At last, the rumble of artillery fire could be heard distinctly, as each of the battalions of Pals of the 30th, 32nd and 34th Divisions were moved by route marches to villages behind some of the least active areas of the Front.

Deadlock on the Western Front

Following the Battle of the Marne in September 1914, when the German invasion of France was halted, a scramble to outflank each other took place, causing the warring armies to end up at the Channel coast. There they dug in and a line of opposing trenches stretched across Belgium and France ending up at the Swiss border. For the best part of four terrible years the fighting became distilled into a simple mind-set, namely, the invaders hanging on to what they had captured, with an eye to taking up the offensive again at an appropriate time. Of course, the British and French had little option but to take on the offensive role to seek the enemy's dislodgement and effect a breakthrough. An alternative strategy was to achieve something decisive on other fronts that, in turn, would cause the Central Powers to cave in and sue for peace.

Understandably, the strategy of the French was dominated by the desire to recover their lost territory and, during 1915, resulted in them hurling their forces at the German lines in Artois, on the Aisne and in Champagne and along the Woevre. It served to prove that the invaders were adept at trench warfare and the art of defending fortified positions. In February and March

French infantry attack under cover of a smoke screen in the Champagne area.
French gun firing on German positions in Champagne.

1915 the French lost 50,000 men clawing their way forward a mere 500 metres into the German defensive system in Champagne. The following month the French High Command hurled its men against the St Mihiel salient and suffered 64,000 casualties for no gains. Against a background of the French criticising the British for 'not pulling their weight', there was an attack by the British in March at Neuve Chapelle.

A French first aid post. The French High Command would continue to throw men against the invader until over 30,000 of their troops finally mutinied in April 1917, refusing to attack, but agreeing to defend.

The Battle of Neuve Chapelle was an isolated affair, carried out with insufficient resources. Around 40,000 British and Indian infantry attacked and made some initial progress, breaking through a section of the German line which was secured by only a single division defending Neuve Chapelle village. Although the village was captured there followed supply and communication problems for the British, despite which they managed to hold the ground they had taken – some two kilometres. Further attempts to push on to attack Aubers was a disaster, as the Germans rushed troops to the area and counter-attacked. Casualties suffered were 11,200 (7,000 British, 4,200 Indian). The Germans lost approximately the same number. A shortage of artillery

British dead scattered among the German wire after an attack at Neuve Chapelle.

shells suffered by the British was to cause a scandal and in turn led to a major reorganisation in Britain, including the forming of a Ministry of Munitions under Lloyd George.

In 1915 the British Expeditionary Force received reinforcement of several new regular divisions drawn from foreign garrisons. These, along with the 1st Canadian Division which had recently arrived in France, brought the British strength up to thirteen infantry divisions and five cavalry divisions. In addition there was a number of selected Territorial divisions to add to the army's strength. The increase in British forces brought with it pressure for them to occupy more of the front line. The French commander, General Joffre, became insistent that the British take over the defence of the Belgian town of Ypres with its salient, which formed a defensive curve jutting out towards the east. The move would allow French troops to be moved south in direct defence of their homeland.

Maschinengewehr *MG 08 an efficient killing machine in the hands of a well trained crew.*
GRAHAM STEWART & JOHN SHEEN

Britain lagged behind in adapting to the form of warfare being fought. Even when it was obvious to every fighting soldier that the machine gun was dominating the battlefield, General Headquarters in France was resisting the increase of the scale of two machine guns per battalion, that had been a part of the peace-time complement. Commander of First Army, General Haig, stated that it was 'a much overrated weapon' and that the present scale of two in every battalion was 'more than sufficient'. To the rescue came Lloyd George in his new capacity as Minister of Munitions who, in support of the advocates of fire-power, generously increased the scale to sixteen per battalion. It was also due to Lloyd George that the Stokes gun, a quick-firing mortar, overcame the resistance of the hide-bound militarists and was introduced despite protests. It went on to become an important weapon of the British Army in the Great War.

It was the Germans who, on 22 April 1915, came close to breaking the deadlock with the employment of poison gas in the Ypres Salient. The weird cloud of green coloured vapour crept across No Man's Land and rolled over the French and Canadian troops. Within minutes a mass of agonised victims were writhing in agony and a four-mile gap appeared in the Allied line with not a defender capable of firing a shot. Because the German High Command placed little faith in the new horror weapon they had introduced they

**It was reasoned by some that the Almighty must surely support the righteous. In the wake of the first gas attack one outraged clergyman expressed his feelings:
'We shall win this war because God cannot allow such scum to exist. How can the Kaiser possibly reconcile such things as asphyxiating gases and the slaughter of innocents with Christianity?'**
Julian Bickersteth, May 1915.

failed to have reserves on hand to exploit the breakthrough. Also the German infantryman was reluctant to follow up due to the unknown effects of the new weapon. Canadians on the flanks of the breach, and the speedy arrival of British and Indian reinforcements, saved the situation in the absence of German reserves. During the next four weeks the Allied Forces of Belgium, France and Britain fought to hold off the German advance and to regain the ground that had been lost north of Ypres. The Second Battle of Ypres ended 25 May 1915.

Meanwhile attempts to smash through the German lines between the towns of Lens and Arras were carried out by the French and continued up until September 1915. Failure resulted and there were clamours for more British involvement, which was met with resistance by the British First Army commander General Haig. He maintained that the supply of artillery shells was still inadequate, that until the situation was remedied, it was little use to make plans for major offensives against strong German positions. In June 1915 the British Army still had only seventy-one heavy guns and 1,406 field guns. The factories in England were turning out 22,000 shells a day, compared to France with 100,000, and Germany with a reported 250,000 shells a day. It would be many months before the efforts of the Ministry of Munitions took effect. In the light of failures Lord Kitchener complained about the promises made to him by the French and British commanders,

Commander in Chief Joseph Joffre.

> *Joffre and Sir John* [French] *told me in November* [1914] *that they were going to push the Germans back over the frontier; they gave me the same assurances in December, March and May. What have they done? The attacks are very costly and end in nothing.*

In spite of the abortive attempts to drive the Germans back to their own frontier Kitchener believed that the next planned offensive would succeed. An offensive was planned with two decisive strokes delivered simultaneously by the French at Champagne and the British north of Arras at Lens. General Haig was uneasy about the planned offensive having made a personal reconnaissance of the area. In his opinion the sector was not favourable for an attack. In his view the German defences were so strong that only siege methods would stand any chance of success. The ground was, for the most part bare and open, and would be swept by machine-gun fire once the attacking infantry ventured across it.

Sir John French.

However, Joffre would not accept any arguments for a postponement until such a time as more heavy artillery could be brought up to bombard the fortified villages. Nor would he consider a change of site declaring that 'your attack will find particularly favourable ground between La Bassée and Loos'.

The artillery bombardment began 21 September 1915 with shells being rationed at ninety rounds per heavy gun and 150 to each field gun. Poison gas was released by the British for the first time, but the wind did not fully cooperate, with the result that some British infantry were overcome by the

General Sir Douglas Haig.

release of chlorine. By the end of the first day the British troops were on the outskirts of Lens. However, failure to bring up reserves and strong German counter-attacks forced the British back. When a second British attack suffered heavy losses on 13 October, Sir John French, decided to halt the Loos offensive. The campaign cost the British Expeditionary Force 50,000 casualties. The French lost 48,000 and the Germans about 24,000. Just one and a third German divisions had sufficed to smash up and drive back six British divisions north of Lens. The French fared no better, as their attack by fourteen divisions petered out under the defensive fire of just five German divisions. It was decided that Sir John French had to be removed as commander of the British Expeditionary Force. His failure to ensure that reserves were brought up to exploit the gains sealed his fate. His place was taken by General Sir Douglas Haig.

The Battle of Loos was yet another failure to follow that of the landings at Gallipoli, which had begun with such promise in April 1915 and was in the process of being abandoned in January 1916. The Pals divisions began taking up positions on the Western Front in December and January 1915.

Pals in the firing line

The 14th, 15th and 16th Royal Warwickshire (Birmingham City) Battalions had their first experiences of coming under fire courtesy of two brigades belonging to the 5th Division. As it turned out the temporary attachment was made permanent; the idea being to spread the raw Kitchener units among the

Three officers of C Company, 15th Battalion Royal Warwickshire (Second Birmingham Pals), receive brother officers at their lavish château headquarters near Monflieures during the battalion's acclimatisation period. TERRY CARTER

Regular Divisions. The 5th had fought at Mons in the opening moves of 1914 and was now placed in position at Bray sur Somme, a quiet sector. Author Terry Carter in the *Birmingham Pals* reproduces an officer's letter to his parents in which his impressions and conditions at the front are described. It was December and the weather was the wettest for many years:

> ... *after five miles we landed in the very small village* [Etinehem] *we are in now. I have never seen such mud in my life as we ploughed through the road here. It is absolutely no exaggeration to say that for nearly two thirds of the way there was two inches of liquid mud and such mud as I have never seen before. I might mention that whilst on the way the guns could be heard quite distinctly and whilst on top of a rise we saw two shells burst on a hill about two and a half miles distant. On arriving here we got the men into barns and then proceeded to look for some place for ourselves.*
>
> *We finally found the place I an now writing from. It is a room with a stone floor about the size of our front room with one bed, one table and six chairs in it. Captain Robinson is sleeping in the bed and "Betty"* [nickname] *and I on the floor. The other two have at present gone out to look for provisions...*
>
> *The hindmost trench is about fifty yards outside this village although I understand the firing line is four miles away, but when I look out of the window I can plainly see the searchlights. I have just had reported to me that a "Zep" has passed over here, athough I did not see it myself...*
>
> *Tomorrow we go to another place two miles up, for a bit of instruction I expect, and then on Sunday night we go for our first dose in the trenches. I always thought, when I was in England, that I should feel too excited to do anything as soon as I heard the guns, and know I was going into the trenches, but, although I have heard it, I do not think any more of it than if I were listening to the sound of trams on the Moseley Road... What my feelings will be when I get right into it, of course, I do not know.*

Next day was Saturday, 4 December 1915, when officers and sergeants of two companies of the 14th Battalion Royal Warwickshires moved up and passed through the shattered village of Bray sur Somme. For the men of the First Birmingham Pals it was their first sight of destruction wrought by enemy artillery. Leaving Bray on the road to Carnoy they arrived at Bronfay Farm, where they halted, awaiting the cover of darkness. They were now in easy range of German field guns. They set off along a road deeply pitted with shell holes and covered in clinging mud, inches deep. They stumbled on and fell numerous times until they were filthy and well covered in mud. The trench system in front of the obliterated village of Carnoy bulged out towards the German positions, forming a salient. Star shells were being fired on three sides and, as they reached the road leading to Peronne, they heard the zipping sound of their first German bullets. Just as the small group of officers and NCOs were crossing the brow of a hill a burst of machine-gun fire chattered out a welcome, causing them to take cover in the nearby reserve trenches. They were directed along to the British support trench line where they located Battalion HQ of the 2nd Battalion Kings Own Scottish Borderers (KOSB). Their small party was divided into two; one to stay at Carnoy and the other to enter the firing line.

A guide who was assigned to them led them off, not along the communication trench, but walking across country. After a mile they were within 500 metres of the front line and, much to their relief, the guide jumped down into the communication trench. Upon following him they understood why he had led them in the open for as long as he could – the trench was calf deep in water and mud. Better to risk the odd stray bullet and shrapnel on top than wading through water-logged trenches for over a mile. Taking their stint in the front line were the 2nd Battalion Kings Own Yorkshire Light Infantry (KOYLI), who took the newcomers under their wing. They survived their first night without casualties from enemy fire. However, two officers, Second Lieutenants Higgins and Hingeley were almost buried alive as they tried to grab a few hours sleep in a dugout. Due to the persistent rain the dugout they were sheltering in began to cave in on them. Fortunately for them both, Higgins was not fully asleep.

Birmingham Pals officers manning a listening post.
TERRY CARTER

Two among the party that had remained in the reserve trenches with the KOSBs experienced two firsts: a 'Whizzbang' (light shell) exploded on a kitchen dugout, wounding two cooks and destroying breakfast – first shell fire and first wounded men. Then as they reported to a ruined building to be guided to the front line,

As this was our first shell it naturally upset us a bit and it took an hour or two to get over it. We were next told to go and draw gum boots and directed to a small building in the village [Carnoy] through which the trench ran. By some mistake Betty and I went to the wrong one and our first sight on entering was that of a poor fellow who had been killed the night before. We then found that we had gone into the mortuary.

After the officers and the NCOs had been introduced to conditions in the trenches, it was the turn of the other ranks. On their way through the communication trenches the horror of what they were entering was brought home by the stink of decaying flesh and the sight of corpses, as the walls of rain-soaked trenches disintegrated to expose former French inhabitants of the sector. That first length of stay was three days and three nights. One private soldier recalled his first night:

> At length we reached what looked like an open drain full of mud. This, we were informed, was the front line. Sentries were posted and we began the night's vigil in surroundings completely strange, and with no idea of what might appear out of the darkness. The situation was very different from what we had imagined. We seemed to have reached the depth of misery. It was a cold, dark night, and there we were squatting on a wet fire step with no shelter of any description. Later on we treated such a case as all in a day's work.

There was one among those Birmingham Pals whose first-time experience of life on the Western Front proved too much. A year earlier he, like so many other youngsters, had been carried away by the patriotic fervour sweeping the country and he did what so many others did – he lied about his age when he had enlisted. At sixteen years old Private Alfred Cowell, 14th Battalion Warwickshire Regiment, had seen enough of army life and he wrote to his mother asking her to get him out. Three other under-age teenagers in the battalion were waiting to be shipped back to England after their parents had sent their birth certificates to the War Office. In a letter to his mother he asked her to do the same for him, adding that should he ever get back to England again he would desert, 'I'll chance being shot as it is awful'. At the end of January 1916 young Alfred Cowell was discharged as being under age. Four months later he re-enlisted again, this time in the Lancashire Fusiliers.

Before their first stint in the trenches was over, two men of B Company, First Birmingham Battalion, were picked off by a German sniper. They were Private Arthur Hackett and the Company Sergeant Major, James Kitchen. Hackett had the misfortune of being the first man of the three Birmingham battalions to be killed in action.

As the second Christmas of the war approached all three Birmingham battalions had experienced a stint in the front line. Strict orders were given that there was to be no handshaking, exchanging of souvenirs and playing football with the Germans as occured had the previous Christmas in 1914. Bitterness and dislike of the enemy caused by the year's fighting had made the repeat of the unofficial and spontaneous truce of 1914 unlikely.

The Birmingham Pals were still learning the art of keeping their heads down and a steady stream of casualties ensued. It was decided to take the Germans on at their own game and sniper sections were set up. The very best marksmen were supplied with rifles fitted with telescopic sights and allowed to set up their own positions along the line in cunningly contrived places, usually at the edge of a certain wood. They were soon regaling their comrades with tales of their accomplishments as battalion snipers. Out of the line time was filled with carrying supplies up to the front and cleaning mud off their

Muddy Maricourt. Four officers of the 15th Battalion Royal Warwickshire Regiment with sticks to test the depth of the liquid mud they have to live in. TERRY CARTER

rifles, clothes and equipment. One sergeant described the experience:

I know that it's Sunday because of Church parade. Once again the day of cleaning commences and we are all hard at the scrape, scrape, scrape against our tunics, trousers and equipment etc, not to mention rifles which require a good day's work to get them right again. Turn out for inspection and pass fairly well owing to the energy displayed with our useful friend the jack-knife. Church parade at 3 pm. Would you believe it! My toes have not been warm for days. First one we have had since we landed. Forgot almost that there was such a thing as Sunday in the week. We sing hymns and get colder.

After the service, which took place in a field just behind where our guns were banging away, our CO says a few words about what men on active service get shot for. By the way, the sermon was about peace. It seems to me that quite a few ought to be shot already!

Good things from home served to brighten the festive season as a multitude of 'practical' gift parcels were delivered. They included cakes, woollen jumpers, mittens, socks and helmets. One embarrassed soldier received a chain-mail coat from a well-meaning relative, which when tried on, chafed him severely. Bombarded by merciless ribbing and leg-pulling he finally upped and flung it through the window.

The 3rd Birmingham Battalion spent its Christmas in the front line at Carnoy from the 23-27 December. During which period of 'goodwill' the Germans put down a barrage which killed six men, mostly from one platoon, and injured three others. Among the killed was the fifty-year-old Regimental Sergeant Major, Peter Swain Morgan, of Kidderminster (formerly of the Coldstream Guards). Once the 3rd Battalion was out of the line, had rested and cleaned up, its members were able to enjoy the traditional Christmas dinner and open their parcels from home. With the Birminghams experiencing action for the first time on the banks of the Somme river, the Liverpool Pals also took up position in the extreme south of what had come to be regarded as the Somme sector. Each of the four battalions was assigned a different section of the front. Each Company took turns in 'going up' and was introduced to the experience by one of the Regular battalions holding the line. Author Graham Maddocks recorded the experience of Lieutenant E W Willmer of the 17th Battalion (First Liverpool Pals):

> *Eventually, after a long march at dead of night, we reached the village of Englebelmer, and each company was allotted to a company, much depleted, of the Royal Irish Rifles; a happy-go-lucky crowd, who were extremely kind to us, and taught us a lot. It was a quiet section of the line and nothing had happened there for some months, we were told. A few odd shells came over and an even fewer number were sent back. Buildings which had been damaged were further wrecked and new shell-holes were created, but very few men were hit, and most of the time was spent trying to make the trenches fit for occupation by human beings. The communication trenches were in such a mess that most of them were unusable. One waited 'til nightfall and then walked over the top to the front line. But the front line had to be kept navigable, and that often meant keeping the water level below that of the fire step, and confining the mud to the bottom of the trench itself. With gumboots one waded through it, but the fire step was dry land. Dugouts were mostly rough shelters and were not proof against enemy action.*

All four Liverpool Pals battalions were out of the front line trench in time for Christmas Day.

The brigade commanders, whose units were engaged in the induction of battalions of the New Army, made out confidential reports on how their charges performed. Brigadier General Bainbridge, commanding 110 Brigade, reported on how the Fourth Liverpool Pals performed under his brigade's tutelage. Military knowledge he judged to be average and 'keeness very pronounced', with a good class of NCO which resulted in good military discipline. In his general remarks he reported:

> *This is certainly the best battalion which has been sent to this brigade for instruction. It is well commanded and has a really good tone all through. The men get through their work quickly, thoroughly and cheerfully, and all ranks are keen to learn. This should be a really good battalion in a very short time.*

As a direct result of the excellent report they were considered to be fit enough to be assigned a sector down in the extreme south of the Somme battlefront. In January 1916, with the rest of 30th Division they marched south to Carnoy, on the banks of the Somme. Because it was a sector recently vacated by French troops the trenches were in a poor state. As they had no desire to get comfortable, but were looking to clear the invaders off their territory, the French took little pains with their defensive works.

The Liverpool Brigade was about to experience its first experience of what it was like to be on the edge of a German attack. A strange warning was given by some undisciplined Saxons in the trenches opposite them. The weather was appaling, as usual, and the trenches they were occupying were without duckboards, making for a miserable, sloshy existence. It seemed as if the enemy across No Man's Land was likewise suffering from the continual drizzle of freezing rain. A voice called out to the Liverpools identifying themselves as Saxons and that after the 29th they could have, not only their trenches, but also 'the ******* Kaiser as well'. It was obvious that the Saxons were equally fed up, perhaps considering that, being of the same blood stock as the English and thus sharing some affinity, they would be helpful. Consequently, they blatantly delivered warning of an impending attack, divulging the date. Had the shouted date been passed to Intelligence at Division the British might have been able to work out that, as the 29 January was the Kaiser's birthday, something would probably be in the offing by way of a celebration.

South of the Somme River, at Frise, the French line jutted out to form a salient. Author Jack Sheldon in his excellent book *The German Army on the Somme* records the events from the German side. He informs us that a

German troops having to cope with movement through a quagmire.

German troops attacking over a wintery landscape.

conference was held on 11 January which planned an attack on Frise and postions running southward. It was felt that insufficent resources would permit only a limited operation to straighten the line and thus shorten it for the Germans. It was decided to use gas, which meant that favourable winds would have to be waited for. German Infantry Regiments 38 and 51 would participate. Sixty batteries of artillery were moved into position along with fifty-nine trench mortars. The favourable wind failed to materialise and extra ammunition was hastily brought up. The bombardment increased until on the 28 January, over a distance of one and a half miles, over 35,000 shells were fired onto the British and French trenches. In the afternoon of the 28th deception feints were launched to mislead the French. The main attack was launched at 4.30 in the afternoon and infantry swept over the French trenches round the village of Frise capturing seventeen officers and 1,300 French soldiers. Many French troops were killed and wounded. Casualties suffered by the attackers were eighty wounded and one officer and four men killed. One elated soldier of Infantry Regiment 38 wrote home after the battle was over:

Feeling alert, well and in the best of spirits. I send you heartiest greetings from the French trenches, which we have just captured in a brilliantly successful attack in a slightly late celebrations of the Kaiser's birthday. I am sitting in front of one of the few French dugouts spared by our drumfire. By the way it is a fairly dismal hole. Before me is a magnificient view of the Somme marshes, made more beautiful in the eyes of us soldiers by the warlike sight of the wrecked canal embankments, smashed avenues of popular trees and the great fountains of water thrown up by the impact of heavy shells. The attack was simple, our casualties were light, but the days leading up to it were hard work. For once it was a return to a jolly sort of warfare. this was not just a fight it was a victory.

The defeat of the French on their right meant that the British flank on the river was exposed to enfilade fire. The French counter-attacked on the last day of January and were able to recapture most of the lost ground, although the village of Frise was held by the Germans until July.

For the Second Liverpool Pals in the front line trenches at Carnoy, the Kaiser's birthday attack brought No.3 Company, under Captain Arthur de Bels Adam, into action. In the early hours of 29 January, Captain Adam reported that the area of trenches manned by his company was being heavily bombarded by trench mortars. Within the hour of making his report, approximately one hundred Germans charged across No Man's Land, some having infiltrated past sentries occupying forward saps, and entered a disused section of trench. The only way to oust them was by grenades and hand to hand fighting. Whilst it was still dark Captain Adams led a counter-attack to dislodge the intruders, and there followed fierce hand-to-hand fighting which lasted for fifteen minutes. The Germans then withdrew taking their wounded with them. Captain Adams found that he had lost two men killed and eight wounded. Two Germans were found dead and four were wounded. They were taken prisoner and one them, a junior officer, died later in the day. For leading the successful counter-attack and ousting the enemy, Captain Adam was awarded the Military Cross. A Lance Corporal Cohen was awarded the Distinguished Conduct Medal, the next highest award for other ranks to the Victoria Cross.

Another battalion of the 30th Division, First Manchester City Battalion, had arrived at the village of Hebuterne which was situated half a mile behind the front line and opposite the German held village of Gommecourt. Their arrival at the village in December 1915 could only be described as naive, or even stupid. Scout Sergeant Bert Payne of the First Manchesters would later write:

That's how the stupidity came in, how ignorant we all were. We thought we were clever but we were just damned ignorant – from the top to the bottom – including me. First of all they should not have come through Hebuterne in daylight. They marched through with bands playing and the officers mounted on their horses. Jerry opened fire and I saw dud shells falling there. Captain Behrens lost his leg, he was shot off his horse. I saw dud shells landing right in the square. What would have happened if those shells had have burst? There would have been carnage. We got through, in the end, to the trenches. That was the first time we had been under fire.

After a week's familiarisation in the front lines the battalion marched down south to the banks of the Somme. They joined the rest of 30th Division in the line in the vicinity of Maricourt village and Carnoy.

Another division, the 32nd, took its place in the line and the Salford Brigade found itself in the vicinity of the German-held village of La Boisselle. It was two weeks before Christmas when, following the usual familiarisation, they took responsibility for an area around what was known as the Ilot. Because the two lines of trenches came close together in front of La Boisselle there was a great deal of underground tunnelling by both sides. The practice was that a deep tunnel would be excavated towards, and under, the enemy lines. When it was judged that the correct distance had been reached a chamber was excavated. The chamber was then packed with bags of high explosives; detonators were placed and wires run back along the tunnel to the firing point. The chamber was sealed up, or tamped, so that the main blast force of the mine explosion would go upwards and hopefully destroy the enemy's trench system. It could be timed to explode at a tactical moment, say prior to an attack. After an explosion there was usually a dash by both sides to occupy the lip of the crater. The loosened earth could be worked very quickly to make defensive positions giving the occupiers the advantage of height, through the raised crater lip, to dominate No Man's Land and the enemy's lines. Spoiling explosions, known as camouflets, were set off in counter-mining tunnels to cave in the excavations of the other side. Sometimes tunnellers would break into the workings of the enemy and fierce hand-to-hand fighting would ensue.

Germans engaged in tunneling operations. The ground in front of the village of La Boisselle was pitted with craters from underground explosions.

On 18 December 1915 two German camouflets were exploded simultaneously, caving in some underground galleries and tunnels. Three miners of a tunnelling company were killed along with a man from the 16th Battalion, Second Salford Pals. The following day the Germans blew their own mine under the British trenches at 3.15 in the afternoon. Salford men were crouched in their positions listening to their artillery putting down a bombardment on German positions in the village of La Boisselle when suddenly the ground under a section of trench, named Dunhollow Street, leapt into the air. Three forward listening posts were destroyed and five miners were killed underground. Two Salford men simply disappeared, no trace was ever found of them even though their pals scoured the area for two nights.

Another listening post on the edge of the main explosion had been wrecked. It was Sergeant A Smith who set off crawling across the open ground to help any survivors. He found five dazed and bruised men among the remains of the shattered post. He led them back to the relative safety of the trenches as darkness fell. Then it was that the sound of a voice, as if in pain, called out 'Sergeant!' Once again Sergeant Smith set off in the direction of the voice. Then there was another cry of 'Sergeant!' from another direction and then another. It was then realised that the Germans were, in fact, mimicking an injured man to draw the courageous NCO up to their lines.

Early in 1916 the brigading arrangements of the Salford Pals were altered to incorporate Regular Army units. This was occuring with most of the Pals battalions, as it was considered the course of wisdom to stiffen the New Army formations, ready for the planned onslaught on the German lines. The attack, referred to as the 'Big Push', was intended to break through the German static defence positions and allow the cavalry divisions to sweep through and drive the enemy out of France and Belgium. Plans had been made for this decisive action in December at an Anglo-French conference at Chantilly. Command of the British Expeditionary Force was given to Sir Douglas Haig and the aim was to secure victory over the Germans by the end of 1916.

Every available division in the British Army would be needed for the coming Big Push scheduled for the summer of 1916. It was to include the 31st New Army Division which, in the winter of 1915, was guarding the Suez Canal against possible Turkish attack.

Guarding the Suez Canal

On 5 November 1914 Britain, France and Russia declared war on Turkey, which nation had managed to stay neutral since the outbreak of hostilities. However, she was brought into the fighting on the side of the Central Powers when two cruisers, the *Goeben* and the *Breslau*, were sold to Turkey by the Germans. The German commander, along with his German crew, then promptly bombarded Russia's Black Sea ports. Turkey's neutrality was thus compromised and her entry into the conflict against the Allies brought about new threats for the British Empire. Entry and exit to the Black Sea through the Dardenelles would be stopped; the Suez Canal could be lost, which would create severe problems when communicating and transporting to and from the Dominions; oil fields in Mesopotamia could be threatened. If the Suez Canal was to be attacked by the Turks then the attack would come by way of the Sinai Desert.

As anticipated, just eight weeks into the war British Intelligence warned of a considerable Turkish force gathering on the eastern edge of the Sinai. The orders given to the Turkish commander, Djemal Pasha, were to seize and hold

German postcard depicting the Turkish troops on the side of the Suez Canal in great force. It was to counter this threat that the 31st Infantry Division was sent to the area.

the Canal long enough to render it unusable by sinking ships to block it and thereby deny the use of that important strategic artery to the Entente. 'By the Grace of Allah we shall attack the enemy on the night of 2nd and 3rd February and seize the Canal.'

The troops guarding the Canal comprised only two Indian divisions, but when the attack came they were sufficient to drive the Turks off. The plan was to cross the Canal to the west side on small pontoons, which had been carried across the desert for the purpose. However, the Turks were discovered, despite attacking under cover of a sand storm. Some who managed to get across were despatched by a bayonet charge. Supply problems were pressing and the Turks withdrew the way they had come. With the British and French operations in the Dardanelles in February 1915 the fight was taken to the Turks. The attack on the Canal, however, served to demonstrate what might happen again in future, thus causing troops to be tied up in its defence.

The 31st Division was sent to bolster the Suez Canal defences and eleven troopships were required to transport it. The first transports sailed on 8

December and the last on the 29th – it was a voyage of three weeks. The journey was memorable for the majority of men, because most had never travelled more than 100 miles from home before.

Some of the transports left an English port to the accompaniment of the battalion band and cheering onlookers. The Sheffield City Battalion received a send off which was recorded by authors Ralph Gibson and Paul Oldfield. On 21 December 1915 Devonport seemed to have turned out in force to say farewell to the men on HMT *Nestor*. Harbour tugs blew their whistles, naval guns fired salutes and men in the naval barracks and crews on other ships cheered their departure. On the *Nestor* the regimental band played 'Keep the Home Fires Burning' and 'Auld Lang Syne', then the National Anthem. The Sheffield men cheered themselves hoarse in response to the send off.

The First and Second Barnsley Pals sailed on 29 December following the same course as their Sheffield comrades. Perhaps the send off was a little more subdued for them, yet just as emotional, as recalled by Frank Lindley, 14th Battalion, York and Lancaster Regiment (Second Barnsleys),

> We went down the Sound at the side of the Hoe and there were some folks there who had got the whiff that we were going. They were waving their handkerchiefs at us. We all waved our pith helmets. If you had have seen that ship, full of these pith helmets all going round. You couldn't see anything on that ship but pith helmets all over. It was a sight to be seen. And then it started – someone singing 'Homeland' and it was ringing and echoing over the Hoe:
>
> > Homeland, homeland, land of my birth.
> > The dearest place on earth.
> > It may be for years.
> > It may be forever.
> > Dear homeland goodbye.

And as Frank remembered and commented in an interview in 1985, 'And there weren't many of us came back'.

What is surprising is the way in which troop movements were published in this country during the First World War. Enemy secret agents would only have to buy certain provincial newspapers in order to gather important intelligence concerning British troop movements. Take for example the report in the *Barnsley Chronicle* newspaper dated 1 January 1916 in which the reporter describes the departure of the Pals for the paper's readers:

> There is a nasty wind bringing in a choppy sea. The transport is now rounding Drake Island and dropping the hawser from the tug. I can see your lads crowding the bulwarks, having a look at the beautiful bay – perhaps the most beautiful and the most interesting in England. They are passing the very spot where Drake played his famous game of bowls; sailing on the very sea where Howard gathered the fleet to smash the Armada. They can see the monuments commemorating both, and three centuries of English history look down on them. They are so near I could almost speak to them. But now she is heading for sea. No – she turns – she is dropping her anchor in the bay. Why? "Some trouble" says a tar, "for see, one of the destroyers told off to escort her returns and speaks to her. Perhaps a submarine knocking about – perhaps

waiting for orders." But as dusk came she made for open sea.

The *Andania*, packed with 2,212 troops, was still at sea and off the coast of Spain when that account was published in the *Barnsley Chronicle*. Some useful information that could be added to other gathered intelligence that would, in turn, provide a picture of British troop movements and could be transmited to U-boats operating in the Mediterranean. A far cry from the 'Careless Talk Costs Lives' policy of the Second World War.

As the English coastline grew fainter the 13,000 ton vessel began pitching and rolling. It was a new experience for the Barnsley men, mainly miners, and at once seasickness gripped the majorityof them. A 13th Battalion man, First Barnsleys, told me that the furthest he had been prior to that sea voyage to the Middle East was to Cleethorpes. He remembered being violently sick and laying on the upper deck of the *Andania* for three days. 'I remember the first day I went down, I got to the top of the gang way steps and met this fellow carrying a trayful of Quaker Oats... that was enough, I went back.' Some who soon got over their initial queasiness were able to eat as much as they liked, there was always plenty to spare.

Innoculations against cholera were carried out early on the voyage when most of the men were weakened by seasickness. Frank Lindley 14th Battalion, Second Barnsleys, recalled the miserable event,

> *When we got out into the Bay of Biscay it was really rough. The best of it was they decided to innoculate us on the ship. We had to go down below near the engines. Talk about hot down there, with the ship pitching and them jabbing needles in. Oh! Crikey! There was a bathroom at the side and that bath was full of spew. To top it all we then had to line the deck and watch for submarines. You could see an odd destroyer nipping about as if they were looking after us. And there were all these porpoises going like hell up and down in front of the ship. It*

For most of the men in the 31st Division it was the first time they had been at sea, with the inevitable results. DAVID BILTON

As the troops ships sailed through the Mediterranean the Pals began to build themselves up following the bouts of sea sickness. DAVID BILTON

was a good sight, but with us staring out at the water it made you ill.
Once the troop ships passed through the Straights of Gibraltar and entered the warmer waters of the Mediterranean life aboard ship improved.

Some weeks earlier, under the cover of night, the *Empress of Britain*, transporting most of 93 Brigade, comprising two Bradford Pals battalions, Leeds and Durham Pals, sailed into the Mediterranean. Some days later they collided with a French steamship which was on a mail run from Salonika to Malta. Both vessels were blacked out and following a zig-zag course, which was the usual procedure with German submarines operating in the area. The French vessel was struck amidships and sank within half an hour. Apart from two French crewmen who lost their lives in the collision, all aboard were picked up and saved. The *Empress of Britain* with a buckled prow, was able to carry on to Malta which was reached the following day. As the ship entered the Grand Harbour, Valletta, the Leeds Pals band put on a show of Imperial majesty playing stirring national songs and marches. It took three days to repair the damage caused by the collision during which time the ship was re-supplied and coal taken on board.

Not long out of Valletta, on the way to Port Said, enemy submarines launched an attack. It was a two and a half day voyage from Malta to the Suez Canal and U-Boats operated in that stretch of water. A torpedo passed close astern, but, apparently its deathly course was diverted by the wash from the troop ship's propellers. The single gun aboard the *Empress* went into action when the U-Boat was sighted on the surface. The Germans made another attempt in the early hours of the next day missing again with another precious torpedo. With superior speed on the water than the submarine the *Empress* sped away making a series of course alterations to throw the aim of the U-Boat captain.

The *Empress* arrived safely at Port Said on Tuesday, 21 December 1915, disembarking the Leeds, Bradford and Durham Pals of 93 Brigade. Before the end of December five ships had brought 92 Brigade, Hull Pals, to the Suez Canal. It would be over a week later that the *Andania,* carrying 94 Brigade, Sheffield, Accrington and Barnsley Pals arrived. Because they missed the cut-off date of 31 December, it meant that the men of 94 Brigade did not reach a war zone until 1916. Thus they would not be entitled to a service medal - the 1914/15 Star. A small point, but one which rankled with many men of 94 Brigade from that time on.

The 31st Division was to be in Egypt for two months as part of the Imperial Strategic Reserve – the only division of the New Army to serve on the Canal. It was there to protect the vital communication link, however, the threat from the Turks had fallen off, although a contingent of Turkish troops led by a German general was hovering at the eastern edge of the Sinai. With the withdrawal of Allied troops from the Dardanelles, following the failure of the Gallipoli Campaign, it would mean that the Turks could turn their attentions to

Port Said showing the offices of the Suez Canal Company. DAVID BILTON

the Canal. On the other hand it also freed Allied troops for use in the Canal's defence. The Pals were to be employed constructing a new defensive line across the path of any possible Turkish incursion. The line of posts, barbed wire and trenches, would be at sufficient distance out in the desert to put any Turkish field gun out of range of the waterway. It was designed to be a defence line 100 miles in length.

With the arrival of 94 Brigade at the beginning of January there was a cultural shock awaiting both the pit lads of Barnsley and the native Egyptians. Charlie Swales, 14th Battalion, Second Barnsleys, in an interview in 1985, described one incident that happened when the two cultures collided,

> When the boat stopped at Port Said some of the natives were coming on rowing boats. They wore fezes and they had like a long smock on down to their ankles. One of the lads said,"Are they lads or lasses?" Then it was that one of the lads had a bright idea. "There's only one way to find art," he said "let's tipple one of the buggers upside darn!" So one of 'em was up-ended to see if it was a lad or a lass. It worra lad. It was all in fun – they were just typical collier lads.

Everywhere the men went they were pestered to buy items of one sort or another by children. Tomatoes, oranges, dates, figs, sugar cane and cakes were offered for sale. In the Arab quarter, and on visits from native peddlers to the tent lines, the Pals mastered the art of bartering for goods. On every street there were bars managed by French, Turkish or Egyptian proprietors. Some establishments offering more than merchandise and drink for sale. Frank Lindley, Second Barnsleys, recalled,

> I went into one place and these lasses were dancing round with bits of lace on and not much else. There'd be a bowl of monkey nuts on the table and we'd sup a glass of wine while these lasses danced all around us.

Some parts of town were out of bounds to the soldiers as the natives in some quarters were not in sympathy with the English presence. There were stories circulating of brutal murders carried out against the unwary, or foolish, who happened to end up in the wrong part of town. One man in the Second Bradford Pals saw a grisley sight when he was swiming in one of the many shallows at the entrance to the Canal. A rowing boat containing the body of a British soldier with his tongue partly cut out was rowed past. The man's body had been discovered in the Arab Quarter.

Both Barnsley battalions left the Rest Camp in Port Said and were transported forty miles along the Canal to El Ferdan in the south. They were then ferried across to the eastern bank. Private Tom Bradbury, E Company 13th Battalion, First Barnsleys, was a regular correspondent to the *Barnsley Chronicle* and the editor dutifully printed his letters so that the town's people could see the life their loved ones were leading on active service.

> I have had my first experience of outpost duty in a hostile country and I have spent a very cold night I can tell you. It makes you feel that you are a soldier when you stand with a loaded rifle and fixed bayonet out in the desert at night, gazing into the sandy wastes towards the Turkish lines. You can guess – daylight comes very welcome. We are indeed roughing it now. We get our

Camels bringing in materials to construct defences on the eastern bank of the Suez Canal.

precious drinking water from a tank-boat and do our toilet and washing in the salty water of the Canal. It is a very funny thing trying to get a lather in sea water. We have a fair number of camels with Arab drivers and they come in very useful for carrying goods. We got a very good view of the surrounding countryside in travelling by train in open trucks. When we stopped at stations the natives came and wanted to sell us all kinds of fruits, such as dates, figs, oranges etc. The fruit tastes surprisingly good out here.

After they had arrived at El Ferdan they were marched off into the desert, and it turned out to be the most difficult march that any of them had experienced so far. Soft, yielding sand swallowed their boots with each step taken. As the sun climbed higher the temperature soared and it was quickly discovered that their thick uniforms were totally unsuited to such conditions.

We went out to a place in the desert called Abu Aruk. We went there digging trenches for quite a while. In the daytime we were roasted, at night time we were frozen. When we were in the trenches we had no cover. We were in the trenches all night you see. Didn't see any tents until we got back to Kantara. We had a few dugouts where we got in to have a sleep and we could hear the wild dogs howling all night, we couldn't shoot them. When we were digging the trenches we had matting to hold the sand back and we used to peg that down. If we had any machine gun emplacements they were built up with sandbags, built up like brickwork.

Ernest Bell, 13th Battalion, First Barnsley Pals

By the end of January fresh troops began to arrive from Gallipoli and the time would soon come when the 31st Division would be relieved of guarding the Canal. The division would be shipped to the Western Front ready for the Big Push planned for the summer of 1916. However, there were some who had come to be among the rank and file who should not have been there at all.

There were a great number of under age soldiers in the Pals battalions and one evening an Australian officer called Best, who was inspecting one of the posts manned by a section of Second Barnsleys, asked them outright, 'Now come clean boys, I know damn well that there's not one of you old enough to be here!' After assuring them that there was nothing he could do about it anyway, each one admitted his true age. All of them apart from one was under the age of twenty-one. The exception was a man called Kilner who was over age to be in the British Army. When asked by the officer if he would rather be with men of his own age, Kilner replied, 'I'm all reight wit young uns, they look after me'.

If army regulations had been followed that entire section of ten men belonging to C Company, would have been taken off active service and returned to England. However, practically every man in Kitchener's New Army was there because of a strong desire to be a part of the great adventure and, regulations or no, it was an experience not to be missed. They reasoned that they were not career soldiers, they were merely civilians in khaki for a temporary period – a few months – until the Germans and their allies could be soundly defeated. After the victory parades were over battalions would be disbanded and the citizens would return to the mines, mills, factories and offices from where they had come. That any of them might be killed, gassed, blinded, maimed or taken captive, was rarely contemplated. That sort of thing happened to others. But injuries and fatalities were already occurring, and not from enemy action. From the Leeds Pals, in February 1916, out in the desert from Kantara at one of the defence posts, one soldier accidently discharged his rifle

Three Leeds Pals watch a Dutch steamer passing through the Canal. Holland remained neutral and the flag painted on the side was to alert U-Boats to the ship's nationality.
LAURIE MILNER

while cleaning it and killed his best friend. A few days later further careless handling of firearms resulted in the wounding of two more Leeds men. Also in the month of February an Accrington Pals officer, Lieutenant Harry Mitchell (a former insurance broker from Blackburn), was seriously injured in an accident and died two days later.

The Pals may not have been professional soldiers but they considered themselves to be every bit as good as the Regulars and Territorials they were to fight alongside. The men were already friends in their civilian occupations, but after training, travelling and sharing common hardships, they were the equal of any. An example of their *esprit de corps* and comradeship is seen in an insobordinate comment called out by an Accrington man during a march. Z Company, 11th Battalion East Lancashire Regiment, was passing a camp of a Regular battalion at El Kantara. They could see that two of the Regular soldiers had been tied to the wheels of wagons in the full glare of the sun, undergoing Field Punishment No.1. That humiliating and uncomfortable act was carried out twice a day for one or two hours each time. It was usually accompanied by strenuous manual work or exercise throughout the day. In extreme cases the punishment could last for as long as three months. The Accrington officer in command of Z Company, Captain 'Potty' Ross, called out to his men,'That's what happens if you misbehave!' Someone in the Accringtons yelled back, 'It won't tha knows, if you did that to any of us, t'others would cut him down!' Proud talk, but sincerely meant by the one who voiced it.

One under age Barnsley soldier (fifteen years old), Frank Lindley, suffered Field Punishment No.1 whilst in Egypt. He had been giving some 'lip' to one of the NCOs and was put on a charge. Frank recalled,

I was fastened to the back wheel of a limber on the sand and another fellow was fastened on the other side of me. He scraped all the sand away to let his wheel down so that he could sit. I was propped up on my wheel and my bloody hat fell off. It was only a couple of hours, but with the sun, I couldn't see for three or four days after – only blue lights. I hadn't done anything really bad. I admit I was a bit arrogant against the 'stripeys' because I'd dressed some of them when they were first in. Then they got a stripe and they worked it at you. They had to show their authority.

A few weeks later in France another Pal died while undergoing the archaic form of punishment. Tying to an object, usually a wooden stake or waggon wheel, in full view of the rest of the battalion was meant to be a deterent to all as well as a punishment. It had taken the place of

Frank Lindley.

flogging which was discontinued in the British Army in 1881. The soldier who died was in the 17th Battalion The King's (Liverpool Regiment), First Liverpool Pals. One day in March there was a surprise kit inspection and eleven men of C Company were found to be without gas respirators. Lieutenant Colonel Fairfax sentenced them all to one day's Field Service Punishment No.1. Each man was examined by the medical officer to make sure that he was fit enough to undergo the ordeal. One man, Private S B Heyes, who had worked as a clerk in Liverpool Corn Exchange, was found to be unwell but the opinion was that he was 'quite able to be tied to a wheel'. Unfortunately, on this occasion, the punishment involved the digging of a large hole to bury some spoiled food. Following that, the men had to double round the village square for ten minutes before being tied to a wheel for ten minutes. They were untied and made to march at the double again. After two hours Heyes, being tied for a period of ten minutes and released for the second time, began staggering when made to double march. He collapsed to the ground in front of his pal, Private Dunn, crying out 'I can't go on' and died in his friends arms. He had suffered a severe heart attack from the exertions.

When the circumstances of his death became public knowledge there was an outcry and questions were asked in the House of Commons. Certainly

General Erich von Falkenhayn, believed that if the French Army could be bled white in a battle of attrition the war could be won for Germany. The place selected was Verdun. A group of French soldiers meet the guide who is to take them to their positions in the front line.

*neral Erich von
Falkenhayn*

commanders became more circumspect in awarding the punishment. In 1923 Field Punishment No.1 was finally abolished.

At the beginning of March 1916, battalions of the 31st Division began to move off from the bases alongside the Canal and head for Port Said. The Division's sojourn in North Africa was at an end.

The Great War would be settled once and for all in France and Flanders, the Gemans had seen to that by launching a massive offensive against the French army at Verdun. The German Chief of the General Staff, General Erich von Falkenhayn, believed that if the French could be bled white in a battle of attrition it would cease to be an effective ally to the British. Therefore a concentrated attack on some city, dear to the Gallic heart would cause the French General Staff to pour men into the fray. In Falkenhayn's 'December Memorandum' he stated:

...the French General Staff would be compelled to throw in every man they have. If they do so the forces of France will bleed to death, as there can be no question of a voluntary withdrawal, whether we reach our goal or not. If they do not do so and we reach our objectives the moral effect on France will be enormous. In an operation limited to a narrow front, Germany will not be compelled to spend herself completely.

It is difficult to imagine a more callous disregard for the lives of his own men than Falkenhayn's strategy to win the war. A deliberate plan to bring about the slaughter of hundreds of thousands so that the will and wherewithall of the enemy to carry on melts away; along with the optimistic view that the attacker's losses, somehow, would be sustainable. The German attack towards the city of Verdun began 21 February 1916. The continuation of the Battle of the Somme into the early winter of 1916 was to relieve pressure on Verdun, which was the sort of fighting that Falkenhayn had planned – that of attrition.

Still on a wave of naive patriotism and high morale, men of the 31st Division headed for the transport ships at Port Said. The 13th Battalion, First Barnsleys, went by rail. Their less fortunate sister battalion the Second Barnsleys marched twenty-seven miles with their commander, Lieutenant Colonel Hulke on his horse ahead of them. Two ships, the *Briton* and the *Megantic,* sailed for the South of France with the Sheffield City Battalion and the two Barnsley battalions. The other battalion of 94 Brigade, Accrington Pals, sailed on the *Llandovery Castle* and they, like the rest of 31st Division, had happy memories of a pleasant voyage through the Mediterranean to the port of Marseilles on the south coast of France.

Tynesiders at the Front

The Tyneside battalions, belonging to 34th Division, began their life at the Front in the first week of February 1916. A quiet section of the trench system, where so many others before them first experienced 'holding the line', was to be their proving ground. They were assigned, by companies, to the oversight of those of Regular battalion companies. Once shown the ropes they could then be moved to sections of the line ready for the Big Push.

Towards the end of the month the 26th Battalion , Tyneside Irish, took over part of the line in battalion strength, for the first time. Patrols were sent out at night to inspect the wire and work was done on damaged trenches. During one night members of the Third Irish looked on in fascination as a German Zeppelin flew low over the British trenches heading eastwards. It may have been in trouble as it came to earth behind the enemy lines.

'Daily wastage' was a term used to describe the everyday killing and wounding of men caused by enemy shelling and small arms fire. Three men were killed in three days and ten men were wounded. On the night of 15/16 March a German flag appeared in No Man's Land in front of the 27th Battalion's trenches. Not the sort of thing that the Tyneside Irish wished to have fluttering away before them. The battalion snipers shot at the pole supporting it and managed to bring it down. What a fine souvenir the flag would make, it was decided. There was no shortage of volunteers to attempt its recovery and that night a Lieutenant Ervine set out with two men of his platoon to capture the trophy. The three-man patrol got to within twenty-five yards of the German flag when a machine-gun opened up on them from one quarter and rifle fire from another. The Germans had been expecting them. The Tynesiders managed to escape the trap and return to their own lines unscathed. In the early hours of the morning, on Saint Patrick's Day, Lieutenant Ervine made another attempt, but on this occasion he went out into No Man's Land alone. Men of his platoon peered into the night, out into No Man's Land, trying to catch a glimpse of him. After a while the Platoon sergeant crawled out through the wire to try and locate him. Then he was spotted, the Germans had fired a star shell to illuminate the area. The usual procedure was to freeze whenever a flare lit up shell-torn ground between the opposing lines. However, the figure of their officer could be seen as he slowly made his way to the safety of his own lines. When he rolled into the front line trench he was seen to be covered head to foot in mud. He had fallen into a flooded disused trench. As his men gathered around him he suddenly dipped inside his muddy jacket and pulled out the German flag. His company commander, Captain Davey, and another officer erected a stout pole and nailed the trophy to it. Above it they secured the battalion battle ensign, a green flag with a golden harp upon it. The Irish flag had been presented to the Company before leaving the country. With that day's dawn the Germans were greeted with the sight of their ensign fluttering away under that of the Tynesiders. As can be imagined, the sight drew rifle fire from the enraged Germans for the rest of St Patrick's Day. Visitors from other parts of the British lines arrived throughout the day to admire the sight and congratulate Lieutenant Ervine. (The German Ensign was presented to the regimental museum in 1959 by Lieutenant Ervine's brother. Lieutenant Ervine was fatally wounded shortly after the incident.)

In the firing by the Germans to bring down the pole with the flags, two Tynesiders were hit and wounded. One of them, Private William Brown, was mortally wounded. A letter to the man's next of kin, in this instance his wife, is an example of the hundreds of thousands written by officers when a man was killed:

German sniper takes aim. Note the well constructed trench with armour plated sniper position. GRAHAM STEWART & JOHN SHEEN

Dear Madam,

It is with very great regret that I have to inform you that your husband lost his life on Friday March 17th at about 4.15 in the early morning. He was on sentry in his bay in a trench very close to the Germans, when a bullet struck him. His comrades took him to the dressing station as fast as possible, but the wound proved fatal.

I have not been in charge of this platoon for a very long time, but during the short time I had you husband under my charge, I was able to see that he was a good soldier and a fearless man. He did his duty thoroughly and died bravely for a worthy cause. I hope that you will be given health and strength to bring up your family and that you will bear up as well as can be expected during this great trial.

I am, yours faithfully,

E J Blight, Lieut.

Two days later snipers of the 24th Battalion claimed two Germans shot, and on the same day the 25th Battalion claimed one Geman cyclist. Awards for gallant conduct began to be made around this time, the Military Medal for the other ranks and the Military Cross for officers. The first Military Cross awarded to the Tyneside Irish Brigade was to the bombing officer, 27th Battalion, Northumberland Fusiliers (Fourth Tynesiders), Lieutenant J W Marshall from South Shields. A sergeant from West Hartlepool, James Burke, had been seriously wounded and got caught up in the German wire. Lieutenant Marshall brought the NCO in under heavy fire.

The Tyneside Brigade was withdrawn from the line on 10 April 1916. They handed over the 'quiet' sector of the line to the 2nd Australian Division which had arrived in France from Gallipoli. Home leave was being granted to a few and reinforcements arrived from England. At the beginning of May the Tyneside Irish Brigade was on the way to the Somme by way of route marches and trains.

The Tyneside Scottish, another brigade of New Army Pals in the 34th Division, Tyneside Scottish, also began travelling south to the area where the Big Push was to be launched. In a letter to his father Private William Hall gave brief details,

> *Well we have had a torturous week last week. We have been marching three days and mind we got some stick with distance, pack and heat and eating rich food, such as nice cake and fruit (dog biscuits) and then we rode twenty-four miles in cattle trucks.*

Albert, the principal town behind the Somme front, scene of constant activity in the lead up to the Big Push. GRAHAM STEWART & JOHN SHEEN

The Tyneside Scottish Brigade was at first employed in helping to bring up material and supplies to the massive supply dumps in the area behind the town of Albert. In the coming all-out offensive the Division had been allocated the line in front of and either side of La Boisselle. The beginning of June found the four battalions in training. A mock-up of the German trench system around the village of La Boisselle had been constructed and the battalions practised attacking. The village of Heilly had been selected to represent La Boisselle and movement of troops took place in the fields either side of the road leading to the village. As well as training and providing working parties and carrying stores, they took their turn in the front line.

It was not a quiet section of the line. The Germans were well aware that a massive attack was iminent and, in an attempt to obtain information, they launched trench raids. They were highly successful one night in June when, after an hour-long bombardment, they swept into the centre positions of the 21st Battalion (Second Tyneside Scottish) and succeeded in capturing nineteen men. Within a matter of days the Germans allowed one of the prisoners to write home:

> My dear wife,
>
> Just a line or two hoping to find you well, as it leaves me at present. You will see I am a prisoner here but going on all right. But we are getting treated all right up to now. There is... of us here so keep your heart up and I hope I will see you again before long. Tell the children I am kindly asking after them. So good day from
>
> Your loving husband XXXXX to you all.

One of the surprising accounts to be found in the book *Tyneside Scottish* by Graham Stewart and John Sheen is the story of the spies.

At the end of June the Divisional Trench Mortar Officer, Captain James, was making his way to the Brigade Trench Mortar positions when he met an officer (referred to as Lieutenant Z) and a private (referred to as Private X). Lieutenant Z was quite excited and explained that Private X had just caused a German spy to be exposed and caught. The spy had been dressed in the uniform of an officer of the Tyneside Scottish and had suddenly appeared round a bay in the trench and started questioning Private X. 'Where is your battalion HQ located?' the officer had asked. Then he had noted that Private X was wearing the insignia of the trench mortars and had inquired as to where the battery was located. Private X was uneasy and gave an evasive reply and made as if to carry on down the trench. The officer became angry and demanded that the soldier answer him. However, in doing so his English slipped when he said, 'Your battery position, where is? Answer me – where are the guns?' At that moment, and much to Private X's relief, another Tyneside Scottish officer appeared round the bay. Private X blurted out, 'Oh Sir! He's been asking me questions – I don't think he's one of our officers. I think he's acting strange-like.' At once the newcommer whipped out his revolver and covered the bogus officer, 'You're right, I've been looking for him – hands up!' He ordered the spy to march off ahead of him down the trench. The Tyneside officer thanked Private X and said that he needn't worry himself and that he would take care of the matter. Private X had reported the incident to Lieutenant Z. The Lieutenant handed a detailed report of the whole incident to Captain James, who added his comments and a commendation on the good work done by Private X.

Captain James considered the matter of sufficient importance to scribble out a report to Divisional Headquarters, hoping that further details would be forthcoming concerning the arrest of the spy. In the event he was summond to report to General Ingouville-Williams at 102 Brigade HQ regarding the German spy. There was no record of an arrest. No Tyneside Scottish officer had made a report or turned up with a prisoner. An officer was assigned to look into the matter and accompanied Captain James back to the front line where they questioned both Lieutenant Z and Private X at some length. But the more they checked the more it became clear: one officer had arrested another, both were wearing Tyneside Scottish uniforms and they left that part of the trench in a particular direction. When the investigating officer and Captain James visited that section of the trench with Private X and followed the direction taken by the prisoner and the arresting officer, it led in the direction of No Man's Land, the trench petering out in a maze of shell holes.

To be captured and found wearing the uniform of the enemy, would certainly have meant the firing squad. The two German spies were very brave, risking certain death as they infiltrated the British trenches and worked together to gather information on the coming attack.

Planning and preparing for the Big Push

Although the area north of the River Somme had been chosen by the Allied commanders, mainly Joffre, for the main offensive of 1916, it had not been Haig's first preference. He would rather have attacked the Germans in Flanders assisted by a landing on the Belgian coast. That plan had to wait until the following year and Messines, minus the inventive, amphibious part of the plan.

Tyneside Scottish officer Lieutenant Raines. The two Germans spies who entered the British trenches were attired in Tyneside Scottish uniforms.

The British held a continuous eighty-mile front from Ypres almost to the banks of the Somme. It had been decided to launch a joint operation in the area where the French and British lines met. In the event, the German's own offensive and the bloodbath taking place at Verdun meant that French involvement was reduced. Originally their front of attack was to have been twenty-five miles launched against the German lines by forty divisions. With French strength draining away the number of divisions available for the Somme offensive fell to sixteen. When the day of the Big Push arrived, just five French divisions took part. From Verdun onwards the British were to pick up the main burden for the Western Front campaign. Another reason why 1 July 1916 was a crucial date and landmark in the history of the Great War.

The newly formed British Fourth Army, under the command of Rawlinson, had taken over the section, some fourteen miles in length, between the villages of Hébuterne and Maricourt, situated near the Somme river. Eleven divisions were to lead the attack with five in reserve. Three cavalry divisions would be on hand to exploit the breakthrough and charge into open countryside. The British High Command had planned events in four stages. The first stage, was to break through the German lines along the entire fourteen miles length, from the German village strongpoint of Serre in the north to Maricourt; the second stage, to secure the high ground between Bapaume and Ginchy. The third stage was to wheel to the left and roll up the German line and the fourth stage, was to march across country to Cambrai-Douai. There were no surprises in store for the Germans, no subtle plans, apart from a diversionary attack to be launched a couple of miles north of Serre against the fortified village of Gommecourt by two divisions of the Third Army. Artillery fire would soften up the Germans by caving in their dugouts and blowing away their barbed wire defences. In order to accomplish this it had been estimated that a week's bombardment would suffice. A total of 1,537 guns were spread evenly along the front to do the job.

General Rawlinson commander of the Fourth Army charged with breaking through on the Somme.

From the time that the British had taken over former French areas of the line, hostile activity had increased. Except when engaged in active operations the French followed a policy of 'live and let live'; not needlessly bombarding and raiding the opposition. With the British policy of continually harrassing the enemy, came the inevitable strengthening of the German defences. Consequently the Somme front changed from a relatively weak defence system in the autumn of 1915 to an impregnable fortress bristling with machine-gun nests, thick belts of wire and supporting artillery. It seemed that everywhere the Germans were looking down from vantage points over the ground chosen for the British attack. Preparations had to be carried out under the binoculars and telescopes of the watchful Germans. Surprise was out of the question and the art of camouflage was being learnt along the way. In February 1916 the construction of hutments on both sides of the River Ancre provided the Germans with their first clue and from then on indications multiplied showing where the attack against them would be launched. So obvious were the British preparations that the German commander, Falkenhayn, believed them to be for a preliminary attack and therefore, a diversion from the true British attack which would take place in the north. There was, therefore, a divergence of opinion in the German command, which should have afforded the Allies an advantage, but they had their own differences. Joffre and Rawlinson viewed the forthcoming battle as one of attrition, whilst Haig believed in a breakthrough.

The Official History, while showing that a breakthrough would not have been decisive in defeating the Germans, even suggests that it could have resulted in a dangerous salient.

Artillery advisers told Haig that he was dispersing his line too much and Rawlinson also expressed concern that a great deal was being expected of the artillery forces available. Nevertheless, at conferences and on other occasions Rawlinson was adamant that, 'nothing could exist at the conclusion of the bombardment in the area covered by it' and he would add later, 'the infantry have only to walk over and take possession'. Officers in the trenches, who were in a position to observe the effects of the shelling, found that their observations and reports that the artillery was not destroying the machine-gun positions and that wire remained uncut, were ill-received. The Official History records that battalions 'which reported that the enemy machine-guns had not been silenced were told by the divisional staff that they were scared'. Many among those who reported the true situation as to the effect of the week-long bombardment would soon be killed, or wounded, by those very machine guns. They were justified in being 'scared'.

To have any chance of successfully reaching the German trenches some commanders 'desired that at least the assault should be made at the first streak of light, before the enemy machine-gunners could see their prey'. It would seem that Rawlinson saw the sense in the suggestion and 'pressed his Fench neighbours to agree'. However, as they had double the quantity of heavy guns in their sector they wanted good light for their artillery observers. He conceded to their requirements and so the attack was to start at 7.30 am in bright summer sunshine.

For the British plan to stand any chance of success the barrage would have to be effective. Further, for the plan to succeed the 100,000 infantrymen would have to cross No Man's Land before the barrage lifted, and before the Germans could race up the steps from their deep dugouts carrying their machine guns with them. There was little chance, for they were hopelessly handicapped by the weight they were carrying. The average weight carried per man was 66 lb which made it difficult for him just to climb out of his own trench. They were to line up and walk towards the German lines (they could do little else, but walk). There could be no running, dodging or taking cover in the initial stages of the attack. The battalions were under orders as how to proceed: they were to attack in four or eight waves, not more that a hundred yards apart, the men virtually shoulder to shoulder in a well dressed alignment as if on parade. They had been drilled to advance steadily, upright, at a slow walk with their rifles, bayonets fixed, held at high port.

Had they been advancing against the muskets of Napoleon's army everything might have turned out differently.

Sniping, Mining and raiding

By the beginning of April the 31st Division was moving into position at the northernmost part allocated to it for the Big Push. The Sheffield City Battalion marching up to the village of Colincamps, which was two miles from the front lines, in front of the German fortified village of Serre – it was 2 April 1916. Over the previous days batches of men had been sent into the front line trenches for instruction by the 1st Battalion, Worcestershire Regiment. Apart from a few women who hung around to sell eggs to the troops, the villagers of Colincamps had departed. British guns were sited nearby and the German batteries were trying to hit them. The village was well on its way to total destruction. It was at this time that the steel shrapnel helmet was issued, the head protection that was to become so familiar for the next thirty years. Also gas masks and rubber capes made an appearance. The men of Sheffield marched off into the trenches in the blackness of the night weighed down with kit and equipment. Once in position they found that they had the Second Barnsleys holding the trenches on their left.

After a British artillery bombardment a smashed German trench in front of the village of Serre. JACK SHELDON

Before them, up the sloping ground, and dominating the area was the village of Serre. It had been occupied by the Germans since 1914 and they had made good use of their time turning it into a stronghold, with three lines of trenches protecting its front. The French had attempted to take the village in 1915 and the Germans had been driven out of some of their trenches at the bottom of the slope. The positions they had been forced out of were zeroed-in and shelled accurately by German artillery. The German dugouts, now occupied by British troops, were well constructed and deep, but were cut into what was now the parados, rather than the parapet. Consequently, shells could, and did, lob right into dugouts before exploding.

Frank Lindley, 14th Battalion York and Lancaster Regiment, Second Barnsleys, described conditions in the trenches in front of Serre,

> There was a job for everybody, repairing, repairing all the time repairing. When we first went in we took over what had been French lines, and they were in a terrible state. We had to start straightaway with the old pick and shovel to straighten things up. We had to deepen the trenches and build the parapets up, get sandbags and square 'em up. We had to make the front line zig-zag and build fire steps. It was continuous dig, dig, dig. The French had wickerwork sections on the sidea of their trenches and sometimes when you pulled the wickerwork down you pulled out a [dead] 'Froggy' as well. And if you were digging in the trench bottoms you'd sometimes come across one there. There was plenty of mud and you'd be plodding about in the trenches. You'd dig a sump and stick a board across it, but there was still that slimey sludge all around, and the stink and the rat holes. You could hear the rats gnawing at bones inside their holes. They'd plenty to feed on.

Four copses marked out where the British front line ran in front of Serre. The four clumps of shattered trees had been named after the four apostles: Matthew, Mark, Luke and John, and appeared named that way on military

The German fortified village of Serre was behind the trees on the horizon. The photograph was taken from the British second line when the position was taken over from the French in 1915.

Serre

maps. Frank recalled the ground in the vicinity of the four clusters of shattered trees,

> The trees in the copses didn't have leaves on them, they were just bits. Our trenches were more or less on the edge of the copses. The main trenches were just in front. communication trenches came up to the copses, but the copses themselves were open. The Germans had them marked though because they could drop a few shells into them. The 'Jerries' had been there before and they'd had a dugout in one of the copses. It had been steep down under their parapet with steps leading into a chamber with bunk places in it. They had been there long enough to do all that. They'd probably been shifted out by the French and gone on to the higher ground above us. They could overlook us all the time with their observation balloons and they could spot everything that went off in our lines. They knew every inch of that land, for the reason that they had been ploughed in there a long time before we appeared.

Behind the four copses were the communication trenches and it was from that ground behind the front line that the sniper teams operated.

A batch of sniperscopes arrived for the use by the Sheffield men on 8 April. The best shots were equipped with them and the German marksmen began to be given a 'taste of their own medicine'. It was noted that in no time at all the enemy's sniper action slackened in that sector.

Sniping had developed into a deadly art form, especially on the Western Front, and battalion snipers were trained at special sniper schools. Marksmen were selected for their initiative as well as their shooting skills. They had a certain autonomy and freedom to operate, thus avoiding the back-breaking labouring, digging and carrying which was an everyday part of the infantryman's life. The single sniper was considered such a nuisance that sometimes an artillery barrage was called down to silence him. In an interview in the 1980s, one former sniper in the Second Barnsleys, Charlie Swales, gave an insight into the operations of a battlion sniper:

> We were in our second line and we were shooting from there, about 400 yards. We were in a dugout with a curtain at the back so that no light showed

Sucrerie of Bihucourt

through. The sniping position at the front was covered by an iron plate which had two apertures, one for the rifle and one for the observer. There were two of you, one with the rifle and one with a pair of binoculars. You used to catch them early before daybreak.

This 'ere day we could see smoke rising from the German lines where they were cooking and we could see the head and shoulders of this chap bobbing about. I told Elijah Wright, who was with me, to slip back t' dugout and fetch t' telescopic rifle. When he came back he told me that one of the lads was sleeping on it and he didn't like to disturb him. "Tha should ev kicked the bugger awake then!" I told him. "Anyway, there's only one thing to do 'Lijah, we'll use what we've got. I'll aim at the smoke and thee just tell me when he bobs up agean." I took first pressure ont' trigger and waited while 'Lijah used t' binoculars. Suddenly he shouted "Reight!" I squeezed the trigger and t' bullet went. 'Lijah slapped my shoulder and yelled out "Thas gorrim!" He'd seen the bullet skim the parapet kicking up the dust. He was still peering through t' binoculars when he suddenly swore, "Bloody 'ell!" He's waving thee a weshart!" [During target firing in the British Army, a 'miss', or 'washout', was signalled by the waving of a red and white flag commonly referred to as 'strawberries and cream'.] *In a split second the German had jumped up and waved a white cloth and bobbed back down again. I told 'Lijah, "He deserves to get away with it for his blasted cheek!" I bet that I'm the only man in the British Army to be waved a washout by a German. We must have done some damage though, because the Germans tried up with dummies, but you could always tell that they weren't the real thing, it was one of those things that we were taught. They were trying to see where we were firing from. We moved further up the trench and started shooting from there. They must have pinpointed the section of trench we had used at first because they shelled and destroyed our sniping post, but no one was hurt.*

It was a single bullet that caused the death of the first man from either of the two Barnsley battalions. Within forty-eight hours of taking up their positions in front of Serre a single bullet penetrated the steel helmet of Private Thomas Burns, a former miner.

Because most Barnsley men had been coalminers the 13th Battalion, York and Lancaster Regiment, (First Barnsleys), was used to assist in tunnelling operations under No Man's Land and the German positions in the area of VIII Corps. The ground in front of the German-held village of Beaumont Hamel had been transformed into a stronghold named, by the British, Hawthorn Redoubt. It was the stronghold that was to be blown up at the beginning of the Big Push, otherwise, it was reasoned, there was no hope of capturing the village. The Pals of the 13th Battalion, working with Royal Engineers of 252nd Tunnelling Company, supplied labour each day; three shifts of 100 men, removing spoil from the galleries.

Our lot were occupied in mining under the German lines. They were going to blow Beaumont Hamel up. The Germans were mining as well. At one time during the process I was down there and you could hear the Germans working. I didn't think much to that.

First Barnsley Pals were involved in tunnelling activities on the Somme.

It was chalk, but it wasn't easier than coal mining because it was all hand moved. There were no tubs to bring the muck out, it was all damned hard work for our chaps. We weren't digging, there was a special company to do that.

Ernest Bell, 13th Battalion, York and Lancaster Regiment

The shaft known as H.3 was seventy-five feet deep and from it a tunnel was being driven towards the German strongpoint some 1,050 feet away on Hawthorn Ridge. By the end of May the gallery had been driven out eastwards 900 feet. It was hard going because the chalk was tightly compacted and large amounts of flint were being encountered. As the 1,000 feet mark approached there was the need to work in near silence. At the gallery face the chalk was drenched in water and digging was done by bayonets. In June the drive reached its objective and a chamber was constructed. A charge of ammonal amounting to 40,600 lbs was placed in the chamber and it was tamped in readiness for the big day.

Further digging operations were underway in front of Serre, but with a difference. The engineers of 252nd Tunnelling Company were busy driving shallow-depth tunnels, called 'Russian Saps' out under No Man's Land. They were intended to become communication trenches once the German defensive positions had been captured. They were only a foot or so below the ground and were designed to be broken out to the surface prior to the attack. In addition to their use following the first assault, the saps were planned to assist the attack itself. At the ends nearest the German trenches, branches were being built and complete emplacements constructed for the housing of trench mortars and machine gun positions. Thus the attacking infantry would have close support on hand. Nine Russian saps were dug across No Man's Land in front of Serre. Despite great care not to alert the enemy to the digging operations they did discover one sap which led from John Copse. The Germans fired a small charge in one of the emplacements killing seven men. In the following week a second charge was placed in the sap and blown. Gas cylinders that were being stored there to

be used in the attack were damaged and two men died from gas poisoning. Eight others were badly gassed.

Frank Lindley of the Second Barnsleys recalled being out under No Man's Land:

> I was on a listening post right up against their wire and under ours in, like, a sap. I don't know just how long I was stuck there, but I thought that they had forgotten about me. There was no system, you were on your own. You could smell their cigar smoke wafting across, and you could could smell their booze. They were playing accordians and piccolos, and you could hear them rattling their beer bottles. They were "hoch, hoching" but I couldn't understand a dickie-bird of what they were saying.

It is good to keep in mind that when Frank was experiencing front line dangers he was just sixteen years old. He had joined up to seek revenge for the death of his brother, who had been killed at the outbreak of war when his ship, HMS *Hawke*, was torpedoed in the North Sea. More of Frank's story, including his joining and then deserting, the Royal Artillery, can be read in Jon Cooksey's ground breaking book, *Barnsley Pals*.

In order to maintain an aggressive policy on the Western Front the British generals ordered the policy of raiding German trenches. It was by this means that Kitchener's New Army formations were 'blooded' into carnal wafare. Former church attending, God-fearing civilians had to be transformed into killers if the war was to be won. The citizens' army included entire contingents of the Church Lads and the Boys Brigades. The 16th Service Battalion of The Highland Light Infantry, was recruited entirely from the Glasgow Battalion of the Boys' Brigade, for Kitchener's New Army. It was obvious to the military powers that putting rifles into youngsters' hands, teaching them to shoot and getting them to bayonet charge sacks of straw would not, in itself, produce effective killers. Raiding the German trenches would serve as the ideal initiation to blood letting and would encourage the offensive spirit. British Army officers and NCOs were fully aware that many among the rank and file were under age boys. Of course, it did not matter, there was a job to be done and, it was reasoned, that by the time the Germans had been

> '...for the most part they are not wildly enthusiastic about shoving a bayonet into the stomach of a fair-haired German boy about their age and imbued with much the same ideas of war as themselves. Why would they be? They know little and care less about the great Prussian Evil which we are fighting'
>
> The Reverend Julian Bickersteth MC. Senior Chaplain 56th London Division

defeated, the youngsters would have made the transition from boys to men anyway. So raiding was the ordered procedure for the battalions taking up sections of the line ready for the Big Push. Raids were intelligence gathering exercises and prisoners, trench maps and documents snatched from German positions could serve to inform the Allied planners.

Documents describing a trench raid by the 14th Battalion York and Lancaster Regiment, Second Barnsleys, were discovered in Barnsley Public Library where they must have been lodged by an officer after the war. Author Jon Cooksey located the German records of the 5th Company, Infantry Regiment 169 for the very same raid, and Barnsley men who were there were interviewed. The result is that we have the detailed anatomy of a Great War British Army trench raid, its planning, execution and outcome. The detail, plans, lists and diagrams appear in *Barnsley Pals*. Nine weeks after the raid Barnsley folk were able to read all about it in the local paper, as could any foreign agent for that matter.

> We have raided the German trenches with glory. We should be proud to think we were chosen out of the whole division, especially as we are the youngest battalion in it. We have added to the glory of the York and Lancasters, our name being decorated with one Military Cross – earned by Lieutenant Quest for devotion to duty and self-sacrifice when wounded in three places. And two Military Medals earned by Privates Clarkson and Russell for gallantry, which consisted of leaving the trenches in broad daylight to bring in a wounded comrade who had been left during the raid.

The Germans almost always reacted vigorously to a raid and their artillery pounded the British trenches in the sector where they expected the raiders to be returning.

The seventy-two-strong raiding party of the Barnsleys launched their attack from trenches occupied by the 10th Battalion, East Yorkshire Regiment, (Hull Commercials). The leader of the raid, Captain Wood, had requested that the Hulls vacate the front line in order to allow the raiders easy passage. The officers of the Hull Commercials, knowing the German tendancy to retaliate with great force to a raid on their lines asked Division for permission to pull their men back until the raiders had returned and cleared away from the area. The request was denied.

Author David Bilton in *Hull Pals* records the results experienced by the Commercials of raids carried out by 94 Brigade. He tells of how, as darkness fell, a large party of raiders their faces blackened, began filing into the 10th Battalion trenches. The fearsome looking lot were armed with revolvers, Mills bombs, cudgels, hatchets and a variety of stabbing weaponry. At the appointed time, midnight, the British guns – sixty in number, consisting of 18 pounders to 9.2 inch howitzers – opened fire. An under age Hull's soldier, Private Tait, was within a few days of being sent out of the line and transported home when he experienced a German counter-barrage:

> We were warned beforehand of the bombardment and we were all compelled to Stand To. No one who has ever been through such a hell

Preparing to raid the German trenches.
DAVID BILTON

An Army chaplain conducts a burial service.

can possibly conceive any idea of its devastation. It was a very Hell on earth. The shells screech overhead creating a weird sensation. B Company was in the Second Line and we had many narrow escapes. You hear an approaching shell screeching through the air. It comes overhead and then one calls up one's utmost nerve power to withstand the shock. There is a flash across the eyes, then a deafening report, followed by part of the parapet tumbling on top of one. I think several times that it is the last time that I shall see daylight. The strafing was appalling. This lasted for an hour and then we rushed down to the front line to dig the poor fellows out. What a sight! Dead and wounded are strewn everywhere. The front line is blown to hell. Soon wounded were being carried out – some on stretchers and some struggling along with the help of a comrade. Very few stretchers were available. The dead are thrown aside until the wounded are all away. It was a veritable nightmare.

Casualties – twenty-six killed and about sixty wounded.

We are relieved at 6 pm but parties remain behind to bury the dead. The burial ground is under a typical French avenue, just behind the Third Line. Everyone presents a sad aspect and how keenly we all feel the loss of our comrades!

On 24 June the preparatory Allied bombardment began. Shells raining down on the German lines produced a continuous series of explosions that rolled like the beating of drum. The term *Trommelfeuer* [drum fire] was used by the Germans to describe barrages of such extraordinary intensity. They knew that the British and French were about to assault their trenches in the area of the Somme River – but where and when exactly?

Chapter Four

THE HOUR APPROACHES

H E HAD SEEN ENOUGH, and experienced enough, to become totally disenchanted with the way the war against Germany and her allies was being conducted. Private Josef Lipmann decided to desert to the enemy. Lipmann was born a Russian of Russian parents and had been living in England just two years before the outbreak of war. He was twenty-one years old, and worked as a carpenter in Coventry when war broke out. He had enlisted in August 1914 and was posted to the 2nd Battalion, Royal Fusiliers. As part of the initial assault battalions of the 29th Division he took part in the landings at Cape Helles, Gallipoli. Unfortunately for him 86 Brigade, of which the 2nd Battalion Royal Fusiliers was a part, was involved in some of the bloodiest fighting of the whole mishandled campaign. By 10 May 1915 when the battalion moved to rest bivouacs its strength was down to five officers and 384 men. Another forty casuaties followed when the battalion returned to the fighting twelve days later. Church of England

Allied invasion fleet gathered at Lemnos prior to the landings at Gallipoli.

Men of the 2nd Battalion Royal Fusiliers at Gallipoli.

Chaplain of 86 Brigade, The Reverend O. Creighton recalled the attack of the 2nd Battalion:

> *The leading company went forward at 8.30. The men seemed to feel that it was a counsel of despair and the officers knew that they could expect no support. With three officers hit the men rushed forward magnificently, almost officerless. there was a perfect hail of bullets, and then the Turks started throwing hand grenades, which did most of the damage, making ghastly wounds.*

At the beginning of the month of June, another attack by W Company (Lipmann's) brought the strength of the battalion down to just two officers and 278 other ranks. The battalion was brought up to strength by replacements and on 29 June was involved in a night attack on the Turkish trenches and some hand-to-hand fighting took place. Three officers and twenty-seven other ranks were killed; three officers and 175 other ranks were wounded; an incredible fifty-seven other ranks were missing (lying dead and undiscovered or captured). During August the battalion took part in landings at Suvla Bay and again suffered heavy casualties. By 8 September the men had been under continuous fire for six weeks. Total casualties since the first landings in April amounted to 279 killed, 954 wounded, 103 missing and 400 sick. No officers remained of the original members of the battalion that had set out from England, and only 166 other ranks. Private Josef Lipmann was one of these. However, suffering and privation was not over for men of the 2nd Battalion, on 26 November a great storm of torrential rain was unleashed against the Gallipoli peninsula and a reported seven foot high wall of water crashed down from the hills and flooded the trenches of both Briton and Turk. Several men were drowned and the battalion area was transformed into a huge lake. A severe freeze followed and two men of W Company were found to have frozen to death. Exposure and frostbite took its toll and at a roll call following the disaster just eighty-four men answered their names.

After eight fruitless months the Allies slunk away from Turkey in a masterful withdrawal without sustaining a single loss of life.

It was all about to happen again; 29th Division was in position before Beaumont Hamel ready to launch its battalions once more against a far more prepared opponent than 'Johnny Turk' had ever been. When volunteers were called for to patrol No Man's Land on the night of 27 June, Lipmann stepped forward. Four strong fighting patrols had been ordered out by Divisional HQ with the task of snatching a prisoner for interrogation by Intelligence Corps officers. One of the patrols was supplied by the Canadians in the Division, 1st Battalion Newfoundland Regiment.

Lipmann was part of a seventeen-man patrol that slipped through the British wire and headed across No Man's Land. The other three patrols also snaked across the desolate ground towards the German wire. The night was suddenly lit by flares and the Newfoundland patrol came under attack from machine gun and rifle fire. Then shells began to rain down on No Man's Land and Captain Butler, who was leading the Newfoundlanders, was wounded and subsequently taken prisoner along with three of his men. Two of them divulged information concerning the coming offensive to their interrogators. However, it was the deserter who proved the most cooperative to his captors.

Lipmann had slipped away from his patrol in the darkness and when the firing and shelling started he had laid low. Eventually the German guns fell silent and the patrols had returned to their own front line. Abandoning his rifle and steel helmet he had crept to the German wire and called out in makeshift German, 'Ich einen Kameraden', and that he was coming over with friendly intentions.

According to his German interrogator, once Lipmann had become aware of the date for the attack he had sought an opportunity to desert. Lipmann explained to his captors that the British bombardment that was raging all along the front had been scheduled to last five days and four nights. That the date and time for the attack was Thursday morning between 5.00 am and 6.00 am German time. (Because of the weather it was put back to Saturday 1 July.) Lipmann supplied detailed information concerning the names of the attacking formations of 29th Division, colour coding of flares which were to be used to signal the artillery and the tactics that would be employed by his own battalion in the assault. Further updated and accurate information, date and time for the attack was later supplied by a German 'Moritz', listening station, at Contalmaison. The information gathering patrols put out by 29th Division had proved to be a catastrophe to the British and an unexpected and welcome windfall to the Germans.

Author Jack Sheldon in his book *The German Army on the Somme*, from which this information is taken, has opened up a whole new area of fascinating information on the Great War.

Preparing for death

Probably the most difficult letter to write is the one that will only be read by close family members after the violent death of the writer. Prior to the Somme offensive 'last letters' in their thousands were penned by British soldiers. One such letter that survived over the years appeared in Jon Cooksey's *Barnsley Pals*. Second Lieutenant Frank Potter had been transferred from the 14th Battalion York and Lancaster Regiment, Second Barnsleys, and placed in command of the Brigade trench mortar battery. His final words to his parents were as follows:

France 27/6/1916

My dearest Mother & Father,

This is the most difficult letter I have ever sat down to write. We are going into an attack tomorrow and I shall leave this to be posted if I don't come back. It is a far bigger thing than I have ever been in before and my only hope is that we shall help in a victory that will bring the war nearer to a successful conclusion. I am hoping to have the nerve to keep my end up and to do my share – that is all that worries me at present. Of death I haven't any fear. I have no premonition of anything happening to me, I have every faith that I shall come out safely, but the chances are against one in a big attack and it is as well to be prepared.

The worst of war is that one's people at home have to bear all the sacrifice and suffering. For my part I am content and happy to give my services and life to my country, but it is not my sacrifice, Mother and Dad, it is yours. The one great thing of this war is that it has taught us to appreciate our homes, and to realise our duty to you more, and also the enormity of your sacrifice in giving your son to our country. At a time like this I couldn't be anywhere else but here. We have all been brought up at home, in school, and church, to a creed which places our duty to our country next to our religion, and I should not have been a true son had I stayed at home instead of coming out here.

Second Lieutenant Frank Potter wrote a letter that he hoped would never be sent.

And so Mother, I don't want you to grieve over me, we have done our duty. I hope Eddie and Dick never have to face the horrors of war and that they will realise that we are fighting now so that they will never have to do, and that they will grow up to be better sons than perhaps I have been. We have been so long in peace in England that this war has come as a big shock to us all, but I am content and happy Mother that I have done my duty.

I have made a will which as a soldier's will I think is legal and will perhaps save some trouble. I only want you to let Ruth have any of my belongings she may want, and I know that you will do anything in the world you can for her.

My fondest love to all at home

Your loving Son

Frank xxxxxxx

Shortly after the attack began Frank Potter received a bullet in the head and his last letter was sent to his parents.

31st Division

Four divisions of the New Army mainly comprised of Pals battalions were to be involved in the opening assault: 31st Division, (Barnsley, Sheffield City, Accrington, Leeds, Bradford, Durham and Hull Pals) attacked Serre; 32nd Division, (Glasgow, Salford, Newcastle and Lonsdale Pals) was to attack Thiepval; 34th Division, (Tyneside Scottish, Tyneside Irish, Edinburgh City, Grimsby Chums and the Cambridge Battalion) attacked La Boisselle; 30th Division, (Manchester, Liverpool and Oldham Pals) on the extreme right flank of the British attack, was to capture Montauban. Regular divisions, brigades and battalions were sprinkled about throughout the Fourth Army to stiffen the new formations with experienced troops. Although few of the Regular and Territorial formations were any longer comprised mainly of veterans. For example the 29th Division, as we have seen, suffered such losses in 1915 as to no longer represent a seasoned and experienced division.

On the night of 30 June 1916 the assault battalions of 31st Division were making their way through the communication trenches to the front line. The commander of 94 Brigade, Brigadier General Rees, had complained to VIII Corps commander, Lieutenant General Hunter-Weston that the Germans would know exactly where the flank of the entire British attack was. He pointed out that between his Brigade and the subsidiary attack two miles to the north at Gommecourt, there absolutely no preparations had been undertaken. No assembly trenches had been dug to mislead the Germans. Rees had taken over temporary command of the brigade from Brigadier General Carter-Campbell and immediately saw the glaring mistakes. To make matters worse, in the opinion of Rees, no effort at wire cutting by shelling had been undertaken in the two mile stretch of

Brigadier General Rees, commander of 94 Brigade.

Pals Battalions on the Somme 1 July 1916

31st Division
ACCRINGTON
BARNSLEY
LEEDS
DURHAM
BRADFORD
HULL

GERMAN SECOND ARMY

36th (Ulster) Division
BELFAST
COUNTY ARMAGH
ANTRIM
COUNTY DOWN
COUNTY TYRONE
DERRY
DONEGAL

32nd Division
GLASGOW
SALFORD
LONSDALE

34th Division
TYNESIDE
EDINBURGH
GRIMSBY CHUMS

7th Division
MANCHESTER
OLDHAM

30th Division
LIVERPOOL
MANCHESTER

BRITISH FOURTH ARMY

David Hemmingway

ground between his brigade and Gommecourt, 'A child could see where the flank of our attack lay to within ten yards.' he lamented. It meant that the German *Infantry Regiment 66*, knowing that there was to be no direct assault on their trenches, would be ready and prepared to pour enfilading fire into the flank of the his brigade. The Sheffield City Battalion and Second Barnsleys would be on the receiving end of that. Nevertheless, so confident were the British planners that the bombardment would take care of the defending Germans that General Rees' observations and concerns were discounted.

Nairne Street was the flanking communication trench and main thoroughfare for the Second Barnsleys, and on 30 June it was crammed with heavily laden men trudging towards the shattered trees of John Copse and the front line.

We all filed up Nairne Street. We were all cheek to jowl because we'd had a stoppage. As we stood there one of their 'coal boxes' dropped on the ground and the explosion covered us all. We scattered ourselves about a bit. My knees must have been red raw with the soil hitting me. The next bloke to me started shaking, he was absolutely unhinged – he couldn't do a thing. We had to get round him and travel on because they were shoving us forward, butting us in the rear. I was next to one of our sergeants, Sergeant Jones, and this salvo of shrapnel came right over the top of us and rattled against our 'tin' hats. Some must have gone down the back of this sergeant and he was done for. I don't know if he died, but he was certainly badly wounded. blood was coming out of his back between him and his haversack. He had to be shoved back.

Frank Lindley, 14th Battalion York and Lancaster (Second Barnsleys)

Nairne Street was being systematically obliterated, as German guns concentrated on what they knew to be the northern flank of the British attack. There were other communication trenches and the assault battalions had each been assigned a route to their jumping-off points. A signaller in the 12th Battalion, York and Lancaster Regiment, Sheffield City recorded his journey to the front line:

It was still daylight when we set off, round about 7.30 pm, all loaded up like pack mules with all the extra equipment we had to carry. By the time we had reached the communication trenches it was quite dark, apart from the gun flashes lighting up the sky. It was a struggle moving down the trenches loaded up like we were. We signallers knew this section of the trenches like the back of our hands, as one of our jobs was to find broken telephone lines at night and repair them. We couldn't climb out of the trenches with all that weight of equipment, so we had to sweat and toil in the mud and water that was knee deep in places. The going was difficult and it took us much longer to get into position than planned. We got there just before first light.

Lance Corporal Reg Glenn, 12th Battalion York & Lancaster (Sheffield City)

The British assault held few surprises for the Germans; they knew the day and the hour and acted accordingly. At first light the German guns opened fire. There were over three hours for the troops to wait, crouched in the trenches waiting for the whistles to blow. The Sheffield men were to attack in four waves, A and C companies were in the front line and would lead, making

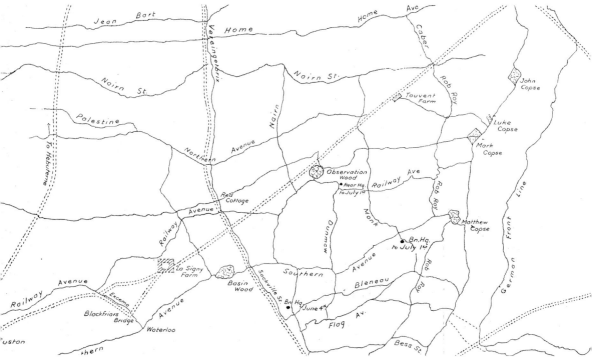

British trenches in front of Serre.

up the first two waves. Behind them, crouched in Campion and Monk trenches were men of B and D companies.

In the trenches to the right of the Sheffield men was 11th Battalion, East Lancashire Regiment, Accrington Pals. The day before they had been at Warnimont Wood and had been busy with their final preparations. Small triangles had been cut from biscuit tins and each man had attached one to his small pack (carried high on his back between his shoulders). Three inch wide strips of coloured material identifying each wave of attack were tied to the mens' shoulder strap. The theory was that the tin and coloured cloth would assist brigade and divisional headquarter staffs accurately to plot the progress of the waves as they advanced across enemy lines. The planners had tried to think of every eventuality; an example being the marking with a yellow arm band the two men in every company who had been detailed to carry a huge mallet. The attackers were to want for nothing. The planning was based on the assumption that the Germans had been all but wiped out in the week-long barrage and that the men had nothing to do but walk across No Man's Land and occupy his strongpoints and trenches. The British plan was also based on the assumption that the German barbed wire would have been completely destroyed by the bombardment.

The Accringtons began their march to the front following a route marked by white tape. Along the way they received additional equipment, two men were given a spade to every one given a pick and some were given a roll of barbed wire to carry in the coming attack. Each bombing party, comprising eight men, collected 100 Mills bombs and twenty-five rifle grenades. At last, with all the extra issues made, the battalion with its commander, Lieutenant Colonel Rickman at its head, marched out from the village of Courcelles as light began to fade. The battalion entered the trench system at the shattered remains of a *sucrerie* (sugar factory). The men were in fine spirits and exchanged good-natured remarks with the crews of an 18-pounder artillery battery. They joked with each other about having a drink in the village of Serre and discussed what souvenirs they would be looking for – the *pickelhaube* being a firm favourite. A dampener to their high spirits appeared when they passed the Royal Army Medical Corps Advanced Dressing Station, sited at Basin Wood. Large mass graves had been dug in readiness alongside the ADS by the division's pioneer battalion, the 12th King's Own Yorkshire Light Infantry. Outside a wooden hut were stacks of wooden crosses.

The men fell silent wondering about the assurances given that it was to be a walk-over. Earlier that day they, along with 8,000 others of 31st Division, had been addressed by the Commander of VIII Corps, Lieutenant General Hunter-Weston, when he had told them that they had every chance of success, 'that not even a rat would be left alive in the German trenches'. He had spoken of their superiority of numbers in men and guns, and quality of equipment and then reminded them of their duty:

> Your lot is a very heavy one and a huge responsibity is shared by every individual. No individual soldier may say he has no responsibility. The 29th Division performed glorious feats of arms in Gallipoli, the 4th Division on your right did wonders in the great

Commander of VIII Corps,
Lieutenant General Hunter-Weston

retreat from Mons. The feats of these divisions will never be forgotten as long as the world endures. You are Englishmen even as they, and now you have your opportunity to shine. You will have to stick it. You must stick it. I salute every officer NCO and man.

It may not have been lost on some at the time, that the two examples held up by the general had not been participation in victories for the two named divisions, but rather their involvement in defeats for the British Army. The General did point out that should any 'funk' the attack and didn't advance they would be shot, and that military police carrying drawn revolvers and under strict orders would be scouring the assault trenches looking for shirkers. Many report how thoroughly sickened they all were by that threat. Hunter-Weston's assurance that God was on their side did nothing to assuage their anger. After all, they were not conscripts but all volunteers to a man; consequently they considered death threats totally out of place.

Author David Raw in his book *Bradford Pals* reproduces the complete contents of a letter from Hunter-Weston to his wife written that same evening. The General's letter reveals the conceit of the man, a part of which said, 'They have never yet been in battle and I therefore went and gave them an inspiriting address, with most excellent results. I felt I had got them... I was given the power to strike the right note and to enthuse the men. It is a valuable gift to be able to speak fairly well'. David Raw records one man's reaction to the 'inspirited' address and leaves it for the reader to judge.

The last thousand yards from Observation Wood to the shattered remains of Matthew and Mark copses was on a downward slope and the going was easier. It was 2.40 am when the battalion reached its destination at the blown in trenches at the front. Lieutenant Colonel Rickman formally took over from Lieutenant Colonel Daniel Burgess, commander of the 10th Battalion, East Yorkshire Regiment (Hull Commercials). On inspection of the state of the front line Brigadier General Rees decided that it was too badly damaged to accommodate the first wave and ordered the whole attack force to move back one trench. Near chaos ensued as the grumbling, exhausted men picked up their loads and moved back. It took until 4 am when dawn was lightening the sky before everyone was in place. At that point there were 720 Accrington Pals men spread along a frontage of about 350 yards; they were organised into four waves. Two officers and sixty men were in reserve. With three and a half hours to wait before the attack the men had nothing to do but try and grab some sleep in the chilly dawn of Saturday 1 July 1916.

To the right of the Accringtons was 15th Battalion, West Yorkshire Regiment, (Leeds Pals) of 93 Brigade. Behind Leeds were the First Bradfords, 16th Battalion, West Yorkshire Regiment and D Company of 18th Durham Light Infantry, (Durham Pals). Forming the Third and Fourth waves was 18th West Yorkshire Regiment, Second Bradfords. Bringing up the rear were the remaining companies of the Durham Pals.

Travelling south the next division to the 31st New Army in the line facing the Germans was the 4th Division, Regular Army, which was to attack a bulge named the Quadrilatral Redoubt – *Heidenkopf* to the Germans. However, it

Stretcher bearers bring up the rear as British infantry move up a smashed communication trench to the front line.

was a strongpoint that the Germans had decided not to hold in the event of an all-out attack. They had placed four mines to be exploded once the British had occupied it. From the Quadrilateral to the German-held village of Beaumont Hamel was the Redan Ridge which was to be taken by the 4th Division. Further south the 29th Division was tasked with the capture of Beaumont Hamel. The deserter, Josef Lipmann, three days previously, had divulged detailed information concerning his division's assault. A huge mine was to be blown on Hawthorn Ridge at the outset of the British assault on Beaumont Hamel.

The opposing lines curved southeastward and were cut by the River Ancre and the Ancre valley and became X Corps area; attacking in that sector was the 36th (Ulster) Division. Infantry of the 36th had been provided by the Ulster Volunteer Force, which pre-war, had been organised into district armed units. Conflict with the Catholics over Home Rule was put to one side until Germany had been defeated. Kitchener had asked the UVF if they would allow the younger members of their military force to be taken into his New Army. The response from the youth was immediate and they were organised into battalions belonging to the Irish regiments which normally recruited in Ulster.

The strongpoint known as the Schwaben Redoubt, and Stuff Redoubt (*Feste Staufen*) in the German Second Line, were their objectives for the first day's advance. The 36th Division's battalions attack was launched from Thiepval Wood.

32nd Division

The 32nd had set out as an all Pals type formation. However, while in France in January 1916, it had left its 95 Brigade, which comprised three Birmingham Pals battalions (14th, 15th and 16th, Royal Warwickshire Regiment) and its one Bristol's Own (12th Battalion Gloucestershire Regiment), for 14 Brigade in the 5th Division. The exchange for the four Regular army battalions would, it was reasoned, bolster the four Salford, three Glasgow, two Newcastle and one Lonsdale New Army battalions. The 32nd Division was part of X Corps along with 36th and 49th Divisions.

The plan for X Corps was that its 36th Division would break through towards the village of Grandcourt, sweeping over the village of St Pierre Divion and the Schwaben Redoubt. In the meantime 32nd Division was to overwhelm the Thiepval defences and advance to Mouquet Farm ('Mucky' Farm), which was on the German Second Defence Line. 96 Brigade's two assaulting battalions were the 15th Battalion, Lancashire Fusiliers, (First Salfords) and on their right the 16th Battalion, Northumberland Fusiliers, (Newcastle Commercials). In support was the 16th Battalion Lancashire Fusiliers, (Second Salfords). On their right was 97 Brigade, its leading assault battalions were the 16th Battalion Highland Light Infantry, (Glasgow Boy's Brigade) and 17th Battalion, Highland Light Infantry, (Glasgow Chamber of Commerce). 14 Brigade was in reserve and was intended to pass through the other two brigades when they had taken their front line objectives.

There were no contingency plans made should the Germans resist and

Thiepval Chataeu in the German trench system.

throw back the attackers. Optimism ruled the plan-makers' deliberations – failure was out of the question. Forty pages of detailed instructions covering every aspect and timing of a successful operation was compiled. For example, within an hour and forty minutes Mouquet Farm would be captured by 97 Brigade. Then 14 Brigade would take the Second Position of the German defences. As a result of French insistence (they required light for their artillery spotters) it was all to be achieved on a bright summer's morning, rather than in the darkness before dawn as some officers had requested.

As darkness fell on 30 June, the two assault battalions, First Salfords and Newcastle Commercials, began moving up from the village of Bouzincourt and entered the badly battered trenches. At the same time the Second Salfords moved about 300 yards to their rear. Captain Tweed, Second Salfords, wrote:

> There was a ruined village [Authuille] to traverse, where shells had set fire to one of the houses, and the red glow added a further awesomeness to the scene. Leaving the village we proceeded along the communication trench leading to the assembly trench. This lay through a thick wood [Thiepval], and enemy shellfire had brought down heavy trees, which partially blocked the way and made progress slow. We were almost at our rendezvous when a crash in front warned those behind that things were not well. The party halted and the order was passed down: "Officer wanted at the front at once." An officer started off crushing past the crouching men, and then whizz crash, a whizz-bang fired enfilade along the trench fell amongst us, followed by others.

A sergeant and three men were killed outright and two officers and five men were wounded. Captain Tweed had no option but to take command of both support companies, and the Big Advance had not yet started.

There was one Regular Army division, the 8th, between the 32nd Pals division and the next Pals division in the line, the 34th Division. The 8th Division was to attack up Mash Valley and capture the village of Ovillers. On their right flank were the Tynesiders.

34th Division

Tyneside Scottish, 102 Brigade, with its four battalions, would attack up Mash Valley north of La Boisselle and south of the village, avoiding the mine cratered ground (nicknamed 'The Glory Hole') directly in front of the village. 101 Brigade comprised of 10th Lincolnshire Regiment, Grimsby Chums; 15th and 16th Battalions Royal Scots Regiment, Edinburgh City and 11th Battalion, Cambridge Battalion, Suffolk Regiment. The brigade of Tyneside Irish, 103, would follow up. Again the plan for the assault by this division's brigades was timed to the minute. The first objective of the leading battalions was the capture of four lines of trenches. The Second Position German was 2,000 yards away and was scheduled to be reached at 8.18 am, forty-eight minutes after the attack began. The second objective was the trench line passing in front of the the two villages of Pozières and Contalmaison, and was to be reached at 8.58 am. At this point the two assaulting formations, 101 and 102 Brigades, would halt and consolidate their gains. Following up would be 103 Brigade which would pass through the other two and capture Contalmaison village.

Having accomplished that task, it was to proceed to the final objective for that morning – a trench line behind the two villages, which would be reached by 10.10 am.

An added risk taken by the Commander of the 34th Division, Major General Ingouville-Williams, was to order his battalion commanding officers, along with their headquarters' staff, to advance with their men. It was to prove disastrous.

Patrol activity was maintained by the Tyneside Scottish up to the day of the Big Advance. The 21st Battalion, Second Tyneside Scottish, sent out two officers and twenty men to raid the enemy trenches on 29/30 June but enemy fire was such that they had to abandon the patrol and return to their own lines. Likewise the 23rd Battalion, Fourth Tyneside Scottish, attempted a raid with forty-five men and were driven back, losing an officer. Engineers were going out to cut the enemy wire and a covering party of platoon strength went with them. One of the officers was cut down by a German sniper and an NCO had to take over command. He

Major General Ingouville-Williams, commanding 34th Division.

brought all the men back safely and was later awarded a Military Medal. The Third Tyneside Scottish, 22nd Battalion, also attempted to carry out a raid but must have been spotted, because flares calling for artillery fire were sent up and they were thwarted by heavy German fire. Undetered, they tried again with a smaller number, one officer and five men, who were to report on the state of the German wire and approximately how many of the enemy were occupying the their front line. They were also ordered to capture a prisoner. The patrol left the British front line at 1.55 am but as it neared the German wire it was fired upon and grenades were thrown, one falling among them. The officer and two men were wounded. Three of them managed to crawl back to their own lines and another patrol sent out to find the other three and bring them back, was unsuccessful. They had disappeared and were never found. It was obvious to the officers and men at the 'sharp end' that the Germans defending this sector of their line were far from cowed by the week-long British barrage – it was an prelude to disaster for the imminent British attack.

In answer to the intense British barrage the Germans put down defensive fire on the British trenches hoping to catch troops assembling for the assault on their trenches. Private Elliott of the Tyneside Scottish recalled,

> *The guns seemed to be all round us, it's then you begin to wonder. As the night wore on we knew it was going to be tough, but it was in the early hours that I was scared stiff. I wasn't afraid to die but I didn't want to be maimed or left lying in agony. I was more scared of the heavy guns than of going over, those big guns would be turned on us.*

Between the 34th Division and the southernmost Pals division were three Regular divisions the 21st, 7th and 18th. On the right flank of the entire British line on the Western Front was the all-Lancashire Pals division – the 30th.

30th Division

With its eight battalions of Liverpool and Manchester Pals along with two Regular battalions (2nd Battalion Royal Scots Regiment and 2nd Battalion Bedfordshire Regiment) this division was in the position of honour. The extreme right of the British Army, next to the French was considered to be the most prestigious position. The French *39me Division* was a formation of the *20me Corps* which had a fine fighting reputation and bore the name 'Corps de Fer' (Iron Corps). Relations between the British and the French were excellent and there was fine cooperation between the fighting units.

The Division was to attack with 21 Brigade on the left: 18th Battalion The King's (Liverpool Regiment) Second Liverpool Pals and 19th Battalion Manchester Regiment, Fourth Manchester Pals. 89 Brigade was next to the French *3me Bataillon* and comprised the 20th and 17th Battalions The King's (Liverpool Regiment), Fourth and First Liverpool Pals. 19th Battalion The King's (Liverpool Regiment) Third Liverpool Pals would advance behind the 2nd Battalion Bedfordshires. The two assaulting Brigades were to capture the Glatz Redoubt. The redoubt, like every other German strongpoint on the Somme, was a warren of trenches laced with machine gun posts which provided overlapping fire. Once the first objectives had been taken the other brigade in the division, 90 Brigade, which comprised First, Second and Third Manchester Pals, would sweep through and capture the village of Montauban.

The day before the attack the commander of 89 Brigade, Brigadier General F. C. Stanley, sent the following message to all four battalions under his charge:

> *The day has at last come when we are to take the offensive on a large scale, and the result of this will have a great effect on the course and the duration of the war.*
>
> *It is with the utmost confidence that we go forward, the battalions of which the City of Liverpool is justly proud, determined to make a name for themselves in their first attack, and the 2nd Battalion Bedfordshire Regiment to add still more to their glorious record.*
>
> *89 Brigade occupies the most honourable position in the whole of the British Army, because not only are we on the extreme right, but we are fighting side by side with the celebrated French* Corps de Fer.
>
> *One and all will strive to prove ourselves worthy of this distinction, and to show our French neighbours what the British can do. That being so, success is assured.*

Manchesters attending Church Parade the day before the Big Push.

British trench mortar bombs, 'plum puddings', during the Somme offensive. Trench mortar pit with crew preparing to fire a 9.45-inch 'flying-pig'.

A British 8-inch howitzer and some of the empty cases from the week-long bombardment.

Shells bursting on the German front lines the last week of June 1916.

German barbed wire, in this instance blasted flat. It was intended that this should be the case along the entire front of the British attack allowing the infantry to walk through to capture the German positions.

With these words I wish you the best of luck and a glorious victory.
There is no doubt that the men were confident of success. They were keen to get to grips with the enemy and although they recognised the possibility of their being maimed or killed the following morning they remained buoyant. After all they had seen the German trenches pounded day and night for a

week – how could they possibly fail? Author Graham Maddocks recorded in *Liverpool Pals* the words of Private Winn, Third Liverpool Pals:

> We had watched the preparations for advance for several weeks. Less than a month ago the valleys were ablaze with colour of an endless variety of wild flowers. Gradually the smiling valley became dissected and now, in place of the wild flowers, one noticed gun muzzles glinting mischievously and menacingly out of their evacuated emplacements. The valleys simply bristled with them – guns of all calibres. There must have been thousands of them and each had a stack of 'Kultur' – Kultur of a German kind – waiting to be pumped into the enemy's lines.
>
> The earth trembled and quaked when the bombardment commenced. Shells whistled and screeched through the air in a perpetual groan; the valleys reeked with the smell of smoke and powder. At night the darkness was rent by myriads of lightning-like flashes which seemed to dance joyously along the surrounding hilltops. The din on one side of the line was deafening, on the other side it must have been nerve-shattering. For days the cannonade lasted with indescribable intensity. The German trenches were severely battered and their earthworks swept completely away.
>
> At last the artillery had done its preliminary work, and done it well, and now it was the turn of the infantry.

How close to their knees did the week-long bombardment bring the Germans? Judging from information collated by Fourth Army Intelligence Corps it was a close run thing.

Effects of the British Bombardment

Captured correspondence, messages, despatches, reports, private letters and interrogation of prisoners reveal that the German infantryman was reaching the end of his endurance. The following are some previously unpublished reports supplied by Bill Turner, author of *Accrington Pals*. They indicate just how close the plan to neutralise the German effort to put up a defense came to success.

> Every one of us these five days has become years older. Bechtel said that in these five days he has lost ten pounds. Hunger and thirst have also contributed their share to that. Hunger would be easily borne, but the thirst made one almost mad. Luckily it rained yesterday and the water in the shell holes mixed with the yellow shell sulphur tasted as good as a bottle of beer.
>
> **109th Reserve Regiment. XIV Reserve Corps. Mametz/Montauban Sector 30 June 1916**

> We are quite shut off from the rest of the world; nothing comes up to us, no letters. The British keep up such a barrage on all approaches, it's terrible. Tomorrow it will be seven days since the bombardment began and we cannot hold out much longer. Everything is shot to pieces.
>
> **111th Reserve Infantry Regiment. XIV Reserve Corps. Fricourt Sector, June 1916**

> I have the impression that the artillery could not give sufficient support. Enemy mortars have been systematically firing at each of our dugouts with the aid of aerial observation. (Less so today). They have been able to handle their mortars as if on the practice range and have not been engaged at all by our

Germans repairing a damaged trench.

artillery. I also noticed today that when artillery fire was called for on our left
the artillery reply was late and, in comparison to the enemy fire, very weak.
Report of a Leutnant Cazarus to Officer Commanding 9 Company 109th Reserve
Regiment. XIV Reserve Corps. Mametz/Montauban Sector, June 1916

Likewise, Jack Sheldon in his book *German Army on the Somme* records similiar
reactions to the British bombardment. In the area where the Salford, Lonsdale
and Glasgow Pals were waiting to assault the village of Thiepval an
unteroffizier, Friedrich Hinkel, of the *7th Company Reserve Infantry Regiment 99*
recorded his experience of the bombardment in the History of RIR 99:

The enemy began to hammer at our trenches and links to the rear with an
hail of fire of all calibres. Artillery fire! Seven long days there was ceaseless
artillery fire, which rose ever more frequently to the intensity of drum fire. Then
on the 27th and 28th there were gas attacks on our trenches. The torture and
the fatigue, not to mention the strain on the nerves, were indescribable! There
was just one single heart-felt prayer on our lips: "Oh God, free us from this
ordeal; give us release through battle, grant us victory; Lord God! Just let them
come!" And this determination increased with the fall of each shell. You made a
good job of it, you British! Seven days and seven nights you rapped at our door!
Now your reception was going to match your turbulent longing to enter!"

Had the Big Push been put back for a few more days and, as a consequence
the bombardment extended, would the Germans have been battered into
submission? In the sector of the line allocated to the 30th Division where the
attackers benefitted from the French artillery, the attack went according to
plan.

Chapter Five

1ST JULY – THE AWAKENING

ROWS OF STEEL HELMETS and glittering bayonets were to be seen all along the front line. It was 7.20 am Saturday 1 July 1916 and a mist shrouded the countryside mixing with the smoke from exploding shells. In his observation post near Maricourt Wood, Lieutenant Colonel Fraser-Tyler, commanding 89 Brigade Royal Field Artillery, was in an excellent position to view the historic events unfolding before him. The mist began to clear and at 7.25 am precisely, hundreds of scaling ladders were placed in position in the forward trenches and waves of men climbed out over the parapet and stood in the grass before their own barbed wire. When their ranks were complete they proceeded to dress-off as if on the parade ground. Then at 7.30 signallers among the ranks dropped their flags, whistles blew, and all along the front waves of khaki surged forward. The Big Push was underway. Over on the right Fraser-Tyler could make out lines of French infantry belonging to the *39me Division* and to the left men of the British 18th Division.

The commander of the 17th Battalion (King's Livepool) Regiment, First Liverpool Pals, Lieutenant Colonel B. C. Fairfax stepped over the parapet at the extreme right of his troops. He made his way to where the commander of

British infantry forming up ready to attack the German lines. JOHN SHEEN

French troops prepare to attack.

French *153me RI*, Commandant Le Petit was standing in front of his men. The two commanders linked arms and stepped out across No Man's Land. C and D Companies of the First Liverpools had moved out early in order to avoid a German counter-barrage that was landing shells on the British assembly trenches. They, like the French infantry, were moving at some speed towards the German trenches. The German first line was named Faviere Trench and behind that was Faviere Support Trench. Both were taken with few casualties as the defenders, men of *Infanterie Regiment Nr.62*, had either fled or were still in their deep dugouts. The mopping up troops of the 2nd Battalion Befordshire Regiment rooted out some 300 prisoners. In the cluster of trees dubbed Germans Wood by the mappers, A Company received the surrender of thirty Germans who had been holding it. The Pals continued their advance and overran Casement Trench. British artillery was softening up Dublin Trench, which linked Glatz Redoubt and Dublin Redoubt. Once the barrage lifted both the French and the British entered Dublin and worked towards each other. When Dublin Redoubt fell the two commanders, Fairfax and Le Petit, met up and embraced each other in a spirit of comradeship. Everything was going according to plan.

All that remained was to consolidate the gains and, with the arrival of picks and shovels, carried forward by men of the Third Liverpool Pals, new trenches were dug away from the captured German ones. This was done in anticipation of a German counter-barrage, which would fall, inevitably, on all the captured Geman positions. Sure enough, when the German shells began to fall, hitting with some accuracy the zeroed-in positions, many lives were saved. Lieutenant E. W. Willmer, First Liverpool Pals, witnessed the action first hand:

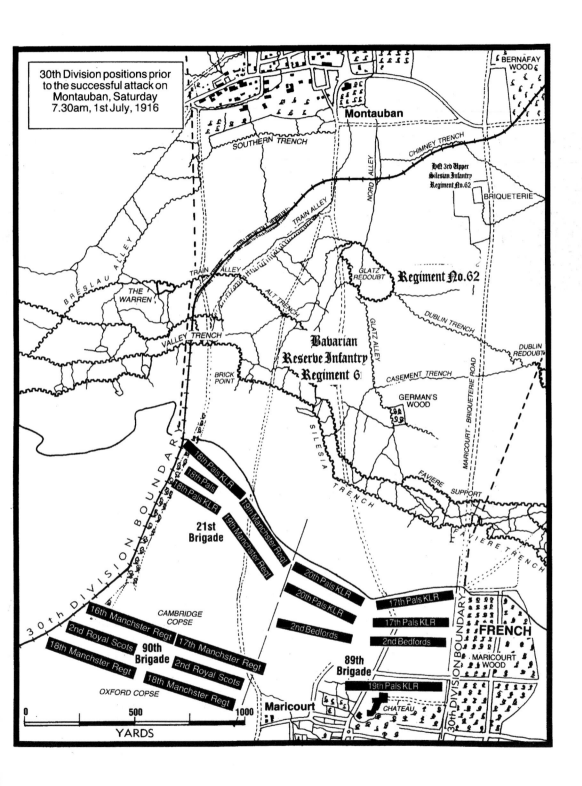

30th Division positions prior to the successful attack on Montauban, Saturday 7.30am, 1st July, 1916

On the first day I was in the support line and got a marvellous view of all that happened. It was a lovely sunny morning and promptly at 7.30, our barrage lifted from the German front line to their support line, and waves of British troops left the trenches and walked out into No Man's Land, in extended line, with bayonets fixed and rifles at the carry. There was no hurry and, so far as our battalion was concerned, very little resistance. Our casualties were small and we gained our objectives without trouble, and dug in at our new position. Further north of course, things were very different, and the casualties were appalling!

In a little over an hour the 30th Division had taken all its objectives. All the battalions had faired reasonably well in the attack. Lance Corporal J. Quinn of the Fourth Liverpool Pals described in a letter the advance on the left flank of the division.

We halted at the first German trench which had practically been evacuated. The men in front of us had by this time reached the German second line. Whilst at this halt many of us lit cigarettes and viewed the situation generally. We were now in possession of three lines of German trenches, and it all seemed so easy – much easier than when we practised it behind the line. Of course shells were dropping all around us, but we took them philosophically. By this time the 19th Battalion, who were reserve carriers for us, had now come over too and we watched them from the battered German trench as they came on with coils of barbed wire, ammunition etc, over their shoulders... Of course what made it so easy was that Fritz had made a strategic retreat – that is to say that he had run like the Devil a few miles back.

There were great numbers that gave themselves up as prisoners, and they did it in anything but a manly sort of way. When our line pushed on further we found that the German fourth line was too congested and so had to dig ourselves in. The shelling was very bad just here, but not many of our fellows got hit. It was later on, when we were holding the trench we had dug,that we had a hot time, for the German artillery picked up the range very quickly, and were soon dropping shells right over the parapet. Most of us out here have a great respect for their artillery.

At around 11.50 am orders were received to implement the second phase of the attack. An abandoned brick-making works – Briqueterie – was to be

Southern part of the Somme battlefield with the ruins of the Briqueterie on the skyline.

captured in the second phase. After a briefing at the north-west corner of Germans Wood, No.4 Company, commanded by Captain E. C. Orford, began the attack. There had been a thirty minute softening up bombardment by the Royal Field Artillery. After a brief fight Orford and his men were able to overcome the garrison occupying the Briqueterie, capturing five officers and forty men, along with two machine guns. Many documents and maps fell into their hands and were dispatched forthwith to the Division's Intelligence officers, and on to Fourth Army HQ.

The long-expected German counter-barrage descended on the former German positions in the early afternoon and carried on into the night. This added to 20th Battalion's total casualties for the first day of the Battle of the Somme until they amounted to twenty-three of all ranks killed and seventy-seven wounded.

The 18th Battalion (King's Liverpool) Regiment, Second Pals, although on the extreme left of the Division, had also benefitted from the intense and accurate French bombardment. The German wire in front of their first line, named Silesia Trench, had been blasted away. The assaulting infantry had 500 yards of No Man's Land to cross before reaching Silesia Trench. When Second Lieutenant E. Fitzbrown, leading his men over the cratered ground that had recently consisted of thick belts of barbed wire, reached Silesia Trench he found it vacated. The Germans were retreating to their support line.

A German machine gun continued to fire on the attackers from some high ground but it was outflanked and charged by Corporal T. T. Richards. The crew carried on firing right to the last minute and then attempted to surrender. They were all shot down or despatched with the bayonet. Bombing parties then proceeded to work along the support trench until it too was subdued and thirty prisoners of the *Bavarian Reserve Infantrie Regiment 6* were taken.

At around that time Glatz Redoubt fell to men of the Second Liverpool Pals and there they began to consolidate their position. Private Gregory described the capture of the German strongpoint:

> When we got to Glatz Redoubt it was in a right mess. There were bodies everywhere, in all kinds of attitudes, some on fire and burning from the British bombardment. Debris and deserted equipment littered the area, and papers were fluttering around in the breeze. There were only two of us at the start, and then we met with others coming in. Then a Geman came up, we thought, out of the

Germans killed during the Somme fighting.
Clearing out German dugouts.

ground but he was coming up some steps. They were proper wooden steps, about twelve or thirteen. They led down to a huge dugout, with wire beds in three tiers – enough beds to take about one hundred people. This little German came out and put his hands in the air – I couldn't shoot him. I just indicated for him to go over the top to our lines and he just scampered off.

Then we went down into the dugout to do a bit of 'souveniring'. The Germans must have left pretty quickly because they hadn't even taken their coats with them, so we went through the pockets. I got a German soldier's pay book, some buttons and a spiked helmet. One souvenir I collected from a German officer's tunic was a diary, which I later handed over to an officer at a dressing station. The remainder of the 'loot', like tunic buttons, I found a ready market for at the base at Rouen, where the Army Service Corps blokes, who were on 7/- a day pay (ours was only 1/-), would pay anything for these small souvenirs. The German spiked helmets, *Pickelhaube*, were especially sought after as souvenirs, but there were dangers in wearing them, as Private Gregory's account shows. Apparently one of his mates was larking about with one of the helmets on his head and was still wearing it when he climbed up out of the dugout into the trench above. At that point one of the Manchesters from a follow-up battalion rounded the traverse and shot him dead. An easy enough mistake to make in the heat of battle.

German helmets, Pickelhaube, were much sought after as souvenirs.

When the commanding officer of the 18th Battalion, Second Liverpool Pals, Lieutenant Colonel E. H Trotter, received reports of the casualties suffered in his battalion's attack he was shaken – especially at the news of the deaths of his fellow officers. As night fell on that terrible day, 1 July 1916, he attempted to estimate his losses. With seven officers and 164 men killed outright he calculated that with those wounded being stretchered off to various dressing stations, the 18th Battalion had suffered around 500 casualties. He had lost around half of his command.

The task of 90 Brigade was to press the attack across the ground taken by 21 Brigade and capture the village of Montauban. The British Artillery barrage lifted from the front of Montauban and began falling on the rear of the village. The 16th and 17th Battalions Manchester Regiment, First and Second City Battalions, advanced into the ruins. So intense had been the barrage that the German garrison of around 100 survivors surrendered readily. Major Macdonald, Second City Battalion, recorded that,

> There was no opposition to the entry. Bombing parties proceeded to clear Nord and Train Alley and C. T. in orchard north-east of B strongpoint. The enemy met with in these places surrendered without opposition and the leading waves pushed on through the town. The rear waves, consisting partly of carrying parties, arrived in rather an exhausted state, due chiefly to their desire to be 'in at the finish'. The town was practically deserted and was completely in ruins. It was almost impossible to trace the run of the streets.

Second Lieutenant Kenneth Callan-Macardle described what he found among the ruins of Montauban:

> Inside was all wreck and ruin, a monstrous garbage heap stinking of dead men and high explosive. Down in deep dugouts, a few of which had survived our heavy shells, (for the Hun builds perfect dugouts), cowering men in grey were captured, living with old corpses. A Brigadier Colonel [sic] and staff of six officers were captured in one that was fitted with electric light and push bell; large parties laughing and dancing like demented things full of mad joy went streaming back to Maricourt unguarded, holding their hands up and calling

'Miracle of the Madonna at Montauban'. This photograph was released to the newspapers shortly after the capture of the village with the caption: *The only thing left intact in the village of Montauban and this large German shell lying at her feet which did not explode.*

While the plaster effigy survived, flesh and blood did not. The village was observed to be littered with dead and dying Germans scattered among the brick dust and the place reeking of decaying corpses.

"Mercy Kammerade!" They had thrown away their equipment and arms and looked utterly demoralised in filthy, stinking grey uniforms. The village was full of the terrors and horrors of war; dying Germans among the brick dust and rubble – horrible wounds and reeking corpses.

As night fell on the most terrible day in the history of the British army up to that time, the men of the Manchester City battalions who had taken Montauban, occupied the trenches on the northern side of the village. They were desperate for water and exhausted, not having slept for thirty-six hours, and were short of ammunition. They had repulsed one counter-attack and, with darkness pressing all around, could well expect another. German artillery began to systematically blast the ground that had been lost to their infantry.

The German High Command were none too pleased that they had been bested in the area either side of the Somme River. Commander of the German Second Army General von Below:

> *Secret Second Army*
> *July 1916*
> *Ia/802*
>
> *In spite of my orders forbidding the voluntary evacuation of positions (General Order Ia/575, Secret) certain positions of our line appear to have been abandoned before any attack had been delivered by the enemy. Every Commanding Officer will be held accountable if the units under his command do not fight to the last man in the sector allotted to them. Any infraction of this order will immediately render the officer concerned liable to Court Martial.*
>
> *This order will be communicated to every commanding officer.*

A further communique from von Below was sent to all regiments under his command exhorting them to stand fast until reinforcements could arrive:

> *Second Army*
> *3 July 1916*
>
> *The final decision of the war depends upon the victory of the Second Army on the Somme. We must win the battle despite the enemy's temporary superiority in guns and infantry. The important ground captured by the enemy at certain points will be retaken from them by our attacks after reinforcements have arrived. For the moment it is essential to hold our present position regardless of cost and to improve them by small counter-attacks. I forbid the voluntary evacuation of positions. This must be made known to every man in the Army. I hold Commanding Officers responsible for this. The enemy must be made to pave his road with corpses. The rapid organisation of advanced defensive positions, of intermediate positions behind the principal salients, and of positions further in the rear must be carried out by every possible means. The organisation of these latter positions must be begun on reverse slopes, so that their situation and construction may be hidden from the enemy. I direct that Commanding Officers shall ensure the maintenance of order behind the line with the greatest energy.*

The Germans were shaken but were far from considering a general withdrawal in the face of the Big Push. Apart from some loss of ground in the south their defence system on the Somme had proved itself and remained intact.

Between the 30th Division, with its Liverpool and Manchester Pals battalions, and the next division containing Pals battalions on the Somme front was the 18th Division. The next division in line, heading north, was a mixture which contained, among others, four Pals and two New Army battalions.

7th Division

The 7th Division, formally an all-Regular division had received four Pals type units, 20th, 21st and 22nd Battalions, Manchester Regiment. The Divisional Pioneer battalion was 24th Battalion, Manchester Regiment, Oldham Comrades. This hybrid division was detailed to attack the villages of Fricourt and Mametz. Its organisation was as follows,

20 Brigade:

> 2nd Battalion, Border Regiment (Regular)
> 2nd Battalion, Gordon Highlanders (Regular)
> 8th (Service) Battalion, Devonshire Regiment (New Army)
> 9th (Service) Battalion, Devonshire Regiment (New Army)

22 Brigade:

> 2nd Battalion, Royal Warwickshire Regiment (Regular)
> 1st Battalion, Royal Welsh Fusiliers (Regular)
> 2nd Battalion Royal Irish Regiment (Regular)
> 20th (Service) Battalion, Manchester Regiment (Pals)

91 Brigade:

> 2nd Battalion, Queen's (Royal West Surrey Regiment (Regular)
> 1st Battalion, South Staffordshire Regiment (Regular)
> 21st (Service) Battalion, Manchester Regiment (Pals)
> 22nd (Service) Battalion, Manchester Regiment (Pals)

Divisional Pioneers:

24th (Service) Battalion, Manchester Regiment, Oldham Comrades (Pals)

At 7.30 the 7th City Battalion, 22nd Manchesters, with the South Staffs on its left, set off into No Man's Land. The air was thick with chalk dust from three huge mines that had been detonated under the German trenches. Despite the fact that a number of German posts in the front line had been destroyed by the exploded mines, the Germans in positions further back were able to pour fire into the advancing ranks.

After twenty-five minutes they had taken their first objective and the South Staffs were fighting through the village of Mametz. A great many of the casualties suffered by the two battalions, had been caused by a single machine gun placed in a house at the southwest corner of the village. It was found to have been protected by a four-inch-thick sheet of armour plate.

By 11.15 am it became known that a stronghold called Pommiers Redoubt had fallen. Machine guns at Pommiers had been causing casualties among the 7th City Battalion, 22nd Manchesters. By early afternoon both the 22nd and

Mametz following its capture.

21st Battalions were holding the trench called Danzig Alley. By 5 pm the whole village of Mametz was cleared of Germans and Lieutenant Colonel Norman, commanding 6th City Battalion, 21st Manchesters, was placed in charge of the village defences. The Oldham Comrades began constructing barbed wire defences along 7th Division's gains. Had there been a drive on to Mametz Wood while the going was good it might have saved bloodshed later. However, it would have had to have been undertaken by Corps reserve troops as the assaulting battalions were incapable of further effort. The 7th City Battalion was broken, with 472 casualties, dead, wounded and missing.

Against the village of Fricourt was launched the 20th Battalion, Manchester Regiment, 5th City Battalion and, at the end of the day's fighting, they were in the village, but at a great price. Private Pat Burke had watched them set off on that sunny Saturday:

All those weary hours the lads had remained calm, but very eager to get it over. They did not go over after a strong ration of rum as some people imagine these affairs are carried out. No, they went over feeling themselves. The colonel watched them mount the steps and his last words were, "Isn't it wonderful?"

The way they extended to six paces and walked over at the slope, one would have thought they were at Belton Park, or our other training quarters. Our reserves were calling out, "Bravo Manchesters!" and "Good luck!" and "Cheerio!" and every other word of praise that such calmness could bring to their minds.

Down they fell one by one, but no excitement occurred until they closed on the German front line.

As evening fell on that first day the 5th City Battalion was down to 250 men. They had not made great progress but they had achieved just enough to justify their near annihilation, in the eyes of the British commanders. Their attack along 22 Brigade frontage marked the end of progress along the southern arm of the Fourth Army's attack north of the Somme.

The 21st Division, adjacent to the 7th and a New Army formation, had been able to gain a few yards of enemy line at heavy loss. Alongside them was the next Pals Division.

34th Division

In some sectors of the German line the week-long bombardment had done little to dent the men's determination to hold. One German soldier wrote to a comrade in Bapaume,

> *Heavy fire since 24th inst. Our casualties are, I am glad to say, quite small. In our Company for example there have been none killed. No attack so far; anyway we are prepared. Our artillery is doing splendidly. If the shell fire does not drive you out of Bapaume there is no need to move on account of the English, they won't get as far as that.*

> *111th Reserve Regiment. XIV Reserve Corps. Fricourt Sector, June 1916*

The above was written by a soldier holding the line which bordered the sector designated for the attack by Tynesiders in the 34th Division. On the frontage of their attack there were found printed instructions on how to communicate with British soldiers who broke into their trench system

> *Expressions to be learnt by heart:*
> *When Englishmen are met in the trenches, shout out, "Hands up, you fool! Arms away!" To be pronounced "Hands opp ju fuhl, Arms ewa!"*
> *At the entrance of a dugout, cry out, "Is anybody inside?" "Is anibodi inseid!"*
> *After throwing in a hand-grenade, shout out, "Come all out, quick, quick!" "Kom ohl aut, quick, quick!"*
> *If the Englishmen come out, shout at them, "Hands up, come on Tommy!" "Honds opp, kom on Tomy!"*

> **Document found in a dugout at La Boisselle. XIV Reserve Corps General Command**

Whether or not the instructions were followed we cannot be sure, but certainly there would have been the opportunity as the Tynesiders descended on their front line.

Brigadier General Ternan watched the ground over which the attack was to take place from an observation post on the forward slope of the Tara Usna ridge. With one eye on his wristwatch he observed the approximate area where he knew mines were about to rip open the earth. The enemy-held village of La Boisselle projected towards the British lines and had seen much underground fighting and the blowing of mines. Heralding the British offensive two further mines were exploded each side of the village at 7.28 am. To the north of the village, near the destroyed Albert-Bapaume road, one mine blew a crater 165 feet in diameter destroying a Geman position called Y Sap. However, the Germans had evacuated the position and only a few soldiers

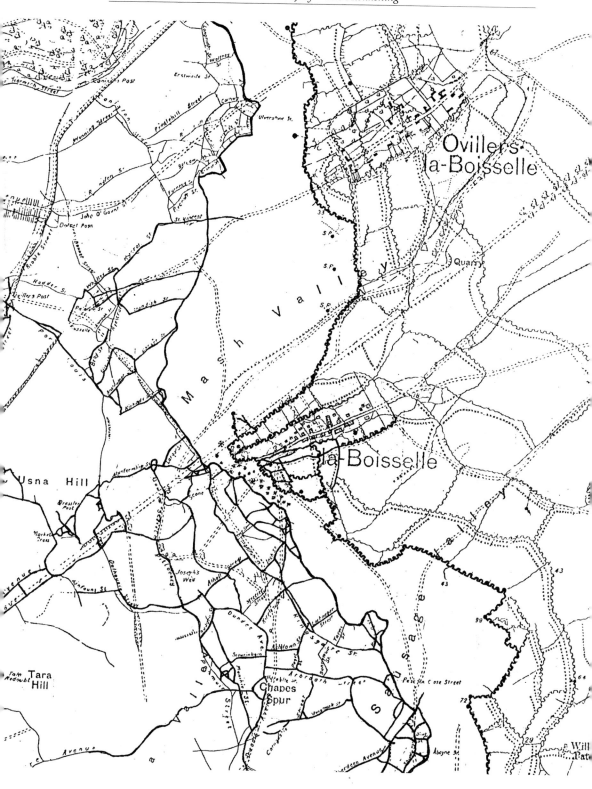

7.30 on the morning of 1 July and the first wave of Tyneside Irish begins to walk towards the German lines.

were killed. It was a different outcome with the exploding of the Lochnagar mine to the south. A German strongpoint, *Schwaben Höhe*, was blasted to oblivion. some 350 feet of the enemy's front line just disappeared. A German officer and thirty-five men were taken from a dugout just beyond the damaged zone; he was able to inform of nine other dugouts in the vicinity each containing around thirty to forty men. They have never been found. A crater 450 feet across had been created by two mines being exploded simultaneously in two separate chambers. Brigadier General Ternan recorded the scene:

> As the watches marked the half hour [7.28] *the two huge mines on the flanks of La Boisselle exploded with a concussion that shook the ground for miles around, and the attack began. The mine on the right [Lochnagar] had been charged with thirty tons of ammonal, and that on the left with twenty tons, so that the effect of the explosions was terrific. The bottom of the valley was quickly obliterated from our view from the dust thrown up and the countless shells, so that one could see little or nothing except the movement of the companies of the reserve Brigade as they went forward.*

One observer in the 8th Division which attacked alongside the Tyneside Scottish reported what he saw:

> *The pluckiest thing I ever saw was a piper of the Tyneside Scottish playing his company over the parapet in the attack on the German trenches near Albert.*

The Tynesiders were on our right, and as their officers gave the signal to advance I saw the piper – I think he was the Pipe Major – jump out of the trench and march straight over No Man's Land towards the German lines. The tremendous rattle of machine gun and rifle fire, which the enemy at once opened on us, completely drowned the sound of the pipes. But it was obvious he was playing as though he would burst the bag, and just faintly through the din we heard the mighty shout his comrades gave as they swarmed after him. How he escaped death I can't understand for the ground was literally ploughed up by the hail of bullets. But he seemed to bear a charmed life and the last glimpse I had of him, as we too dashed out, showed him still marching erect, playing furiously, and quite regardless of the flying bullets and the men dropping all around him.

Authors Graham Stewart and John Sheen, have identified the brave piper and include a photograph in their book, *Tyneside Scottish*. Another piper, George Griffiths, gave his account of leading the attacking infantry, whilst playing his pipes:

At the given signal we jumped from our trenches and struck up our pipes. It was like all hell let loose. I got so far and then got caught on some barbed wire. after I got disentangled I had to abandon my pipes and take up my rifle. Fellow piper Willie Scott, a shipyard worker from Elswick in Newcastle, was still ahead of me playing. When I reached the German trenches and jumped in, the first man I saw was Willie – dead, but still holding his pipes. If ever a man deserved the VC Willie did.

Attempting to fight their way into La Boisselle was the Brigade Bombing Company armed with Mills grenades. This was observed by Private Elliot who was pinned down in No Man's Land with the rest of his section:

Over in the village you couldn't see much of what was happening because of the dust and smoke, but I could see some of our lads chucking bombs. They were beckoning towards us, trying to get us to come forward. They couldn't see that Fritzie boy had a machine gun on us. Billy Grant, the sergeant, wanted to get forward to the crater to support them. He said that if we didn't get forward the barrage would paste us. We waited until the machine gun had passed. One... two... three! We tried to get to our feet to charge but as soon as we rose, that gun was on us. Billy was caught in the side by machine-gun fire. That was it, we durst not move, it was belly down for the rest of the day after that. I often wonder if we could have done more to get forward, but we were possed, well and truly possed. The lads up in front must have put up a good fight because we could hear bombs and shouting and Lewis guns well into the afternoon. So if the lads in the front went down, they went down fighting.

The bombers had managed to gain a toe-hold but the Germans drove them out, captured or killed them.

In the area of the Tyneside Irish the situation was much the same. After overrunning the German first and second lines the attackers were faced with fierce counter-attacks and machine-gun fire. CQMS Gavin Wild, 26th Battalion, Third Tyneside Irish, was later to write concerning the death of Private Jack Hunter from Bowburn:

We got to their second line and the Germans gave us lots of machine-gun fire, and I got to within about twenty yards of a Geman machine gun. A bullet went through my hip and another through my arm. Jackie dragged me about ten yards to a shell hole and just as he pushed me into the safety of the hole, he was shot through the head. A shrapnel shell bursting overhead lodged a piece of shrapnel in me, but I managed to crawl into the hole. I was there abaout sixteen hours and all the while a lovely sun was burning down. Poor Jackie and I lay all that long burning day together in that shellhole. You can imagine my feelings, lying there with one of my best chums who'd given his life to save mine.

Commanding a German machine gun position, defending against the Tyneside Irish attack on their lines, was *Oberleutnant* Kienitz, Reserve Infantry Regiment 110. He recorded the events he and his men experienced:

Silently our machine guns and the infantrymen waited until our opponents came closer. Then, when they were only a few metres from our trenches, the serried ranks of the enemy were sprayed with a hurricane of defensive fire from the machine guns and the aimed fire of the individual riflemen. Standing exposed on the parapet, individuals hurled hand grenades at the enemy who had taken cover to the front. Within moments it seemed as though the battle had died away completely, but then, initially in small groups, but later in huge masses, the enemy began to pull back towards Bécourt, until finally it seemed as though every man in the entire field was attempting to flee back to his jumping-off point. The fire of our infantrymen and machine guns pursued them, hitting

German machine gun crew operating a captured Russian machine gun on the Western Front.

them hard; whilst some of our men daringly charged the British troops capturing prisoners. Our weapons fired away ceaselessly for two hours then the battle died away in Bécourt Hollow [Sausage Valley].

By midday the situation was stable from the German point of view. Apart from a few men hanging onto the lip of Lochnager crater, the British were back in their own lines. The attack had not been a surprise and the large distance the attackers had to cover before reaching the German front line, ensured failure. It certainly hadn't helped that the attackers were loaded down with equipment and ordered to walk.

Another Pals battalion in the 34th Division, the 10th Battalion, Lincolnshire Regiment, Grimsby Chums, had also suffered heavy casualties. This Service battalion had been formed around a neucleus of ex-boys of the Grimsby Municipal College cadet force. Recruits for the battalion had come from as far afield as Nottingham, Worksop, Sheffield and Wakefield. As the first day of the Battle of the Somme ended it was realised that the Grimsby Chums had lost over 500 men out of a fighting strength of 842. Subsequently, it was established that 187 had been killed. The Battalion war diary records the problems encountered in retrieving the wounded:

Owing to the continuous rifle and machine-gun fire great difficulty was experienced in getting in the wounded, many of whom lay out in No Man's Land for over thirty hours, but through the constant exertions of all ranks

The crater caused by the mine explosion under the German position known as 'Y Sap' is next to the German front line. Very few of the attackers ever reached the crater.

during the nights of 1st/2nd and 2nd/3rd as far as could be ascertained all the wounded belonging to the battalion had been brought in before the battalion left the fighting area. Any attempt to reach them by daylight was immediately met by machine-gun and rifle fire from the enemy's trenches and all our wounded, when seen to move, were immediately fired on by the German snipers.

Continuing north the next village fortified by the Germans was Thiepval with its defending strongpoints of the Leipzig Salient and the Wundt Work. This was the objective of the next Pals formation, the 32nd Division.

32nd Division

As on other sections of the front, the Germans were ready for the big attack when it came. Instructions on how the German soldier was to conduct himself under attack were issued to all units on the Somme.

Notice for each dugout in the Front Line

Our infantry is superior to any enemy, we either resist to the utmost or die.

Our dugouts are proof against the heaviest and longest artillery bombardments. However, you must leave them at the correct time just before the enemy arrives and hurry to the parapet. Anyone remaining in them will be killed by hand grenades or rendered unconscious by gas. Therefore, get out!

Rifles and hand grenades are not to be stored in entrances to dugouts. They might easily get buried there. Therefore take them with you into the dugout. Also the machine guns.

Don't fear a gas attack, even when it darkens the air. The gas soon wafts behind. Put on protectors, place wooden boxes before you and set them alight.

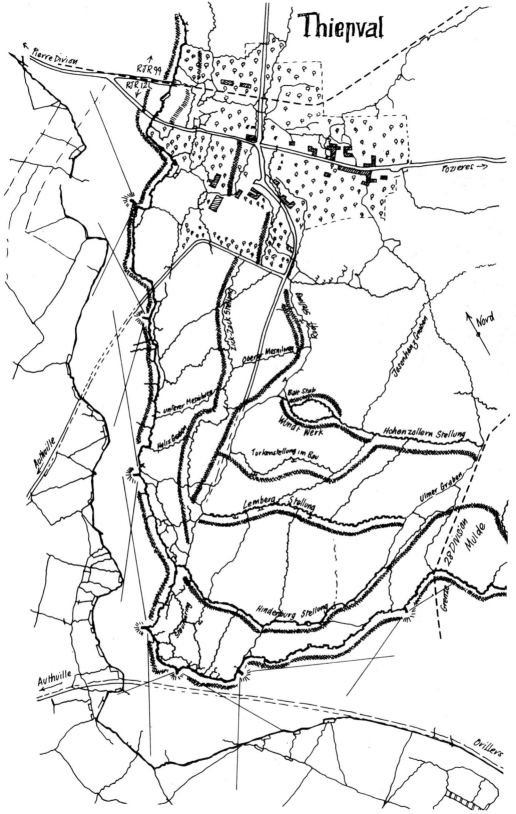

Thiepval defences taken from an original German map showing the location of front line machine guns, their angles of fire and effective range.

Only those troops who lose their heads during a gas attack have been beaten by the enemy. Steadfast troops have repulsed attacks.

Don't use the rifle before you are at the parapet, nor hand grenades until the enemy is near. They are often thrown too early.

I. If the enemy gets into the trenches, continue to fight with hand grenades. Help will come at once from behind and the sides. Everyone in the neighbouring trenches must also stand to if the enemy break in.

II. If the enemy break through don't lose your head! Only weak-kneed troops surrender. Brave troops continue with rearguard actions. In this way brave troops have taken thousands of prisoners in recent battles.

III. Rations and water will always be supplied to the troops even in battles lasting several days. **The Commanding General v. Stein**

The Germans knew what to do once the shelling of their trenches ceased. The British had been told by their generals that it was to be a walk-over.

At 7.23 am the 17th Battalion, Highland Light Infantry, Third Glasgow Pals, raised from the Glasgow Chamber of Commerce, left their own trenches and crept forward to within thirty yards of the German front line. At 7.30 am the British bombardment lifted and the Glasgow men got to their feet and charged into the trenches forming the Leipzig Redoubt. The Germans were still in their dugouts and the Scotsmen had won the race of death. They pressed on to the second line called 'Hindenburg Strasse'. However, a well-sited machine gun in the Wundt Work stopped their further advance, forcing them back to the Redoubt. Supporting them on their right was a Regular battalion, 2nd Battalion King's Own Yorkshire Light Infantry, which battalion helped the Glasgow Pals to consolidate their gains in the German stronghold.

German machine gun team.

Glasgow and Salford Pals and Newcastle Commercials attacked across this ground when attacking Thiepval village.

Working with men of the 252nd Tunnelling Company, 32nd Division pioneers, the 17th Battalion Northumberland Fusiliers (North Eastern Railway) began to drive saps across No Man's Land which were to act as communication routes to the captured positions.

Things were not going so well for the 16th Battalion Highland Light Infantry, Second Glasgow Pals (Glasgow Boys' Brigade) on the left. Upon reaching the German wire they found it to be intact and, unable to find a way through, men sought cover in shell holes. Machine-gun and rifle fire effectively cut off their line of retreat and they had to wait for nightfall before making their way back to their own lines. Once back in Authille Wood they were able to establish that their abortive attack had cost them 554 casualties.

When the signal for the attack came for the 16th Battalion Northumberland Fusiliers (Newcastle Commercials), they advanced behind a football as it was kicked ahead of them. They were received by a hail of fire that cut them down in neat rows. Forced to take cover as best they could, the survivors were taunted by German defenders who stood on their parapet inviting the 'Tommies' to come forward. Battalion survivors later mustered at Aveluy Wood and it was found that 378 had become casualties.

Men of the 15th Battalion Lancashire Fusiliers, First Salford Pals, with ten minutes to go before the whistles blew, crawled out into No Man's Land. They were about one hundred yards from the fortified village of Thiepval where the final flurry of explosions from the British bombardment were falling. Incredibly, German machine gun teams, ignoring the bombardment, were already manning their weapons and a steady tack! tack! tack! of machine guns could be heard above the exploding shells. At the signal hundreds of Salford men stood up and began to walk forward. The instant that they cleared a rise in the ground in front of the village bullets began smacking into them. A German counter-barrage began to lay down intense fire on the British front line trenches. All communication between the attackers and their Battalion HQ ceased. Private Hutton was beside his Company Commander, Captain Alfred Lee Wood, and later gave his experience from a hospital bed:

> Barely fifty yards had been covered when he was hit by a bullet which grazed his head, whilst I got one in the arm. Without pausing we went on a little further, when a second bullet struck the captain on the head causing a nasty gash. Almost at the same moment I was shot through the leg. Turning to me Captain Wood asked, "Are you badly hit?" and I replied, "Yes Sir, I can't go on this time." He then ordered me to try and get back to our trench and, although I begged him to come back with me since he was badly wounded, he said "No, I will get that machine gunner."

Because of the neighbouring division's success (the 36th (Ulster) Division had broken through and the attackers had advanced for almost a mile), much of the attention of *Reserve Infantrie Regiment 99* was directed at this breach. Because of this initial success, some Salford men were able to pass through the wire where it had been destroyed and enter the German front line trench.

Follow up companies of 96 Brigade were cut to pieces and, yet, it was still believed that the attack was going to plan. Observation from battalion and brigade headquarters was hopeless and runners were not getting through.

The Lonsdale Pals (11th Battalion, the Border Regiment) faired no better in their attempt to assault Leipzig Redoubt. Machine gunners in a strongpoint called the Nordwerk were able to sweep their ranks with deadly fire, killing Lieutenant Colonel P. W. Machell, along with most of his officers. Casualties amounted to around 500 men killed and wounded out of the 800 men and officers who advanced into No Man's Land on that Saturday morning. An interview with one of the survivors describes the death of the Colonel:

> It was half past seven when we started... we were third in the line, B and C Companies being in front of us. We could see them moving in the open as they passed a wood, until the fire caught them and they went down like grass. I was beside the Colonel in the front trench – I carried bombs. The Colonel was to go with the last line after us, but when he saw our second line cut down that way and then it was our turn, he just said, "Oh damn!" Then he climbed up onto the parapet, "Come on lads!" he yelled, then he was hit and staggered back, and before we could prevent it he fell backwards into the trench again. But we had to go on, I had my bombs. We were all singing 'John Peel' like mad and cheering enough to raise the dead. Then I was hit by a bullet in the arm and stumbled and fell. But I got to my feet again and carried on as I was carrying the bombs. You would have been amazed at the way our lads were singing and cheering, as if they were at a football match.

Three officers and 300 men survived that attack. They got nowhere and, throughout the rest of the day and that night, individuals struggled back to their start lines as best they could. Apart from the next formation, 36th (Ulster) Division, which had made some progress, the story was very much the same.

31st Division

As previously stated, the last division along the Somme front engaged in the Big Push, moving north, was a Pals division, the 31st. The Division's objective was the village of Serre and beyond. Two brigades would lead the attack, 93 and 94. Leading 93 Brigade was the 15th Battalion The Prince of Wales's Own (West Yorkshire) Regiment (Leeds Pals). They would sweep around the southern side of the village of Serre and, turning northeast at Pendant Copse, face Puisieux au-Mont. 93 Brigade had the furthest distance to cover, the Bradford and Durham Pals to pass through the Leeds men once they had taken the Second Objective.

The honour of being first 'over the lid' fell to my own platoon (No. 13) and another, Platoon No. 10. Not a man hesitated: in broad daylight last Saturday morning our lads got the order to advance. No sooner had the first lot got over the parapet than the Germans opened up a terrific bombardment, big shells and shrapnel and their parapet was packed with Germans exposing themselves waist-high above the top and they opened rapid fire. They had machine guns every few yards and it seemed impossible for a square inch of space to be left free from flying metal.

Our guns had kept up a hot bombardment for seven days, and for over an hour just preceding our platoon going over the lid. It seemed as if nothing could live in their first line trench; individual shells could not be heard no matter how big they were, it was one continuous scream overhead, and a roaring and ripping of bursting shells just 'across the way'. But, at the moment of our advance, the Germans seemed to be giving us shell for shell.

'We saw it going sky high – it was just one hugh mass of soil going up!' Exploding of the Hawthorne mine heralded the start of the attack north of the Ancre valley.

British infantry walking towards the German lines. JOHN SHEEN

Young Willey [Second Lieutenant Willey] *led our platoon... He has always shown calm grit and courage in the firing line, and we had every confidence in him, but never has he appeared so noble and courageous as he did last Saturday. At the order every man swarmed out of the front line trench, and doubled out a few yards before extending to twenty paces interval between each man and laid down for nine minutes. At the end of that time Young Willey jumped up and, waving his revolver, shouted "Come on 13! Give them Hell!"*

We were repeatedly struck by fairly large pieces of spent shrapnel, but when the moment came for the advance and we saw the calm and steady way in which our lads climbed over the trenches onto the parapet and made for their positions in regular order, we felt inspired. **Private Arthur Hollings 13 Platoon, D Company**

Within minutes many of the leading waves were gone and those who tried to follow suffered the same fate. Every Leeds officer who went into the attack was either killed or wounded. Other waves waited for the order to go, but by this time it was becoming apparent at Brigade headquarters that a massacre was taking place. Battalion runner, Private Charles Cryer, was ordered to find out exactly what was going on:

I was sent over to find out how the first wave of attack had gone on and what advance they'd made, and there was no actual sign of anybody, they'd all been wiped out.

On 94 Brigade front they were taking the full effect from enfilade firing being poured into them by machine gunners of *Infantry Regiment 66*. As Brigadier General Rees had feared, with nothing happening on that sector of the front the Germans knew exactly where the attack ended and were free to add their weight of fire in support of their comrades defending Serre.

Lieutenant Colonel Rickman, commanding 11th East Lancashire Regiment, Accrington Pals, made his report to Brigade HQ, (situated in Observation Wood), just twenty minutes after the attack had got underway. He had looked on in despair as his battalion was cut down in No Man's Land. He had taken

Leeds and Accrington Pals in the first wave of the attack found that the wire had not been cut in sufficient places.

over the battalion at Caernarvon on St David's Day 1915 and from that time on had been devoted to its well-being, not just as a New Army formation, but as a family-like brotherhood forged in pre-war days in factories, mines, offices, church organisations and sporting clubs. Now he had to report that the attack was floundering and that heavy casualties were being incurred. All that he had worked for was disappearing before his eyes. He could now only wait for reports from his 'waves' of infantry. Private Clark later told of what it was like that Saturday morning:

> While we were walking in line my section came to a shell hole. We had to decide which way to go round it. Some went to the left and I went to the right. Just then a shell came over and I was thrown to the ground by the blast of the explosion. When I picked myself up I realised that I had a flesh wound in the leg. I looked around and to the left of me there was nothing – not a man. For fifty yards on either side of me no other man was going forward, there was only dead and wounded on the ground. I went forward about twenty yards and was wounded again, in the arm this time. The wound was quite bad as my arm had dropped and was useless – it felt cold. I thought, "I'm not going forward with this hand, I had better get back and get a dressing on it." Then another shell burst and knocked me over.
>
> I was still lying prone on the ground when a piece of shrapnel hit me behind the ear and I slipped into a shell hole about twenty-five yards from the German front line trench. Wiping away the blood I pulled the piece of shrapnel out, then creeping forward I spotted some Germans. I fired just one shot and then suddenly there was a 'thud', it was as if my head had been blown in two, and I was blinded by blood.

During the morning it was observed that men were dashing from one shell hole to another in their attempts to return to the British front line. However, some Accrington men did manage to get through the German wire and into the enemy's front line trench before retreating. Corporal Hale was a signaller

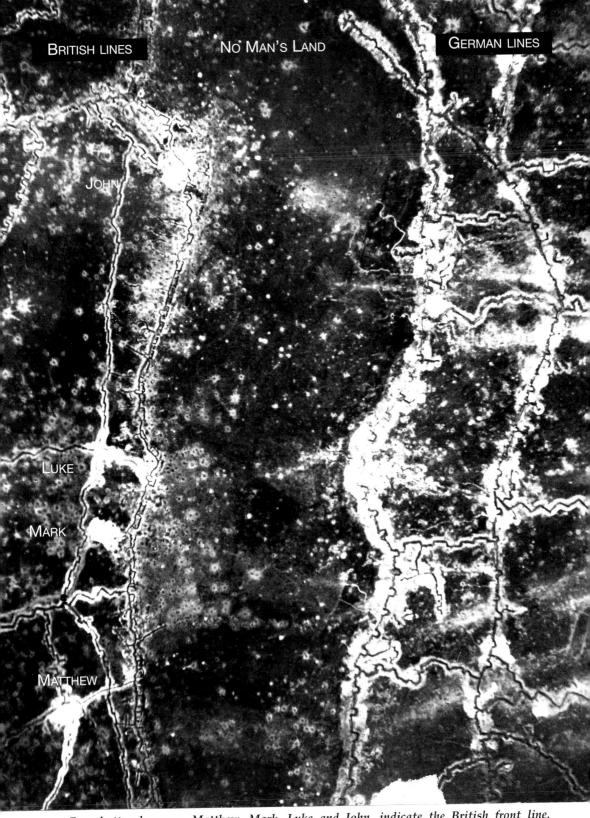

BRITISH LINES   NO MAN'S LAND   GERMAN LINES

JOHN

LUKE

MARK

MATTHEW

Four battered copses, Matthew, Mark, Luke and John, indicate the British front line.
Photograph taken by a British aircraft on the morning of 1 July 1916 during the attack.

attached to the fourth wave and he, with another two of his signaller pals, Private Orrell Duerdon and Private Bill Stuart, made it all the way, viewing it almost as a miracle:

> At zero hour we advanced a hundred yards when a shell burst a dozen or so yards from us, the force of which knocked me down. Orrell and Bill asked me if I was all right and if I had been hit. "No, I'm OK" and we carried on. We could see lads dropping all around and we remarked how marvellous it was that we were being missed. When we got to the German front line I was hit in the hand by a bullet. When we dropped into the trench Orrell bandaged my hand and then said, "Will you remove this piece of shrapnel from my head?" It was a surprise as this was the first time he had mentioned that he had been hit. He must have been wounded by the shell that had knocked me over. I removed it from near his temple, it was only a small piece and he didn't seem any worse for it and said that it didn't hurt. Just then a shell came over and blew the parapet in almost smothering us. Orrell and I decided that it was rather unhealthy there so we had to part company, he to go on and keep communication going and me back to the dressing station, for now my left arm was useless. We shook hands and wished each other good luck.

Corporal Hale never saw his pal Orrell Duerden again.

A member of a Lewis gun team also made it into the German trenches, Private Bewsher with some in the first wave and describes the action:

> I was right in front of a machine-gun post and I emptied a drum at a few Germans who were on the parapet. They were throwing potato-mashers [grenades] over my head. I'd got a bit too close to them. Some of them went back down the communication trench (I was surprised to see how wide it was) and I followed. I got almost to their second line before it dawned on me that I was the only one there and so I decided to go back. Still holding the Lewis gun I scrambled back twenty yards into No Man's Land where I took cover in a shell hole and trained my Lewis gun on the communication trench. I waited for the other waves. Suddenly there were Germans coming back up their communication trench. Whether they were looking for wounded or not I don't know, but I let them have it and they disappeared. I was sure that they were going to counter-attack so I ran back towards our own lines. I had some narrow squeaks and one bullet hit my water bottle. I felt the water on my leg and thought that it was blood. Another went through my haversack and broke all my biscuits before lodging in a tin of bully-beef. A piece of shrapnel hit my Lewis gun, bending the barrel and knocking the foresight clean off. There was a dead Sheffield City pal with a Lewis gun alongside of him and I threw mine down and picked his up. I took up position again and started firing at that group of Germans again. Then I jumped up and raced for our front line again.
>
> By a stroke of luck I stumbled across C Sap which protruded into No Man's Land. In there was Lieutenant Colonel Rickman and our Signals Officer, Captain MacAlpine. "Was that you firing that gun out there?" the Colonel asked. Yes sir! I thought that they were going to attack. I didn't know whether they were stretcher-bearers or infantry, but I had a do at them." Then he said, "That's my lad." Then turning to Captain MacAlpine he said "Take his name

and number." I wondered 'What the hell for?' Having your name and number taken was always for a crime.

Colonel Rickman sent Private Bewsher to join the few defenders manning the British trench in front of the four shattered copses, Mathew, Mark, Luke and John. Should the Germans launch a counter-attack there was little to stop them from bursting through the British lines. Within minutes of Private Bewsher setting up his Lewis gun he was hit in the head and woke up at the Advanced Dressing Station at Colincamps.

The 12th Battalion York and Lancaster Regiment (Sheffield City) were positioned between Luke and John Copse and would, as a consequence, bear the brunt of the enfilading fire coming from Gommecourt and the sector occupied by *Infantrie Regiment 66*. Lance Corporal Reg Glenn was a signaller with the Sheffield Pals:

Battalion HQ was in a big dugout in John Copse. You can imagine how hectic it was with all the to-ing and fro-ing, people making last minute arrangements, little nervous reactions wanting to get everything right. Our barrage was still banging away but with the light of the morning the Germans began shelling our trenches. Funny thing about being in a barrage was being afraid and trying not to show it to your mates, while at the same time trying to get used it. The least amount of cover gave you a sense of security – even a sheet of brown paper over your head would have seemed sufficient.

Zero hour was at 7.30 am and just before it the first two waves got out of the trench and laid down in No Man's Land. There seemed to be an uncanny silence, you could even hear the skylarks singing. It was a beautiful morning, then the whistles blew. They all stood up and started to move forward in a straight line. They hadn't gone but a few steps when they all went down again. I thought that they had been tripped by a wire laid across No Man's Land. But it was soon obvious why, we could hear the machine guns chattering away and all hell broke loose. I ducked back down in the trench and moved back to Battalion HQ to await instructions. Things got a little chaotic with the rest of the battalion trying to get forward with the attack and keep up with the timetable. The wounded struggled to get back and John Copse soon became filled with wounded.

It was in the trench that ended at John Copse called Nairne, that the 14th Battalion, York and Lancaster Regiment, Second Barnsley Pals, had the task of advancing into No Man's Land and manning a Russian Sap (shallow tunnelled trench) that had been dug. The plan was to break the sap open and continue it to join one of the German communication trenches, thus providing a new continuous front line facing northwards. However, because of the heavy shelling and machine-gun fire sweeping the flank of the attack and the failure of the division's assaulting battalions to capture the trenches in front of Serre, their progress was bound to be halted.

Both A and B companies of the Second Barnsleys had left Nairne and occupied the sap within half an hour of the start. The tunneling troops assisting the Engineers had continued to dig, extending the sap towards the German lines. An estimated 20% of the two Barnsley companies succeeded in

Right: John Copse, Saturday morning. When this aerial photograph was taken it was becoming evident that the attack on Serre had failed and the British trenches were filling with dead and wounded. Sheffield City Battalion had its HQ in John Copse.

NO MAN'S LAND

NAIRNE STREET

JOHN COPSE

When the British barrage lifted the Germans raced from their dugouts and manned the battered trenches. Within minutes they were laying down fire on the attackers. Note the wooden base for the machine gun, this was so as to make it more manageable when carrying it in and out of dugouts.

reaching the German front line. By 9.05, one and a half hours after the attack began, six platoons of the Second Barnsleys were reported as making good progress with the new trench. Twenty-five minutes later they had all simply disappeared.

At 9.30 am, two hours into the attack, the officer commanding the Russian Sap detail, stumbled wounded into 14th Battalion HQ situated in Roland Trench. He reported to Lieutenant Colonel Hulke that he needed reinforcements to man the Russian Sap – two platoons would suffice. Hulke promptly ordered two platoons from the reserve companies forward. Within minutes the report came back that the reinforcements were unable to locate the sap. Annoyed and puzzled, Colonel Hulke went to investigate for himself. He too was unable to locate the beginning of the sap that should have started as a continuation of Nairne Street, and headed in the direction of the German lines. Indeed, Nairne Street, John Copse and No Man's Land had ceased to be distinguishable, as the terrain was a mass of shell holes and torn up ground. It was being further pulverised as he watched. German guns, situated a few miles away in the Gommecourt area, were joining in the systematic wrecking of the left flank of the whole British attack. It had become clear to them exactly what the British plan was for that particular area.

In the days leading up to the Big Push German patrols constantly reconnoitred the ground in front of the copses. In spite of the vigilance of British patrols the Germans discovered the Russian Sap which started from John Copse. One night they placed charges in one of the emplacements and fired it, killing seven men. A week later they repeated their success, this time killing two men with a release of gas into the same sap. Eight others were rescued with difficulty but all were badly gassed. They certainly knew about the Russian Sap and its line-up with Nairne Trench. They also knew that this section was where the whole British offensive line began. There had been no preparations carried out by the British north of Nairne Street. Brigadier Rees had voiced his concern over this and had been ignored – the Second Barnsleys and the Sheffield Pals were paying for it with their lives. Frank Lindley, Second Barnsleys, recalled what it had been like in that particular hot spot:

As we were waiting for the whistle a bloody great mine went up over to the right. We saw it going sky high – it was just one hugh mass of soil going up. The ground shook all along our line. That mine shouldn't have gone up until we were on the top. As soon as it went off the barrage lifted and the smaller guns lifted too on account of this 'ere mine going up and us going over. Well the Jerries were up and out and they'd got their guns ready.

I was in the first wave on the extreme left, Second Lieutenant Hirst was next to me, just to my right. We were shoulder to shoulder when we scrambled onto the fire step and then we were on to the top of the parapet. It wasn't very long before he got it. I think that it was a machine-gun bullet in the head, but I only took a fleeting glance. We had orders not to bother with the wounded but to keep moving. When I looked around our lads were going well on my right – there was nothing to be seen of any of our men on the left. I could see as far as Gommecourt Wood and the gentle raising ground towards Serre, it was all laid out like a panorama. You could see the lines of German trenches on the gentle slope above, where they were shooting down on us. That slope seemed like a mountain side that morning. There was enfilading fire coming from Gommecourt. It was alright the generals saying 'you will walk across'. Even if we had run across we would have been in the same fix because we couldn't have got through their wire. Only a few managed to get through but what good could they do? You couldn't get to the places where their machine guns were situated in emplacements. What few gaps existed were only a few feet wide and were covered by machine guns.

I remember seeing the lads laid in rows just as if they had gone to sleep. And the sun flashing on them bits of tin on their backs all down the line. Some of the lads I recognised; that's so and so I thought to myself. The machine guns just

British troops crawl into No Man's Land in front of Hawthorn Ridge, 1 July 1916.

laid them out. I was lying in a shell hole and could see piles of dead where they had made for gaps in the wire. Some were caught up on the wire and their bodies were being knocked about by bullets, legs and arms were flying around all over.

An NCO, *Unteroffizier* Otto Lais, belonging to *Infanterie Regiment 169* in the book *Die Schlact an der Somme* (reproduced in Jack Sheldon's *The German Army on the Somme*) gives us some idea what it was like to face the attack by men of the citizens' army raised in the north of England, from Sheffield, Accrington, Barnsley:

Wild firing slammed into the masses of the enemy. All around us was the rushing, whistling and roaring of a storm; a hurricane as the destructive British shells rushed towards our reserves, rear areas and artillery which was firing courageously. Throughout all this racket, this rumbling, growling, bursting cracking, wild banging and chattering of small arms could be heard the steady tack, tack of the machine guns. That one firing slowly, this other with a faster rhythm – it was the precision work of fine equipment combined with skill – both were playing a gruesome tune to the enemy, whilst, at the same time, providing the crews and rest of us manning the rifles and automatic weapons with a high degree of reassurance... Belt after belt was fired, 250 rounds – 1,000 – 3,000. 'Pass up the spare barrels!' Shouts the gun commander. Barrels are changed – 'fire on!' 5,000 rounds and the barrel must be changed again. It's red hot and the water coolant is boiling – the hands working the weapon are scorched and burned – 'Keep firing' urges the gun commander, 'or shoot yourself!' The cooling water turns to hissing steam with the continuous firing. In the heat of battle, the steam overflow pipe slips out of its fixing on the water jacket. With a great hiss a jet of steam goes up, providing a superb aiming point for the enemy. It is a great advantage that they have the sun in their eyes and we have it at our backs.

The enemy draws nearer. We fire on endlessly and there is less steam. A further barrel change is becoming urgent. The water coolant has almost steamed away. 'Where's the water?' yells the gunner. 'Get the mineral water out of the dugout!' 'There's none left Unteroffizier!' It all went in the eight day bombardment.

The British keep charging forward. Despite the fact that hundreds are already lying dead in the shell holes at our front, fresh waves keep emerging from the assault trenches over there. We have got to fire! One of the gun team rushes into the crater with the water container and urinates into it. Another joins him. The British have closed to grenade throwing range and hand grenades fly backwards and forwards. The barrel change is complete, the water jacket is refilled. Load! A hand grenade bursts close to the weapon. Just keep calm and get the tangle sorted out... working parts forward – belt on – working parts back. Then same again. Safety catch to the right! Fire.

18,000 rounds! The other platoon weapon has a stoppage. Gunner Schwarz falls over the belt he is feeding, shot through the head. The belt twists and feeds rounds into the gun crookedly and they jam. The next man comes forward and the dead man is pulled to one side. The gunner strips the feed mechanism and removes the jammed round and reloads. Fire; pause; change barrel; fetch more ammunition; lay the dead and the wounded on the floor of the crater. That is the hard and unrelenting tempo of the morning of the 1 July, 1916.

By the time the fighting ceased on that day that particular machine gun had fired no fewer than 20,000 rounds.

It was all over before noon for the Pals before Serre. A small force of the 13th Battalion York and Lancaster Regiment, First Barnsleys, was left holding the British front line, along with survivors who had crawled back from No Man's Land. A mixture of Accrington Pals and man of the 12th Battalion King's Own Yorkshire Light Infantry (Pioneer Battalion), were manning the second line.

Reports to various headquarters were hopelessly inaccurate and as a consequence, orders being issued were unrealistic. At 10.27 am Brigadier General Rees, commanding 94 Brigade, had received a communique from 31st Division headquarters informing him that the diversionary attack by 56th Division on Gommecourt had been successful. Further, that it had been observed that infantry, under his command, had taken the village of Serre and

that 93 Brigade had reached Pendant Copse and were seen to be about to take on their third objective. General Rees knew at once that the report was nonsense. The reality was that there was little that the survivors of his command could do but hang on to their own positions and tend the wounded. It had been a disaster and yet Major General Wanless O'Gowan continued to order Rees to send reinforcements to assist those who were still thought to have captured the German trenches.

During the afternoon the magnitude of the disaster in front of Serre was beginning to dawn, first on Divisional and then Corps headquarters.

As darkness fell wounded and unwounded Pals crawled and staggered back across No Man's Land. During that night Sheffield City Battalion headquarters were informed that some 150 Sheffielders were holed up in a stretch of the German front line.

Major General Wanless O'Gowan commander of the 31st Division

Hopeful of saving more lives Brigadier Rees ordered the colonel of the 12th Battalion York and Lancaster Regiment to get word to his men to withdraw. But at the Sheffield City headquarters there were only ten unwounded men, runners and signallers. A request was made to the Second Barnsleys to help. Between 1.30 am and 3.15 am a two-officer strong patrol crept into No Man's Land. They were unable to locate any Sheffield men in the German front line. Rather the Germans were manning their own trench and were firing their machine guns into the night in case the British were intent on carrying on with a night attack. The patrol did locate a number of wounded and was able to assist them back to their own lines.

General Douglas Haig was not impressed with the performance of VIII Corps. In his diary he recorded the Fourth Army's efforts and included his criticisms:

Reports up to 8 am seemed most satisfactory. Our troops everywhere had crossed the enemy's front trenches. By 9 am I heard that our troops had in many places reached the "1.20" line. [The line to be reached 1 hour and 20 minutes after the start.] *We hold the Montauban-Mametz spur and the villages of those names. The enemy are still in Fricourt, but we are round his flank on the north and close to Contalmaison. Ovillers and Thiepval villages have held our troops up, but our men are in the Schwaben Redoubt which crowns the ridge of the last named village. The enemy counter-attacked here, but were driven back. He, however, is holding on to positions with a few men in the river valley.*

North of the Ancre, the VIII Corps commander [Hunter Weston] *said that they began well, but as the day progressed, their troops were forced back into the German front line, except two battalions which occupied Serre Village, and were, it is said, cut off. I am inclined to believe from further reports, that few of VIII Corps left their trenches.*

The attack on Gommecourt salient started well, especially the 56th Division under General Hull. The 46th Division [Stuart Wortley] *attacked from the north side, but was soon held up. This attack was of the greatest assistance in helping VIII Corps, because many of the enemy's guns and troops were employed*

General Sir Douglas Haig was not impressed by the performance of VIII Corps.

against it, and so VIII Corps was left considerably free. In spite of this, the VIII Corps achieved very little.

Haig coveyed his concerns to the commander of the Fourth Army, General Rawlinson, who said that he would place VIII Corps under the command of General Gough. Haig agreed, commenting that, 'the VIII Corps seems to want looking after'. As to the amount of casualties suffered, his opinion was that they, 'cannot be considered severe in view of the numbers engaged and the length of the front attacked'. At that point in time General Haig believed the casualties for the day to have been 40,000. But it is doubtful that the more accurate figure of 58,000 (a third of them dead) would have changed his expressed opinion.

An awakening

The hideous reality of 20th century warfare, as experienced on that Saturday morning, served to dismantle the patriotic, Boys' Own, idea of vain glorious conflict that thousands of British civilian workers had embraced in the summer of 1914. The great adventure was turning sour and transforming into a seemingly ongoing nightmare. Never could they have envisaged what lay ahead for them. Their 'blooding' in the trenches leading up to 1 July had given some of them an inkling, as friends were killed here and there by snipers and shelling. Also the night raids across No Man's Land had served to introduce them to the realities, but where the raids proved successful it could still seem to be a bit of an adventure and even prove exciting.

For sixteen-year-old Frank Lindley, dragging himself through the smashed-about trenches behind John Copse, it was a journey he would never forget. A large piece of shrapnel had ripped through his thigh, the explosion

The less seriously wounded having their injuries attended to at an Advanced Dressing Station. Below: This shows a soldier being treated for entry and exit wounds to the upper left arm.

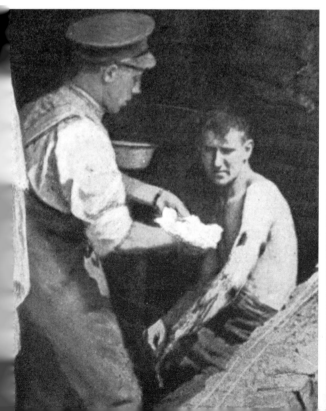

Dead were collected and brought to where mass graves had been dug in the days leading up to the attack.

of the 'whizz-bang' that wounded him blasting away his trousers. He had crawled and rolled his way back across No Man's Land, and then he had the task of making his way through the reserve trenches across the bodies of the slain,

> *One bloke must have been climbing out of the trench and it had done him across the middle. It left his feet and bottom half in the trench and all his insides were hanging down the trench wall. I remember thinking, 'so that's what a human liver and kidneys look like'. It's funny what you think at times like that.*
>
> *I remember thinking, 'How the bloody h... are they going to clear this mess up?' With a disaster on the scale it was you wondered how they were going to shift everyone. There's a lot still there, there must be.*

At the end of the much battered Nairne Street, Frank Lindley received a shot for tetanus and eventually was driven off in an ambulance. He was one of the more fortunate wounded.

Of the assaulting battalions in 94 Brigade, 31st Division, Sheffield City and Accrington Pals had paid a heavy price. Between them they had lost more than a thousand men killed or wounded out of a total of a little over 1,400. The follow up battalions of Barnsley Pals had lost 175 killed with 392 wounded; of these another 35 would die of their wounds during the following weeks.

There were other Pals formations on the Somme that had not taken part in the attack on the first day. They too would experience their disillusionment and an awakening to the realities of warfare.

Chapter Six

JULY TO NOVEMBER 1916

THE FOLLY OF THE PALS CONCEPT became all too evident as entire communities began to receive notification of the death, missing in action, or wounding of their menfolk. The Leeds Pals had suffered the loss of thirteen officers killed, with two more later dying of wounds sustained in the attack. Other ranks killed and died of wounds amounted to 233; whilst wounded came to 267 with another 181 missing, giving a final count of uninjured survivors as just forty-seven. Although this figure has been questioned, and cannot be substantiated from any official sources, it may be safely assumed that less than a hundred men from the 15th Battalion West

Photograph taken at Hall's Corner, West Sleekburn, during the week following the 1 July Somme attack. Women and children wait for news of their menfolk. The postman is there to collect the post from Newcastle. Some of these women will be receiving an official telegram informing them of their husband's wounding or death – eight men of the Tyneside Scottish had been killed and ten wounded from West Sleekburn.

Yorkshire Regiment remained physically unscathed following the 1 July débâcle. There was, of course, the 10% of the battalion held in reserve.

It was the end of an idea; the Pals battalions would begin to lose their identity as reinforcements arrived to bring the formations back up to strength. Wounded men, once fully recovered, would often be sent to any battalion requiring numbers at that particular time.

It has been said that the Pals battalions of the British Army were not unique and that the family/friends idea of mates serving together was first seen in the Territorials. However, it must be kept in mind that the 'Saturday Night Soldiers' as the Territorials were referred to by those who sought to disparage them, consisted of men with an interest in all things military. Parading in uniform, weapons, drill, weekend and annual camps at the seaside held an appeal. The Pals battalions, on the other hand, were raised by numerous local authorities, were made up of men who, under normal circumstances, would never have subjected themselves to the demeaning insults and coarse language of drill sergeants and corporals during the drudgery of interminable drill periods. That was on top of the privations of outdoor living, army rations and exhausting route marches. It took patriotism and national pride on a scale never experienced in the history of the nation, either before or since, to give rise to the Pals' phenomenon. Such was the fervour that swept through the nation's menfolk – and it has to be said through their mothers, sisters and girl friends – that in many cases sufficient numbers came forward to form one or two battalions numbering around 1,000 men each and even complete brigades – even divisions.

Lloyd George was very active in the creation of an all-Welsh division.

The Reverend Julian Bickersteth MC, Senior Chaplain 56th (London) Division wrote to his mother concerning the death of his brother Morris, killed 1 July 1916, leading B Company, Leeds Pals 'over the top' and tried to make sense of it:

> *'I think July 1st will for ever stand in the history of the world as one of the epoch-making dates in all history. It denotes the beginning of the turning of the tide – the turning point in the Great War. If it was necessary and right as I believe it was, of God's all-seeing providence, for our dear Morris to pass on so soon and so young to the Larger Life, I cannot help feeling glad that the day was July 1st and not sooner or later. He found himself among that splendid crowd of glorious men who 'passed over' at the time – a noble company.'*

It still had to be seen as a righteous war and the idea that the Almighty favoured the allies was promoted by the press:

The *Illustrated London News* of 22 July 1916 carried this picture depicting a supposed incident during the opening stages of the Battle of the Somme and posed the question, 'was it a miraculous sign set in the heavens by the Divine power'? and concluded that the combatants would have been set musing 'on the message of the cross and self-sacrifice'.

The Graphic journal commissioned a painting of a dying soldier and a crucified Christ to bring some comfort to its readers who had lost someone in the Great War battles.

Originally, in the heady days of September 1914, it had been intended that Wales would provide an entire army corps for Kitchener. That turned out to be far too ambitious. However, a Welsh formation of divisional strength was soon raised and was, inevitably, referred to as 'Lloyd George's Welsh Army'. The War Office was persuaded by him, to appoint commanders of his personal choice to commands within the division. It too served on the Somme, but was not deployed on the first day of the Big Push.

38th (Welsh) Division

The all-Welsh division crossed to France in December 1915 and faced its first major battle seven months later on 7 July 1916. The formation was given the task of attacking Mametz Wood, the taking of which would allow the next phase of the Somme offensive to proceed. At 8.30 am, on a day that was overcast and showery, waves of troops belonging to the 11th Battalion, South Wales Borderers (Second Gwent Pals) and 16th Welsh Regiment (Cardiff Pals) advanced across the fields towards Mametz Wood. Accurate enfilading machine-gun fire, supported by artillery, stopped the attack and the men dropped and hugged the ground. Some men, ducking and weaving, were able to make it back to their start line. Over an hour later they rose and attempted to advance again, but the result was the same. The divisional commander threw in another battalion, 10th Battalion South Wales Borderers (First Gwent Pals), but again the attack floundered. As the day ended 115 Brigade of the 38th Division had got nowhere and had sustained an alarming number of casualties.

Consternation at the failure spread to the highest level of command and two days later the Commander-in-Chief, General Sir Douglas Haig, turned up at XV Corps headquarters along with the Fourth Army commander, Sir Henry Rawlinson. They made it quite clear that they were disappointed at the performance in action of the 38th (Welsh) Division. The commanding officer, Major General Ivor Philips, friend of Lloyd George, was informed that his services were no longer required. He returned home in some embarrassment with a shadow over his reputation. Before the war he had been Liberal MP for Southampton and ten years before that had served in the army, seeing service in Burma, on the North-West Frontier and China. In their very first major engagement, battalions of the 38th Division had failed miserably. The commander of the 7th Division, Major General Watts, was placed in temporary command of the 38th and he was determined to accomplish something with it, despite its inauspicious start.

Monday 10 July was chosen for the next attack and the operational order simply stated: 'The Division will attack Mametz Wood tomorrow with a view to capturing the whole of it'. The plan was simple: by sheer weight of numbers concentrated on a short front, the attackers would seek to swamp the defenders in a head-on charge. There would be no tactical subtleties to distract the enemy such as feints and diversions. However, there would be support from artillery and heavy trench mortars.

After hearing the plan, the commanders of the assaulting battalions were not impressed. Lieutenant Colonel Hayes, commanding the Swansea Pals, ordered the officers and platoon sergeants to his headquarters; they found him staring out towards Mametz Wood, approximately 600 yards across No Man's Land. He turned to face the gathered officers and NCOs, and met the eyes of each one of them in turn. Then suddenly, pointing at the wood in the distance with his stick, he announced, 'Tomorrow at five minutes past four our battalion is going to take that wood... We shall lose our battalion'.

Likewise, the commander of the Cardiff Pals, Lieutenant Colonel Carden told his men on the eve of battle, 'Boys, make your peace with God! We are going to take that position and some of us won't come back. But, we <u>are</u> going to take it'. The failure of the first attempt was strong in the minds of the colonels.

As dawn was beginning to tinge the sky with grey light the 13th and 14th Battalions The Welsh Regiment, Rhondda and Swansea Pals, were lying on the open ground preparing to move forward. At a given signal bayonets were fixed and men in eight waves got to their feet and moved forward in perfect order:

...Our colonel, who was waiting about fifty yards in advance of our position, took off his steel helmet and, as the artillery raised its fire to another part of the wood, he gave a movement with his helmet to get the first wave to advance. There was not a moment's hesitation – each and every man moved off in perfect order and the colonel repeated the sweeping movement with his helmet each time the line was 100 yards in advance of those still lying down. **Stanley J.C. Williams**

Lieutenant Colonel Ronald James Walter Carden, commanding Cardiff Pals.

Right: XV Corps map for the atta on Mametz Woo

Lieutenant Colonel Carden, advancing at the front of

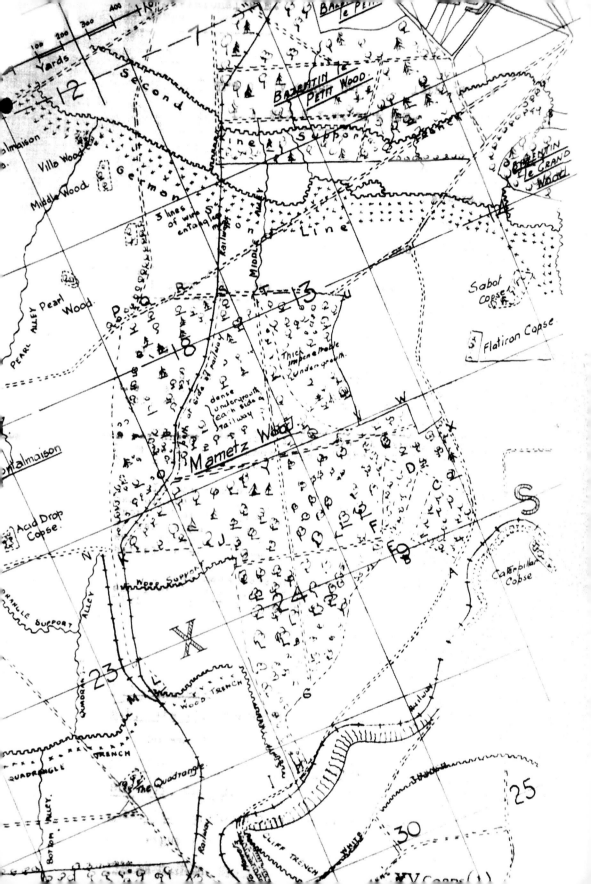

his men, reached the edge of the wood before being wounded. He got back on his feet urging his men on and was finally killed by a well-aimed shot. Sergeant Lyons of the Swansea Pals commented, 'We suffered many casualties particularly among our officers, the Germans were adept at picking them off'.

By 4.50 am the Swansea Pals had reached the second objective deep in Mametz Wood. But progress was slow because of the density of the undergrowth. Shortly after 7.10 am, all 114 Brigade's reserves had been committed to the fight as the Germans had counter-attacked through the underbrush. Then it was seen that men were leaving the wood and retreating and were calling out to advancing follow-up troops to 'retire!' Captain Glynn Jones managed to stop the fleeing men and reformed them in a hollow about 150 yards from the wood. Then he led them back. Lieutenant Colonel Hayes recorded the confused fighting:

> *Direction was most difficult to maintain; it was almost impossible to read a map, and certain troops were found to be following the artillery, which proved to be the enemy's barrage. I personally found two platoons taking cover and firing towards the first ride* [already captured]. *The 14th Welsh did gain objectives, but they were only there in detached posts. I visited them and lost my*

A battalion marches past Mametz Wood on its way to the front.

way doing so a few times. I saw some dead Germans and some wounded, but on my own front there was no organised resistance, with the exceptions of the well placed machine guns. All of them had a dead man in the pit or were deserted. Most of my own battalion's casualties were caused by machine-gun fire and a certain amount of both our own and hostile artillery fire. There was some hand-to-hand fighting at the edge of the wood, but very little.

At 4.30 in the afternoon a final effort was made to clear the Germans out of the wood and by nightfall the commanding officer of 7th Division reported:

Our infantry are holding a line about 150 yards north of the Central Ride, and are apparently well dug in. The undergrowth of the wood is very thick and many trees have fallen. Danger from German counter-attack is therefore not great, as they could only advance by the rides. The enemy placed, for several hours this evening, a very heavy barrage on the rides in rear of the line held and on the road running round the south western side of the wood; shells of 5.9 and of heavier calibre were falling.

The 38th (Welsh) Division had taken the wood and held it as ordered.

The following day both 113 and 114 Brigades were relieved by 115 Brigade. The Swansea Pals had advanced on Mametz Wood with 676 men; by the end of the fighting ninety of them had been killed and upwards of 300 wounded. Some would later die of their wounds making the figure around 100 dead. (See *Swansea Pals* by Bernard Lewis for further information concerning this battalion.)

Other Pals battalions had yet to 'go over the top' for the first time as the Battle of the Somme carried on for another five months.

5th Division

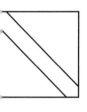

Birmingham Pals, in the 5th Division, had remained part of GHQ Reserve with the intention of employing them wherever gains materialised. On the sector from La Boisselle to Maricourt a breakthrough had been achieved. At dawn on 14 July, 22,000 men of XIII and XV Corps launched an attack over a 6,000 yards frontage from Bazentin to Trones Wood. This time there was no concentrated week-long artillery barrage, just an intense bombardment five minutes before zero hour from all available guns. Six attacking brigades had moved men into No Man's Land during the night and were 500 yards from the German front line. The attack went according to plan and a salient 6,000 yards deep on Bazentin Ridge was captured. In the distance was High Wood, seemingly undamaged thus far by shelling, and the Germans had withdrawn behind it to a trench system called the Switch Line. Had fresh troops been used to advance on it immediately, possibly High Wood would have been taken without too much trouble. As it was the infantry and follow-up cavalry were ordered to remain on the ridge. Eventually an attack was made and a cavalry charge, complete with lances and drawn sabres took place on the German line behind High Wood.

The turn of the Birmingham Pals came on 20 July with an attack intended to capture High Wood. Acting Transport Officer of the 14th Battalion Royal Warwicks, Lieutenant Alan Furse, recalled,

We spent only one night here [village of Meaulte], *but this was our first insight into what a push means. Day and night the road was one long line of ambulances and walking wounded. Occasionally a battalion which had been relieved would march through with a total strength of about 150 instead of 600 or 700. Although we realised what losses these men had, it never seemed to occur to us that we might be the same but then, of course, we had not been blooded.*

On their march up to the front they passed through the shattered villages of Fricourt and Montauban. They rested in Montauban so that they would arrive at the front line under the cover of darkness. They were able to observe at first hand the defences constructed by their resourceful enemy. Sergeant Arthur Cooper, 14th Battalion Royal Warwickshire Regiment, First Birmingham Pals, described his impressions,

We marched through the German old first and second line of trenches towards the present front line. Ye gods! What a maze of trenches they had. We stayed for a time on the side of the road for dinner and to wait until dusk before getting nearer. I dropped off to sleep on top of a filled in shell hole and found when I woke up a little board stuck up explaining that it was the grave of twenty-five Tommies. The smell about this part of the country was simply awful. Hundreds of men had just been buried and the place was littered with equipment and everything else which soldiers usually carry. At about 6 pm we march on again. We got a fairly thick shelling on the way too. A Company was lucky and got through whole, but the other companies lost a few. Of course the Huns knew all the nooks and corners. It was an awful march up to the trenches. The stink from the dead horses and the dead Tommies who lay about was chronic.

Upon reaching their destination the battalions of 13 Brigade deployed along the recently captured trenches that had fallen on 14 July. The feature known as Caterpillar Valley was to their rear and would soon be filled with artillery pieces. Before them the ground sloped down before raising again towards the German Switch line. The brigade deployed as follows:

2nd Battalion King's Own Scottish Borderers took over the first two lines, with the First Birmingham Pals in the third. Digging in behind were the 1st Battalion Royal West Kents, who were in support.

The first part of the attack was made by two battalions of the 7th Division, 8th Battalion Devonshire Regiment and 2nd Battalion Gordon Highlanders. It commenced before dawn at 3.30 am and experienced some initial success. However, the Germans recovered and machine guns situated in High Wood and the village of Longueval put up a deadly crossfire. The Devons and the Gordon Highlanders suffered almost 400 casualties between them.

A feature called the Black Road was where the attack was consolidated and the First Birminghams moved up to relieve the assault battalions. Whilst the general staff made up their minds what to do next the 14th Battalion Royal Warwickshire Regiment stayed on Black Road for the next two days. All the time the Germans were shelling their position. It had been decided that the next attack was to be launched towards Wood Lane, which came out of the top corner of High Wood. The First Birminghams and the 1st Battalion Royal West Kents would lead the assault.

A heavy artillery barrage was laid down in the region of Wood Lane. Unfortunately, it was observed that the exploding shells were missing the line of trenches along Wood Lane. This was to be a night attack and as darkness fell Birmingham men crawled out into No Man's Land. It was to be their first experience of 'going over the top' as an assaulting battalion. At 10 pm the whistles blew and men rose to their feet and charged towards the German trenches at Wood Lane. They were met by a heavy counter barrage and extremely accurate machine-gun fire. The 14th Battalion Royal Warwickshire Regiment suffered 485 casualties, 194 of whom were killed. Private J.E.B. Fairclough commented on the disaster in the book *First Birmingham Battalion in the Great War*,

> The first parade on Pommiers redoubt was a very sad one: a battalion had practically disappeared, leaving a mere handful to carry on its fine traditions. It is comforting to remember that the companies went to the charge in magnificent style, never faltering or hesitating, in face of murderous fire, and Birmingham has reason to be proud of her sons and of the courage they displayed in the face of hopeless odds. Our first attack did not succeed, but in that magnificent effort and failure the City 'Pets' proved their worth in iron manner.

The 16th Battalion Royal Warwickshire Regiment, Third Birmingham, had its turn to come. That opportunity to go 'over the top' arrived on 27 July. There was to be an attack, yet again, on Longueval and Deville Wood by two brigades, one belonging to 2nd Division and the other to the 5th Division.

Four dead British soldiers killed during an attack on German trenches. Stretcher bearers carry a casualty to the rear.

Third Birmingham was to be in close support during the initial stages. A new innovation was to be tried, the creeping barrage. It was to leap forward in three intervals of ninety minutes each. The infantry was then to rush forward and consolidate each time until the village and wood were cleared of Germans. However, the Germans had excavated interconnecting tunnels between the cellars of the ruined houses in Longueval. Cellars had been reinforced providing ample protection. As a consequence we read in the Divisional History:

> Parties of Germans came up from the cellars and dug-outs, and took up positions in the ruined buildings. The Norfolks pressing forward were checked, and the barrage went on in accordance with the time-table, leaving the Germans in the village free of shellfire. The fight now developed into a struggle between the opposing infantry amid the ruins of the village within a ring of artillery fire.

Two hours into the attack and it became Third Birmingham's turn. B Company, 16th Battalion Royal Warwickshire Regiment, was ordered to form a defensive flank on a line running from Longueval's ruined church to the northern end of Trones Wood. Shellfire was continuous throughout the day and into the night. Nineteen-year-old Second Lieutenant Eric Pearman left a record of the fighting,

> We now came into the evening barrage laid down purposely to stop the

Men of the 16th Battalion King's Royal Rifle Corps occupying trenches in Delville Wood shortly after its capture.

supports reaching the line. As we were going forward one could see in front the splintered trunks of what once had been Delville Wood. We were told to enter along the edge of the wood with its blasted trunks and burning shrivelled branches. Here the barrage reached a crescendo; field guns and howitzers... nothing gave protection from the high explosives which rained without cease and which, if it didn't get a direct hit, just buried. We hadn't even the comfort of moving – either backward or forward – and the orders were to stay put until required. Would we ever be required? Would any of us be there to be required, to answer a call?

The Norfolks had taken their objectives and we were all shortly to be pulled out. They didn't want us here. I remember taking what was left of my platoon back to the edge of the wood where there were far fewer standing trees. There we linked up with another subaltern named Rowlands who had survived untouched. He told me that he was quite certain that he was going to be killed and I tried to cheer him up. Shortly afterwards I felt an urge to check up on my platoon further on. When I came back to meet Rowlands he was not there, nor the men who had been there with him. A giant shell had taken the lot, or buried them. I can remember scratching in the earth, calling Rowlands and then losing consciousness. I came to with Jimmy Holme pushing the neck of his whisky flask between my lips. Sadly for him I drank the lot. He could not, or would not, believe me when I said that I was looking for Rowlands but thought I was crazy. And Rowlands could never tell any of us where he was.

For the two days of close support that the 16th Battalion was in Longueval, they suffered 267 casualties, fifty-seven of that number killed and the majority were never recovered.

Throughout the month of August the 5th Division was invloved in heavy fighting, the outcome of which could hardly be termed successful. However, in September, when the village of Morval became the objective for 15 and 95 Brigades, the division experienced success. Bombardment began on the German lines at 7.00 am on 24 September and would last throughout the morning and afternoon, with similiar the following day. Zero hour for the attack was at 12.35 pm in order to suit the French, who would be attacking the village of Combles simultaneously. Assembly trenches were being dug and so the Germans must have been alerted to the fact that an attack was on the way. But with the passing of dawn, the usual time for the Tommies to come at them, they must have concluded that they had another day before it came. Then the bombardment began in earnest and behind a succession of creeping and stationary barrages sixty-four battalions of British and Dominion troops, wave after wave, systematically made their way in leaps and bounds to their objectives. The Divisional History recorded,

On the left 15 Brigade carried the village of Morval with a rush; a halfhearted opposition put up by the Germans still in place was quickly overpowered and, after mopping up the dugouts and cellars in the village, the troops moved out into the open country east of the village. Among the prisoners captured in the village was the German Town-Major, who remained faithful to his post, probably thinking that discretion, in the shape of a strong dugout, was the better part of valour.

By nightfall the final objective running southward from the Moulin de Morval had been consolidated. The whole attack had been carried through exactly to plan and timetable, a truly remarkable feat.

The 14th Battalion Royal Warwickshires had played its part in the text-book advance and capture of the village. The officer commanding D Company, Lieutenant Alan Furse, wrote his experiences of the successful attack down in his memoirs,

...Every gun within miles was firing without ceasing and even by putting your mouth to anyone's ear and shouting you could hardly make yourself heard. Under these conditions it was very difficult to control a hundred and fifty men spread out in a line, with about two yards between each, but I was so excited that I tried to do it by shouting. As a result, by the time we had done the first mile, I was absolutely hoarse and could hardly make myself heard even in a dugout. Whilst covering this mile we had passed through several barrages but we reached our first trenches without a single casualty. On reaching these trenches on the crest we got down into them and were able to see the wonderful results of our barrage on the village of Morval about three-quarters of a mile away, over the valley on top of the next hill.

By this time our front line had taken the first two Hun lines and were getting into the village itself and with the glasses I was able to see the Huns getting up in bunches from their trenches in front of the village and retreating through it. At this point some Brigade machine-gunners put up two guns in our trench and we were able to see the results of their fire on those bunches of Huns. After about twenty minutes in these trenches we got orders to advance to the next line in the valley in front, and in going through the barrage we lost a good few men on the slope. It was during this part of the advance that a German shell hit the ground within a foot or so of me, without exploding fortunately, but the pressure of the wind from it was enough to knock me over.

We spent about twelve hours in the valley... When the Huns are on the retreat like this and are continually taking up new positions, they could only get accurate ranges [for their artillery] *by map references and as that valley we were in was clearly marked up, and they themselves had dug the very trenches we were occupying, they gave us something to be going on with.*

With the attack on Morval being a complete success and casualties comparatively light compared to earlier attacks it was, nevertheless, a near exhausted division which made its way to Citadel Camp near Fricourt on 27 September 1916. The three battalions of Birmingham Pals had lost a mere fifty men killed in action during the three days, 24 to 26, of the fighting for Morval. It was announced that the 5th Division was being moved from the Somme to another sector of the front. The General Officer Commanding Fourth Army, General Rawlinson, sent the division a tribute, thanking them for their conspicuous efforts during the fighting at Delville Wood, the capture of the Falfemont Farm line and Leuze Wood, and finally the storming of Morval.

During their period on the Somme from 20 July to 28 September the three Birmingham Pals battalions lost 785 men killed, 515 of whom were never found, or whose remains were unidentified.

31st Division

This Pals division had suffered heavily on the first day of the Battle of the Somme; however, the four Hull battalions in 92 Brigade had been held in reserve and so missed the slaughter. The division was moved north to a quieter part of the Western Front. Apart from trench raids, the Hull Pals had yet to experience 'going over the top' in a major assault on the Geman lines. In October 1916 the news began to circulate that the 31st Division was about to depart for the Somme. On the 8th of the month the division moved off, first by train to Candas and then a five and a half hour route march by night to the Vauchelles area. Another 'big effort' was being arranged and the 31st Division had been 'invited' to attend.

The attack was scheduled for Monday, 13 November, and now it would be the turn of the four battalions of 92 (Hull) Brigade to lead the assault. The area designated by the planners was the fortified village of Serre – once again. It would start during the hours of darkness, zero hour being 5.45 am. The aims of the attack were modest; it was hoped to reduce the German salient between the Albert-Bapaume road and Serre. The main attack was to be delivered by V Corps (consisting of 2nd, 3rd, 51st and 63rd Divisions) against the German lines north of the River Ancre that had been unsuccessfully assaulted on 1 July. 92 Brigade would cover the extreme north and provide a defensive flank. South of the River Ancre II Corps would attack at the same time.

On the eve of the attack two of the Hull Pals were approached by one of their NCOs, Sergeant Raine, and announced that one of them would not be taking part in the attack as a man was needed to remain behind at Rossignol Farm. The two privates, Surfleet and Bell, looked as if to say, 'well, which one?' The sergeant took a coin and tossed it and Private Bell lost. 'Your're for it Bell!' said the sergeant. Bell shrugged, 'San fairy ann... It doesn't matter!' His pal, Private Surfleet, mentions his friend's subsequent death in his diary. Also in his diary he records events as the battalion moved off into the night leaving him as an observer:

Hull Commercials on the Somme. David Bilton, author of **Hull Pals,** *has identified all of these men.* DAVID BILTON

With sad hearts we watched the main part of the battalion move off to the line. There was an air of artificial jollity about; a joke here, a coarse remark there, a wave of the hand to a pal... "lucky devil staying behind"... "all the best old man"... "get those b... rations up early!"... "We're going back for a rest after this"... "who says we're not a scrapping division?"... "send you a postcard!" All these and many more remarks, but it is the thinnest of veneers, a very feeble covering over the sense of grim reality which I felt the whole battalion was feeling. We stood there whilst the boys, in column of route, marched forward, slid down the hill and turned right and were gradually swallowed up by the mist, mud and confusion. Their sounds died out; only a rumble of guns and the creaking of heavily laden limbers remained in a scene so desolate and miserable that one could not help feeling depressed and sad.

Patriotic fervour had faded away since the awakening to the horrors of war on that Saturday morning in July. Even though the Hull Pals had not until that moment 'gone over the top' in a major assault, each man had seen and experienced enough to dispel the naive 'gung-ho' attitudes of 1914.

The Third (Hull Sportsmen) and Fourth (Hull T'others) battalions led the attack on a 500 yards frontage and succeeded in taking the German front line. However, the taking and holding of the German support line was proving difficult. The inevitable counter-attacks came against them as the defenders, soldiers of *Infanterie Regiment 169*, began bombing along their communication trenches and had to be fought off. A German machine-gunner, staff sergeant, *Vizefeldwebel* Spengler-Hugsweier, was in a position directly in line with the Hull Pals' attack and described what occured:

During the early morning [13 November] fog lay thickly over everything, blinding us. Our eyes strained like needles, trying to pierce the milky wall. There were four of us manning our machine gun, which was located five metres behind our front line trench. Ever since dawn the enemy had been bringing down drum fire. All of a sudden it stopped, just as if it had been cut off with a giant knife. Our hearts were in our mouths, because we knew that they must come now! Outwardly we were calm. One of the gun crew was whistling through his teeth, another was pulling hard on a cigar which remained unlit. I went below into the dugout and made some coffee, without which everyone would have felt faint through exhaustion. At last the brown brew began to boil and I breathed in the aroma in anticipation – suddenly, someone was yelling my name. Taking one last longing look at the hot coffee, which was now boiling over, I was up and out and standing next to the machine gun. Staring into the grey fog I could make out ghostly figures that seemed to be moving all around our position, appearing and disappearing – over to the left – to the right and even behind. They had overrun the first trench and our position.

We opened fire and the advancing figures were checked before falling back, only to rise and come on again with fixed bayonets. At that precise moment I got a stoppage. Was it imagination or did we see the triumphant gleam in the bloodshot eyes of the khaki-clad soldiers who were coming at us. The thought passed through my mind that I might surrender, but this I dismissed, brave soldiers shouldn't think like that. We still had plenty of hand grenades, why had

Germans on the receiving end of a barrage.

we been issued with them in the first place, if not to use? I felt quite calm as I began throwing bombs among the fleeting figures and felt relieved to see them stumbling away as explosions occurred among them. My gun crew laughed out loud at each explosion – we were just four and they were many – I wish I could have seen their faces. Then bullets began zipping into the ground all around us and I wondered if I would be killed instantly if I was hit. My mind was all a-whirl at what might could happen to me – I thought of my life so far. One grenade after another was being pressed into the palm of my hand; pull – throw to the front; pull – throw to the right; pull – throw to the left! Explosion after explosion, were they never going to stop coming at us? Were they waiting for the moment when we ran out of grenades? All at once the wraith-like figures were swallowed up by the fog the way they had come. A feeling of sheer exhaustion descended on me, I couldn't move, I just wanted to sleep. It had been endless torture since June and now it was November.

A new danger began as the enemy began a bombardment that grew in ferocity. There was nothing for it but to withdraw out of the targeted area. We leapt out and ran weaving, tripping and ducking from one shell hole to another. At one point I placed my hand on a red hot shell splinter and burnt my hand as shards of hot iron whizzed past our ears. None of us spoke a word as we were all gasping and out of breath. The wild look in the eyes of my men spoke volumes. Then the race for life or death began once more and we set gasping air in through clenched teeth. Finally we were through the area being shelled and *safe. It was a miracle: May the Almighty be praised.*

At 5.25 pm, 92 Brigade was ordered to fall back giving up the ground they had taken. The attack by the 3rd Division had failed, leaving 92 Brigade with an unprotected right flank. As it became dark the last parties stumbled into the British lines. Prior to this withdrawal, about four hours earlier, Private Surfleet had been called into action:

> *It was five o'clock in the evening when Lieutenant John, who was in charge of us, dashed in and told us to get our fighting equipment on. We were to go up to the line to help, though no one seemed to know what the job was to be. My fingers trembled as I buckled my belt with a mixture of excitement and nervousness – but we were pretty well resigned to anything.*

It was already getting dark as the party, which included Private Surfleet, took the most direct route towards the British front line forward of the village of Hébuterne. The roads were crammed with various types of transport moving up guns, ammunition and supplies, while at the same time ambulances were coming back the other way, 'streams of living going forward while the wounded and dying or dead were coming back'. There were artillery positions to each side of the road in places and the gunners were keeping up a steady stream of shells directed on the German positions.

> *Sometimes we were so near a gun its flash nearly blinded us and the noise was appalling. Some of the lads grumbled for being taken that way, and some fell out wounded by shrapnel, which increased as we went on. We came in for some very heavy retaliation as the German batteries tried to cut off our reinforcements. Three of our party were killed and several others wounded by shrapnel and pieces of high explosive which fell around us. It was particularly bad as we reached the communication trench and our stretcher bearers came along to tend to our wounded. The dead were lifted out and placed on the parapet. We halted at the start of the trench and Lieutenant John went off to get some instructions. It was a very nerve-racking wait and one or two of our party – thank god there were not many – took advantage of the noise and disturbance and slipped quietly down a side trench and stayed there until, all the work done, we were returning. Then the miserable devils slipped back into the file, no one of any importance being any the wiser. There are some things one can understand; I must never sneer at a man who is afraid, for I have been more frightened out here than it is necessary for me to record, that is one thing. Scrounging to the detriment of your pals is another and we who saw those rotters have not forgotten – I don't suppose that we ever shall.*

The Battle of the Ancre brought some success and on 13 November the British took the German fortified position at Beaumont Hamel. However, heavy snow forced Haig to abandon his gains. Haig now brought an end to the Somme offensive. Since 1 July, the British had sustained 420,000 casualties with the French suffering upwards of 200,000. An estimate of German casualties on the Somme were approximately 500,000. Allied forces gained some ground, however, at its deepest point it amounted to only seven miles in depth. The Germans had been pushed back but held and there had been no breakthrough.

Chapter Seven

CHANGING ATTITUDES AND DISILLUSION

COMMENSURATE with the five month period over which the Battle of the Somme was fought runs the story of the Pals battalions and the disillusionment of the members. It is the story of patriotic passion, born of a jingoistic Edwardian society which viewed force of arms as the rightful God-given tool of the British Empire, crushed in a matter of minutes one Saturday morning. It was a rude awakening from an idealism which included absolute conviction of Divine approval. According to Old Testament accounts the Lord of Hosts regularly intervened to assist His people Israel in their conflicts with the surrounding nations. Therefore, as the Germans were the aggressors and the British Church were God's people, logic, reason and

Crowds in Hull, believed to be Hessle Road, waiting for news from the front. Note the shrines to the fallen set up on the street corner. DAVID BILTON

holy writ indicated that He would grant success to the righteous warriors who sought to put that alien nation in its place.

It was St Augustine who outlined the rules for a Just War one of the critera being:

A just war is wont to be described as one that avenges wrongs, when a nation or state has to be punished, for refusing to make amends for the wrongs inflicted by its subjects, or to restore what it has seized unjustly.

The war against Gemany was certainly 'just' most people in Britain, France and Russia reasoned. St Augustine went on to lay down basic guide lines for those engaging in a just war: he decreed that there were two parts to the Just War concept, *Jus ad bellum* (conditions in which military force is justified) and *Jus in bello* (manner in which the war is conducted). Some viewed the war as a crusade against tyranny and the political cartoons of the day depicted that idea.

When General Sir Douglas Haig took over as Commander-in-Chief on 19 December 1915, he brought to the office a religious faith instilled in him by his mother. A week after his appointment he wrote to his wife telling her that those about him expected success from his command of the BEF; that he was 'meant to win' by some 'superior power'. Not that he subscribed to the *crucesignati* (individuals signed with the cross – crusader) idea but rather that, Right would triumph ultimately, or as he wrote in his letter, 'I feel that one's best can go but a short way without help from above'. He was convinced that he was working under Divine Providence and that never left him no matter how bad things went for the Allies on the Western Front.

He sought to have the conviction of Divine backing instilled in the soldiers under his command. He was particularly concerned about the feelings of the huge Citizen Army. Particularly since the blood-letting of the Somme battles had plunged them into experiences which would demoralise professional soldiery, let alone clerks, schoolteachers, warehousemen, shopkeepers and miners. When the Archbishop of Canterbury visited GHQ in May 1916, Haig made two requests of him: Firstly, that the chaplains should preach to the troops about the reasons why Great Britain should carry on with the war; reminding the men that Britain had no selfish motives but was fighting for the good of humanity. Secondly, that the chaplains of the Church of England must cease quarrelling amongst themselves. 'In the Field we cannot tolerate any narrow sectarian ideas. We must all be united whether we are clerics or ordinary troops.' The Church of England was arguing over methods of service whether they should be conducted as a High Church or a Low Church ceremony. 'It seems to me most disgraceful at a time like the present that the National Church should be divided against itself, instead of giving us a noble example of unity and good fellowship. Haig was deeply concerned over the Church's function as a 'nourisher of the spirit'.

In July, at the height of the Battle of the Somme, the Archbishop of York turned up for lunch at GHQ along with Bishop Gwynne. Haig recorded their conversation in his diary:

The Archbishop spoke to me privately about the necessity for opening the

Burial on the Somme in the winter of 1916. The war would last another two years.

'When will this senseless murder end? Is there nobody sufficiently Christian to back up Lord Landsdowne's peace initiative? ...The country is hoodwinked. Facts are distorted or totally misrepresented by the press. Everyone seems to be on the make. My nostrils are filled with the smell of blood. My eyes are glutted with the sight of bleeding bodies and shattered limbs, my heart wrung with the agony of wounded and dying men.'

The Reverend Julian Bickersteth MC, Senior Chaplain 56th London Division. December 1917. (See page 128)

doors of the Church of England wider. I agreed and said we ought to aim at organising a great Imperial Church to which all honest citizens of the Empire could belong. In my opinion Church and State must advance together and hold together against those forces of revolution which threaten to destroy the State.

At the beginning of the year Haig had written to George V and to the King's Private Secretary, Lieutenant Colonel Clive Wigram, requesting that they discourage high dignitaries of the Church from coming to France, 'They only come when the weather gets finer, and then chiefly for the "joy-ride", or self-advertisement'. In spite of the request to 'discourage' them, the Archbishop of York and another bishop had turned up for lunch at a time of the worst disaster ever experienced to date by a British Army in the field. Some 20,000 dead and missing after a single day's fighting.

It was his dissatisfaction with the Church of England that determined the Commander-in-Chief to remain with the Church of Scotland for his periods of prayer and worship. However, he recognised the important part the chaplains had to play in keeping the British soldier fighting on by supplying succour and moral support.

Hull Pals

In February 1917 the Hull Brigade was still in the trenches in the vicinity of Hébuterne. It was on the 27th that information began circulating that the Germans had withdrawn from their fortified village of Serre. Their patrols began to confirm that the Geman trenches had been abandoned. In the weeks that followed they were involved in following the German withdrawal over the desolate landscape. In April they left the Somme.

Accrington Pals

In February 1917 six officers and 200 other ranks joined the battalion which made a total of 700 replacements since July 1916. Again the battalion was at full establishment. In the latter group of new arrivals were some of those who had been wounded on 1 July. In the other groups were many who had been wounded serving with other regiments. It was partly to flesh out depleted battalions with experienced men and partly War Office policy to break up the community based Pals formations whose losses had caused such a terrible blow to the morale of the British public.

With the German withdrawal to the Hindenburg Line men of the 11th Battalion East Lancashire Regiment could walk about freely over the former killing fields in front of Serre. It was then that they were able to discover some of the skeletons of their lost Pals and take part in burial details, laying them to rest.

Sheffield City Battalion

When the Germans fell back to their prepared postions they left countless booby traps some of which are listed in the Sheffield City book:

1. A shovel stuck between timbers in a dugout. When removed the shovel pulled a wire firing a mine.
2. A stove with its pipe left off. When picked up so as to replace it a wire fired a hidden charge.
3. A thin wire stretched across the entrance to a dugout, connected to a heavy window weight. When the wire was broken by a soldier entering the dugout, the weight fell into a box of detonators setting off a large charge next to it.
4. One of the timbers lining the wall of a dugout left sticking out at one end with a nail protruding. Behind the wall was a cartridge percussion cap. When an unwitting soldier hit the nail to repair the wall it set of a hidden charge.
5. A dozen stick grenades attached to a sandbag. The sandbag had to be removed to gain entry to a dugout. When moved it set off the grenades.
6. A charge left up a chimney with the fuze hanging down. When a good blaze was going off went the charge.
7. Lumps of coal had holes cut in them and detonators inserted. When put on the fire they exploded sending fragments of coal into the men warming themselves.
8. A branch placed over the entrance to a dugout as if to conceal it. when moved aside it set off a two minute time delay fuse. This allowed the

searchers to get deep inside the dugout before exploding a huge charge, completely destroying it.

Barnsley Pals
Although the Germans had withdrawn they still mounted surprise raids on unwary troops manning follow-up positions and ambushed patrols. In March, as elements of the 14th Battalion York and Lancaster Regiment, Second Barnsleys, were occupying an outpost near Puisieux a German patrol appeared out of the afternoon mist. Private Ossie Burgess was wounded by a 'tatie masher' in the leg and captured. He had been awarded a marksman badge for the Lewis gun some weeks previously. However he had heard that the Germans were offering money for killing or capturing marksmen and he had removed his badge and discarded it. How relieved he was that he had done so now that he had fallen into their hands.

> I must say this the Germans were very good to me. They picked me up and put me on a stretcher and took me to their aid post. I was interrogated three times at three different places. At the third interrogation there were four guards, two at the front and two at the back. They eventually took me to a Colonel who was using a Belgian interpreter – it wasn't easy. Then the Colonel asked me if I wanted a cigarette and then drew out what looked like a revolver which he pointed at me. When he pulled the trigger a flame shot up and he lit my cigarette. We both laughed [it must have been his party-piece for prisoners. But the relief caused his prisoner to relax, and hopefully talk]. It lasted an hour, but I told him a pack of lies.

Leeds Pals
A stretcher-bearer with the 15th Battalion West Yorkshire Regiment, Lance Corporal Arthur Pearson, recalled the German withdrawal:

> Our boys got safely into Jerrie's lines, consolidated the position, explored his deep dougouts and very comfortable Jerry made himself, with wire beds, chairs and tables looted from the villages and even electric lights.
>
> Souvenirs galore – boxes of cigars and cheroots, caps and helmets – he had either got out in a hurry or was going a long way and had dumped his extras. Now comes the tragic part of that advance. The Bradford Pals had been ordered to come through our company and to probe deeper into the German line. At that time those trenches were a wet, squelchy, sticky mess, mud was knee deep in the communication trench. Consequently the Bradfords who should have gone over before daylight couldn't get through the mud so it was daylight when they climbed out to attack. Jerry had left a few machine-gun posts manned and the poor old Bradfords got the lot, they were cut down before they got far. There were not many unwounded survivors, and we SBs were attending to their wounded and carrying them down to the First Aid Post. All night and every night this went on the whole time we were in the line.

Despite the fact that the follow-up advance was proving costly, by 28 February the brigade was in Rossignol Wood, which had been on the German Fourth Line, about a mile from the British line of 1 July 1916.

Bradford Pals

Under the code name 'Alberich' the German withdrawal had been planned with their usual thoroughness. Haig ordered that General Gough, commanding Fifth Army, should push forward and probe the enemy's front. Private Walter Hare was to experience his personal first time 'over the top'.

We had no idea what our objective was. I expect the officers knew, but unfortunately we soon lost some of the officers. I pressed on over the wire which had not been cut, then across No Man's Land and to the enemy wire which was still intact. We were now having casualties from enemy machine-gun fire, but we kept moving forward as best we could. I got to the enemy's front line where there were a few dead Germans. There was a wood in front of us with a lot of enemy machine guns. We got bogged down but Lieutenant Wilson wanted us to press on in despite of the machine-gun fire. A corporal from another mob had got mixed up with us and he said that we should stay where we were, and so we obeyed him because we thought that his was the best advice.

The fighting for Rossignol Wood for both the Bradford and Durham Pals was their last action on the Somme. A Court of Enquiry was ordered to be set up by the commander of 31st Division, Major General Wanless O'Gowan, concerning the loss of sixty-five men taken prisoner. The inference was that the men had given themselves up too readily. The account of the proceedings and the outcome makes interesting reading in David Raw's *Bradford Pals*.

Salford Pals

For much of January 1917 the Salfords occupied the trenches in front of Serre where 31 Brigade had attacked on 1 July 1916. Well behind the lines a gruesome ceremony was enacted at the end of the month.

The temperature was below freezing on 27 January when, at 7.30 am, a prisoner with his arms bound was brought out and seated on a dilapidated old chair to which he was then secured. A gas helmet, turned back to front, was placed over his head and a scrap of white paper was pinned over his heart. Six men from his own platoon moved to where six rifles were laid out for them; each rifle had a round 'up the spout' – one of which was supposedly a blank. At a given, previously agreed, couple of silent signals, the men took aim and fired. One man more nervous than the rest fired early and the rest followed. Private John Taylor had suffered execution by firing squad at Bertrancourt for the crime of desertion. He had already been under a suspended sentence of death for 'quitting his post'. There had been instances of petty thieving and on the march up to Beaumont Hamel an officer had to threaten him with a revolver. With his record he stood little chance of his sentence being commuted and which General Sir Douglas Haig confirmed. The First Salford Pals Intelligence Officer was ordered to see that the sentence was carried out.

Tyneside Irish

At the end of September 1916 the brigade left the Somme and went into the line at Armentières. The Battle of Arras was launched in April 1917 and during the attack on the 9th the First Irish, after capturing its first objective and advancing on its second, was held up by a machine gun firing on its left flank. A group of around eighty men started to fight their towards the German machine-gun position. An officer and a lance corporal, Thomas Bryan, scouted ahead but the officer was spotted and killed. Thomas Bryan told what happened next:

> On this great day our lads were held up by a machine gun, which was so well hidden we couldn't check its deadly work. I therefore made up my mind to put a stop to its activities, so creeping over the top, I went from shell hole to shell hole. Whilst working my way along, I was spotted by one of the enemy, who letting drive, caught me in the right arm. Following this bit of hard luck I decided to try a bit of rapid fire on the place where I thought the machine gun was placed, and on this being carried out, the gun which had been spitting forth its fire of death barked no more.

Lance Corporal Bryan then went on the say how he shot down two of the gun team who tried to escape. However, eyewitnesses testify that they definitely saw his bayonet flashing as he finished off the gun crew. Bryan, despite being wounded, had located the hidden weapon and rendered it silent by accurate rifle fire. He had then ensured that it would not be re manned by charging the position and finishing the survivors with his bayonet.

With the machine gun out of action the way was clear to recommence the attack. Brigade HQ ordered up the Fourth Tyneside Irish from reserve and the attack got underway again. Lance Corporal Thomas Bryan of Castleford, Yorkshire, became the first Northumberland Fusilier in the Great War to receive the Victoria Cross. The citation mentions that 'The results obtained by Lance Corporal Bryan's action were far reaching'.

Tyneside Scottish

The steady disintegration of the Pals battalions continued, as seen in the case of the steady loss of the north-country identity of the Tyneside Scottish Brigade. Brigadier Ternan complained bitterly:

> The reorganisation of the Brigade was now pushed on and officers and men were sent to us from a variety of units to bring us up to strength. At first few of our own wounded returned to us, and I got letters from men complaining that they had, on recovering from their wounds, been posted to units in which they were entire strangers. As one corporal who had been posted to a south country battalion wrote, "They don't understand what I say, and I can't understand them". I tried hard to get our own men back, and was fortunate enough to enlist the sympathies of the Second Army Commander, Sir Herbert Plumer, with the result that a certain number of our own men did eventually return to us, but in nearly every case the man, to his annoyance, was posted to the wrong battalion, not the one in which he and his friends enlisted and with which he had his home associations.

However, GHQ persisted in its policy – the era of the Pals was over with official blessing.

Grimsby Chums

Disillusionment with the war was manifest in numerous ways. The 10th Battalion Lincolnshire Regiment finally left the Somme 15 August 1916 and the commanding officer, Lieutenant Colonel E Kyme Cordeaux, CBE, had experienced sufficient horror. He asked to be relieved of his command and four months later left for a safer command. That option was an officer-only way of getting away from the awful slaughter that was beginning to seem like an endless commitment to those involved in it.

Author of *Grimsby Chums*, Peter Bryant, cites another way employed by some to escape the perpetual nightmare. A battalion runner, who had been an excellent soldier up to that point, made what he obviously considered to be a small sacrifice. He confided in his chum and fellow runner, that he had had enough and that he was going to do something about it. Shortly afterwards the two runners were sent with a message to a particularly hazardous part of the line. When they were out of sight of the HQ, one of them watched in stunned silence as his companion wrapped his right hand in an old tunic and then fired his rifle into it blowing away two fingers. 'I saw that he was bandaged up in a fashion and he set off walking to a sunken road along which ambulances were rumbling.' Upon his return he reported his fellow runner as a shell-splinter casualty.

Birmingham Pals

Leaving the Somme at the end of September 1916 the three battalions moved north to Béthune where they stayed for six months. In April 1917 13 Brigade was involved with the Canadians in the successful capture of Vimy Ridge.

Author Terry Carter in *Birmingham Pals* tells of his interview with veteran Ted Francis (16th Battalion, Royal Warwickshire Regiment). The worst memory of the war for Ted, who died in March 1996, occured at Ypres. Because of the terrible condition of the ground in the Salient a seemingly heartless order was issued to the effect that should any man fall into the slime and water-filled shell-holes, he was to be left. The reason behind this was that anyone who stayed to try and effect a rescue could end up in the same predicament. Even after eighty years Ted could still recall their cries for help as they slowly sank to their deaths. Captain Arthur Bill, Second Birmingham Pals, described how a party of A Company came upon one unfortunate soldier who had slipped off the duckboard track and was stuck thigh deep in bottomless mud. They tried to help him by placing rifles under his armpits and lifting, but there was no foothold for them. They had to leave him; duty called. Two days later when returning from the line the soldier was still there, but by now only his head was showing and he had gone raving mad.

Manchester Pals

For many of the Manchester Pals the Somme battles meant the end of their active military service. Those taken prisoner experienced life in the enemy's country – a country under Royal Navy blockade with all that entailed in food shortages and rationing. Rowland Heathcote, First Manchester Pals, was captured at Trones Wood along with his entire patrol. Eventually they arrived at Duisberg in Westphalia and were directed to work in a coal mine there:

> We were given clogs and tins as used by miners and marched to the pit 300 yards away. There we refused to take the lamps. We explained that prisoners of war in England were not ordered to work in the pits and that we should not be made to do it. Lipman, the only one of us to speak German, was our interpreter. We were marched back to the prison, lined up and told that we were to be shot, the armed guards marching at the back of us. Lipman was pulled by the ears every time he was wanted to interpret some order. We stuck it out from just six in the morning until late in the afternoon, when only three of the original fifteen were left standing. They were taken to their cells and next day the same thing happened. We were again lined up and prodded and assaulted until several men fainted. We realised that this could not go on and we gave in.
>
> In the pit we were knocked about, but I gave one Gerry a good hiding, and the word was passed round that the Englishmen were not to be struck. After that we had a comparatively good time. Food came regularly from England and we had our own jokes on the Germans.

Liverpool Pals

The Pals moved forward across open country to catch up with the Germans as they fell back on the Somme to the Hindenburg Line. They had been used to static warfare for so long the months of March and April gave the troops the novel experience of being able to advance across open country. It was only when the Pals took stock of the land that had been given up did they realise the utter devastation. Brigadier General Stanley recorded what the Liverpools found:

> It is impossible to convey to anyone who has not seen it the state to which the enemy had reduced the whole of the country. As regards his trenches he has blown up every single dugout, smashed in all his machine gun emplacements, OPs etc. He has demolished everything except his wire entanglements. And of these there were belts without number of extraordinary width and thickness. These were intact, and I can only thank Heaven that we did not have to attack through this wire. It would have taken us months of wire-cutting. Apart from his trenches he had set himself to destroy everything. What had remained of the villages he had blown up; there was not a single house standing higher than three feet. Every tree had been cut down; he had not even spared the gooseberry and currant bushes. The roads and the bridges were all blown up. In fact we have always given him the utmost credit for his thoroughness and this wholesale destruction was one of his masterpieces.

*   *   *   *

The account of the Pals on the Somme must come to a close here. The Battle of the Somme terminated in the rain-washed month of November 1916. By that time, to some extent, every single Pals battalions had lost its original identity. Never again would the like of them be seen, nor indeed would the kind of religiously-fuelled patriotism which spawned them.

BIBLIOGRAPHY

William Turner *Accrington Pals, 11th (Service) Battalion (Accrington) East Lancashire Regiment*, 1987, Wharncliffe Publishing Ltd

Jon Cooksey *Barnsley Pals, 13th and 14th (Service) Battalions, York & Lancaster Regiment*, 1986, Wharncliffe Woodmoor Investments

Terry Carter *Birmingham Pals, 14th, 15th & 16th (Service) Battalions, Royal Warwickshire Regiment*, 1997, Pen & Sword Books Ltd

David Raw *Bradford Pals, 16th, 18th & 20th (Service) Battalions, The Prince of Wales Own West Yorkshire Regiment*, 2005, Pen & Sword Books Ltd

David Bilton *Hull Pals, 10th, 11th, 12th & 13th (Service) Battalions, East Yorkshire Regiment*, 1999, Pen & Sword Books Ltd

Laurie Milner *Leeds Pals, 15th (Service) Battalion The Prince of Wales Own West Yorkshire Regiment*, 1991, Pen & Sword Books Ltd

Graham Maddocks *Liverpool Pals, 17th, 18th, 19th & 20th (Service) Battalions The King's (Liverpool Regiment)*, 1991, Leo Cooper

Michael Stedman *Manchester Pals, 16th, 17th, 18th, 19th, 20th, 21st, 22nd & 23rd (Service) Battalions, Manchester Regiment*, 1994, Leo Cooper

Michael Stedman *Salford Pals, 15th 16th, 19th & 20th (Service) Battalions Lancashire Fusiliers*, 1993, Leo Cooper

Ralph Gibson & Paul Oldfield *Sheffield City, 12th (Service) Battalion, York & Lancaster Regiment*, 1988, Wharncliffe Publishing Ltd

Bernard Lewis *Swansea Pals, 14th (Service) Battalion, Welsh Regiment*, 2004, Pen & Sword Books Ltd

John Sheen *Tyneside Irish, 24th, 25th, 26th & 27th (Service) Battalions, Northumberland Fusiliers*, 1998, Pen & Sword Books Ltd

Graham Stewart & John Sheen *Tyneside Scottish, 20th, 21st, 22nd & 23rd (Service) Battalions, Northumberland Fusiliers*, 1999, Pen & Sword Books Ltd

Peter Simkins *Kitchener's Army, The Raising of the New Armies, 1914-16*, 1988, Manchester University Press

Martin Middlebrook *Your Country Needs You*, 2000, Pen & Sword Books Ltd

Ray Westlake *British Battalions of the Somme*, 1994, Pen & Sword Books Ltd

Chris McCarthy *The Somme, The Day-by-Day Account*, 1993, Arms & Armour Press

JM Winter *The Experience of World War I*, 1988, Grange Books PLC

Liddel Hart *History of the First World War*, 1997 edition, Macmillan Publishers Ltd

John Terraine *Douglas Haig The Educated Soldier*, 1990 edition, Leo Cooper

The Private Papers of Douglas Haig 1914-1919, edited by Robert Blake, 1952, Eyre & Spottiswode

W Grant Grieve and Bernard Newman *Tunnellers*, 1936, Herbert Jenkins Ltd

Thomas Herbert, MA, *The World's Greatest War*, published 1914, Unknown

Julian Putkowski & Julian Sykes *Shot at Dawn*, 1989, Wharncliffe Publishing Ltd

Jack Sheldon *The German Army on the Somme*, 2005, Pen & Sword Books Ltd

Peter Bryant *Grimsby Chums*, 1990, Humberside Leisure Services

K. W. Mitchinson and I. McInnes *Cotton Town Comrades*, 1993, Bayonet Publications

Douglas Sutherland *Tried and Valiant*, 1972, Leo Cooper

Tim Saunders *West Country Regiments on the Somme*, 2004, Pen & Sword Books Ltd

John Bickersteth *The Bickersteth Diaries 1914-1918* 1995, Leo Cooper

Pals Battalions
Order of Battle

The definition of a Pals/City battalion: a unit raised by a local authority or private body which undertook to organise, clothe, billet and feed the recruits. The provision of weapons was the responsibility of the Army. Official acceptance of the battalion by the War Office was when reimbursement for expenditure took place.

Privately raised formations numbered **144** and were broken down as follows:

Pals/City	**96**	battalions
Ulster Volunteer Force	**13**	battalions
TynesideScottish and Irish	**8**	battalions
Public Schools	**5**	battalions
Sportsmen	**5**	battalions
Commercials	**3**	battalions
Public Works Pioneers	**3**	battalions
Empire and Empire League	**2**	battalions
Boys Brigade, Church Lads Brigade	**2**	battalions
Others	**7**	battalions

This information is based on the book, *Your Country Needs You, Expansion of the British Army Infantry Divisions 1914-1918* by Martin Middlebrook.

30TH DIVISION

89 BRIGADE

2nd Battalion
Bedfordshire
Regiment
(Regular Army)

17th Battalion
The king's (Liverpool
Regiment)
(First Liverpool Pals)

19th Battalion
The king's (Liverpool
Regiment)
(Third Liverpool Pals)

20th Battalio
The king's (Live.
Regiment)
(Fourth Liverpool Pa

21 BRIGADE

2nd Battalion
Alexandra, Princess of
Wales's Own (Yorkshire
Regiment)
Green Howards *(Regular Army)*

2nd Battalion
Duke of Edinburgh's
Wiltshire Regiment
(Regular Army)

18th Battalion
The king's (Liverpool
Regiment)
(Second Liverpool Pals)

19th Battalio
Manchester
Regiment
(Fourth Manchester

90 BRIGADE

2nd Battalion
Royal Scots
Fusiliers
(Regular Army)

16th Battalion
Manchester
Regiment
(First Manchester Pals)

17th Battalion
Manchester
Regiment
(Second Manchester Pals)

18th Battalio
Manchester
Regiment
(Third Manchester F

11th Battalion (Pioneers)
Prince of Wales's Volunteers
(South Lancashire Regiment)
(St Helens Pioneers)

31ST DIVISION

92 BRIGADE

10th Battalion
East Yorkshire
(Hull Commercials)

14th Battalion
East Yorkshire
(Hull Tradesmen)

15th Battalion
East Yorkshire
(Hull Sportsmen)

14th Battalion
East Yorkshire
(Hull T'others)

93 BRIGADE

15th Battalion
West Yorkshire
Regiment
(Leeds Pals)

16th Battalion
West Yorkshire
Regiment
(First Bradford Pals)

18th Battalion
West Yorkshire
Regiment
(Second Bradford Pals)

18th Battalion
Durham Light
Infantry
(Durham Pals)

94 BRIGADE

12th Battalion
York & Lancaster
Regiment
(Sheffield City)

13th Battalion
York & Lancaster
Regiment
(First Barnsley Pals)

14th Battalion
York & Lancaster
Regiment
(Second Barnsley Pals)

11th Battalion
East Lancashire
Regiment
(Accrington Pals)

12th Battalion (Pioneers)
King's Own Yorkshire Light
Infantry
(Wakefield/Pontefract Miners)

32ND DIVISION

14 BRIGADE

1st Battalion
Dorsetshire
Regiment
(Regular Army)

2nd Battalion
Manchester
Regiment
(Regular Army)

15th Battalion
Highland Light
Infantry
(Glasgow Tramways)

19th Battalion
Lancashire Fusilie
(Third Salford Pals)

96 BRIGADE

2nd Battalion
Royal Inniskilling
Fusiliers *(Regular Army)*

15th Battalion
Lancashire Fusiliers
(First Salford Pals)

16th Battalion
Lancashire Fusiliers
(Second Salford Pals)

16th Battalion
Northumberland
Fusiliers
(Newcastle Pals)

97 BRIGADE

2nd Battalion
King's Own Yorkshire
Light Infantry
(Regular Army)

11th Battalion
Border Regiment
(Lonsdale Pals)

16th Battalion
Highland Light
Infantry
(Glasgow Boys' Brigade)

17th Battalion
Highland Light
Infantry
*(Glasgow Chamber of
Commerce)*

17th Battalion
Northumberland Fusiliers
(N.E.R. Pioneers)

34TH DIVISION

101 BRIGADE

0th Battalion
ncolnshire Regiment
rimsby Chums)

11th Battalion
Suffolk Regiment
(Cambridgeshire)

15th Battalion
Royal Scots (Lothian
Regiment) *(First Edinburgh)*

16th Battalion
Royal Scots (Lothian
Regiment)
(Second Edinburgh)

102 BRIGADE

0th Battalion
orthumberland Fusiliers
irst Tyneside Scottish)

21st Battalion
Northumberland Fusiliers
(Second Tyneside Scottish)

22nd Battalion
Northumberland Fusiliers
(Third Tyneside Scottish)

23rd Battalion
Northumberland Fusiliers
(Fourth Tyneside Scottish)

103 BRIGADE

Collar badge

4th Battalion
orthumberland
usiliers
rst Tyneside Irish)

25th Battalion
Northumberland
Fusiliers
(Second Tyneside Irish)

26th Battalion
Northumberland
Fusiliers
(Third Tyneside Irish)

27th Battalion
Northumberland
Fusiliers
(Fourth Tyneside Irish)

18th Battalion
Northumberland Fusiliers
(First Tyneside Pioneers)

35TH (BANTAM) DIVISION

104 BRIGADE

17th Battalion
Lancashire Fusiliers
(First South East Lancashire)

18th Battalion
Lancashire Fusiliers
(First South East Lancashire)

20th Battalion
Lancashire Fusiliers
(Fourth Salford)

23rd Battalion
Manchester Regim
(Eighth City)

105 BRIGADE

14 Battalion
Gloucestershire
Regiment *(West of
England)*

15th Battalion
Sherwood Foresters
(Notts & Derbyshire)
(Nottingham)

15th Battalion
Cheshire Regiment
(First Birkenhead)

16th Battalion
Cheshire Regimer
(Second Birkenhead)

106 BRIGADE

17th Battalion
Royal Scots (Lothian
Regiment)
(Rosebury)

17th Battalion
Prince of Wales's Own
(West Yorkshire Regiment)
(Second Leeds)

18th Battalion
Highland Light
Infantry
(Fourth Glasgow)

19th Battalion
Durham Light
Infantry
(Second County)

19th Battalion
Northumberland Fusiliers
(Second Tyneside Pioneers)

36th (Ulster) Division

107 Brigade

8th Battalion
Royal Irish Rifles
(East Belfast)

9th Battalion
Royal Irish Rifles
(West Belfast)

10th Battalion
Royal Irish Rifles
(South Belfast)

15th Battalion
Royal Irish Rifles
(North Belfast)

108 Brigade

9th Battalion
Royal Irish Fusiliers
(County Armagh)

11th Battalion
Royal Irish Rifles
(South Antrim)

12th Battalion
Royal Irish Rifles
(Central Antrim)

13th Battalion
Royal Irish Rifles
(First County Down)

109 Brigade

9th Battalion
Royal Inniskilling Fusiliers
(County Tyrone)

10th Battalion
Royal Inniskilling Fusiliers
(Derry)

11th Battalion
Royal Inniskilling Fusiliers
(Donegal and Fermanagh)

14th Battalion
Royal Irish Rifles
(Young Citizens)

16th Battalion
Northumberland Fusiliers
(First Tyneside Pioneers)

38TH (WELSH) DIVISION

113 BRIGADE

13th Battalion
Royal Welsh
Fusiliers

14th Battalion
Royal Welsh
Fusiliers

15th Battalion
Royal Welsh
Fusiliers

16th Battalion
Royal Welsh
Fusiliers

114 BRIGADE

10th Battalion
Welsh Regiment
(First Rhondda)

13th Battalion
Welsh Regiment
(Second Rhondda)

14th Battalion
Welsh Regiment
(Swansea Pals)

15th Battalion
Welsh Regiment
(Carmarthenshire)

115 BRIGADE

16th Battalion
Welsh Regiment
(Cardiff Pals)

10th Battalion
South Wales
Borderers
(First Gwent Pals)

11th Battalion
South Wales
Borderers
(Second Gwent Pals)

17th Battalion
Royal Welsh
Fusiliers

19th Battalion
Welsh Regiment
(Glamorgan Pioneers)

39thDivision

116 Brigade

th Battalion
yal Sussex Regiment
st South Down)

12th Battalion
Royal Sussex Regiment
(Second South Down)

13th Battalion
Royal Sussex Regiment
(Third South Down)

14th Battalion
Hampshire Regiment
(First Portsmouth)

117 Brigade

th Battalion
le Brigade (The Prince
nsort's Own)
Pancras)

16th Battalion
Sherwood Foresters
(Notts & Derbyshire)
(Chatsworth Rifles)

17th Battalion
Sherwood Foresters
(Notts & Derbyshire)
(Welbeck Rangers)

17th Battalion
King's Royal Rifle
Corps
(British Empire League)

118 Brigade

st Battalion
mbridgeshire Regiment
rritorial Force)

1/1st Battalion
Hertfordshire Regiment
(Territorial Force)

1/6th Battalion
Cheshire Regiment
(Territorial Force)

4th/5th Battalion
Black Watch (Royal
Highlanders)
(Territorial Force)

13th Battalion
Gloucestershire Regiment
(Forest of Dean Pioneers)

INDEX